THE DISCOVERY OF THE GRAIL

Andrew Sinclair is a novelist, historian, critic and film-maker whose published works include biographies of Jack London and Francis Bacon, *The Albion Triptych, War Like a Wasp* and his books about patronage and the arts, *The Need to Give* and *Arts and Cultures*. He has also written previously on Jerusalem and the Grail. He was a Founding Fellow of Churchill College, Cambridge, and has taught and travelled widely across the world. He lives in London and is married to the writer Sonia Melchett.

D1428837

Also by Andrew Sinclair

FICTION

The Breaking of Bumbo
My Friend Judas
The Project
The Hallelujah Bum
The Raker
A Patriot for Hire
The Facts in the Case of E. A. Poe
Beau Bumbo
Gog
Magog
King Ludd

NON-FICTION

Prohibition: the Era of Excess
The Better Half: the Emancipation of the American Woman
The Available Man: Warren Gamaliel Harding
The Concise History of the United States
Che Guevara
The Last of the Best
The Naked Savage
Dylan: Poet of His People
Jack London
John Ford
Corsair: the Life of J. P. Morgan
The Other Victoria
Sir Walter Raleigh and the Age of Discovery
The Red and the Blue
Spiegel: the Man Behind the Pictures
War like a Wasp: the Lost Decade of the Forties
The Need to Give: the Patron and the Arts
The Sword and the Grail
In Love and Anger: A View of the 'Sixties
Francis Bacon: His Life and Violent Times
Jerusalem: The Endless Crusade
Arts and Cultures

THE DISCOVERY OF THE GRAIL

by Andrew Sinclair

ARROW

This edition published by Arrow Books Limited 1999

1 3 5 7 9 10 8 6 4 2

First published in the United Kingdom in 1998 by Century

Arrow Books Limited
Random House UK Limited
20 Vauxhall Bridge Road, London SW1V 2SA

Random House Australia (Pty) Limited
20 Alfred Street, Milsons Point, Sydney,
New South Wales 2061, Australia

Random House New Zealand Limited
18 Poland Road, Glenfield
Auckland 10, New Zealand

Random House South Africa (Pty) Limited
Endulini, 5a Jubilee Road, Parktown 2193, South Africa

Random House UK Limited Reg. No. 954009

A CIP catalogue record for this book is available from the British Library

Papers used by Random House UK Limited are natural, recyclable products
made from wood grown in sustainable forests. The manufacturing
processes conform to the environmental regulations of the country of origin

ISBN 0 0992 7094 3

Typeset by SX Composing DTP, Rayleigh, Essex
Printed and bound in Germany by
Elsnerdruck, Berlin

Contents

Contents

To my Grail on earth, the grace of Sonia

Preface

The Grail is a personal quest. Few who seek it may find it. It is not a treasure hunt, but an exploration of self. The duty is control of the body, then a search for the secrets of creation.

There are millions of paths to the Grail. If we ever reach the end of the road, we will see it in the shape of our experiences on the way. While there is only one Maker of our world, that One may appear in as many forms as nature does. Otherwise, there would hardly be so many religions claiming to know the sole method of approaching the One. The quest for the Grail is the parable of all of our lonely looking for the divine.

Yet there is a geography of the Grail. While the endeavour of this book is to present the first complete history of the Grail, I would also try to demonstrate some of the ways to its discovery. The craft on this voyage, which the Grail romances called the Ship of Solomon, has two sails – Belief and Evidence. The wind must blow fair on both for those who seek to steer their right passage.

I will show many places and many things and many symbols of the Grail. They are signs that indicate the path to each pilgrim. They are pointers to the individual, who must tread or ride or navigate a lonely course towards the One.

The story will become personal to me. Once upon a time, I found the holy chalice carved on tombstones in Scotland. They led me on to the fate of the Knights Templar, named by two of the medieval poets as the keepers of the Grail. They also led me to the history of my own family with the name of St Clair or Sancto Claro, the Latin for 'holy light'. The journey extended over Europe and the Near East and across the Atlantic Ocean.

As a sinful seeker, I only knew the signs. I have not yet seen the vision. Yet I may try to describe how other and better people can achieve that transformation of the senses, that blessed vision of the gifts of all creation.

Chapter One

Sources of the Grail

> But the marvel that he found
> Terrified him time after time.
> No man may speak or tell of it.
> Whoever does so is in trouble.
> For it is the sign of the Grail.

Gautier de Doulens, *The Story of the Grail*

The womb has always made children. The horn and the cup have served drink. The cauldron and the bowl have given food. From these facts of life comes the quest for the Grail.

The earliest records of the West come from the Near East. Water power ruled the first cities and kingdoms of Mesopotamia. A wise god of the underworld called Enki sent up his freshwater Ocean to the *apsû* tanks in the first Assyrian temples. This water was carried in buckets by fish man-gods to humankind. Persian worshippers then poured libations from jars into bowls set before the altars of their gods. In these original scenes of religion, the water tank and the bucket, the jug and the bowl were depicted as the source of life, which should be given back to the divine. They were prophecies of the Grail.

The theocracy of ancient Egypt was equally dependent on the river Nile, which could make the desert green. Thoth was the god of wisdom and science, who invented letters and became the Greek Hermes. Both divine messengers had the serpent of wisdom as their symbol. The Athenian dramatist Sophocles was said to have received in his house the healing

1

god Asclepius in the form of a sacred snake. As Herodotus declared in his *Histories*, 'the names of almost all the gods came from Egypt into Greece'. He then added that the Egyptians were 'the first who introduced public festivals, processing and solemn supplication'. These rites were introduced into the mysteries at Eleusis, the primal ceremonies of birth and death in Greece, while the oracles at Dodona and Delphi provided the prophecies of the future. The very Greek myths of creation also had an Egyptian basis, although some of them derived from the original inhabitants called the Pelasgians, influenced by the primary cults of a goddess of Mother Earth and fertility.

In the beginning was Chaos. Eurynome, the maker of everything, was caught in the coils of the great serpent Ophion. She was changed into a dove, a later symbol of the Grail, and produced the Egg of Creation, which split in two in the serpent's grasp to produce the universe and our world. Later, the great god Zeus was born. His father was Kronos, who had married his own sister, Rhea. Told that he would be dethroned by one of his sons, Kronos swallowed them all except for Zeus, for Rhea had substituted a stone for her son. She gave him to the nymph Amalthea to rear in the shape of a goat. Amalthea kept him fed from Cornucopia, a horn of plenty, so famous in legend that Gelon, the tyrant hero of Syracuse, reproduced it in the fifth century BC in a grotto in his palace garden. Zeus became the cupbearer of Kronos and gave him an emetic, which made him vomit out Zeus's brothers and sisters as well as the substitute stone. Kronos was then defeated with his allies, the Titans, and exiled to farthest Britain: he would later be worshipped in the shape of a black stone. Zeus was said to have given his stone to serve as an altar at Delphi, where the oracle pronounced his wisdom and held the cup that was the mouth and the womb of the gods. Aeschylus, Pindar and Pausanias all wrote that the Delphians considered that divine white stone as the navel and the centre of the world.

In these creation myths, many of the later themes of the

Grail appear: the wise serpent, the split egg-bowl of creation, the stone of prophecy, the Cornucopia, the cup and its godlike bearer, the replacement of the supreme ruler, the divine altar still on earth. In the important mysteries at Eleusis, none of the rituals were foretold. Leaving Greece from there, Demeter rescued her daughter Persephone from the underworld of Hades, only to lose her each year to winter in the everlasting cycle of the seasons. Demeter had made the earth the Waste Land of the Grail Castle fables before she recovered her daughter and allowed again the greenery of spring and the harvests of autumn. 'Happy is he of all men living on earth who has seen these things,' a Homeric hymn declared of the Eleusinian mysteries. 'But he who is not initiated in these holy rites, who has no share in them, he shall never have an equal lot in death in the shadowy depths.'

During the dramas and celebrations over nine days at Eleusis, sacred vessels were shown. Clement of Alexandria and Plato both mentioned a ritual speech of the worshippers: 'I fasted, I drank the potion. I took it from the chest. Having tasted it, I put it away in the basket and from the basket into the chest.' These sacraments were followed on the fourth day of the festival by a procession with a basket containing pomegranates and poppy seeds, cakes and salt, and a live serpent. On the last day, two jars filled with water and wine were placed to the east and to the west. These were overturned to the words *ue kue*, 'rain' and 'conceive'.

These fertility rites were matched in the contemporary Orphic mysteries of Dionysus, the god of wine and the spirit. He was a similar god to the Egyptian Osiris and Attis and the Phoenician Adonis. They all died and were born again to become divinities of life and death, giving human beings an assurance of their own immortality. In Greek legend, the body of the child Dionysus was eaten by the Titans, who boiled and spitted and roasted his flesh. This was a communal and cannibal feast. The Titans were then destroyed by a thunderbolt from heaven, and humanity was born from the ashes. An element of this ancient blood sacrifice would reach the Christian religion.

The celebrants of Dionysus also ate the raw flesh of animals, as he was said to have done: the savage hunter as well as the god of wine. When his follower Orpheus, with his lyre, was torn apart by the frenzied Bacchantes, his sacrifice was a prelude to eating the divine flesh and drinking the blood in an orgiastic mystery, at which some healing cures of the disturbed and the sick were reported by Plato. The singing head of Orpheus was said to have been washed up at Lesbos, an event celebrated by Milton in his *Lycidas* – another version of the speaking heads of the Celtic gods and Christian martyrs. The worshippers at the Orphic ceremonies affirmed the split between the corrupt body and the eternal soul, which descended into Hades and was sent back to this world in an endless recurrence until the spirit might be liberated to join the gods. An Orphic gravestone in southern Italy asserted: 'I am a child of earth and the starry heaven, but my descent is from heaven. This you know yourselves.' Clement of Alexandria again recognised this view of the flesh as the prison of the spirit, when he wrote that ancient theologians witnessed 'that for a punishment the soul is yoked with the body and buried in it'.

The way to heaven was through an ecstatic vision of God. An ascetic life of penance culminated in a religious celebration, in which wine and narcotics were used to induce the vision of the divine. The early ceremonies of the Orphic cult may have included Minoan and Anatolian sacrifices, where the blood of sheep and goats was poured from a jug into a cauldron in the ground. Later Orphics in Roman times were attracted by the Christian communion, when wine was translated into holy blood as a means of absolution, of freeing the spirit from the flesh.

Although the Romans defeated the Greeks, they surrendered their education to their slaves. 'When in Rome,' the saying went, 'do as the Greeks do.' The Mesopotamian, Egyptian and Hellenic myths of creation and rebirth joined the Italian

The Alchemy of the Grail

At the opening of *Perceval*, the first Grail romance about the holy fool, the season of the year was given as 'when fields grow green'. Perceval of Wales picked up his three javelins and met five knights who shone in the sunlight in red, white, silver, blue and gold. The four elements of the classical and medieval cosmos were earth, air, fire and water. Their colours were blue, golden-yellow, red and green. To explain the changes within an alchemic vessel which might convert base metal into gold, earth was seen as blue and lead, air as yellow and sulphur, fire as red and arsenic, while water was green and copper. Beginning with the ancient Greeks, alchemists put lead and copper on ledges above metallic sulphur and arsenic sulphide along with water in a pot over the heated floor of their stills. The fumes made sulphuric acid, which condensed and fell on the copper and lead. The acid and salts first blackened the two metals, then whitened them, and finally made them red, before they were melted into yellow brass, which looked like gold.

The colours worn by the knights in the Grail romances attested to the power of alchemy in the imagination of the Middle Ages. In *Perceval*, the fool's first act after visiting King Arthur was to slay the Red Knight, who had struck him with his lance. He then returned to the travelling court at Carduel, or Carlisle, the gold cup stolen by the Red Knight. This deed was not only a material forecast of Perceval's later vision of the Holy Lance and Grail at the castle of the Fisher King, but also a symbol of the reddening fire of alchemy, which transmuted the base into the precious. Throughout the succeeding Grail romances, the colours of the elements and alchemic changes – particularly green, black and red – appeared in the costumes and heraldry of the various heroes of chivalry. The references culminated in Wolfram von Eschenbach's *Parzival*, where the Grail was revealed as a green stone or wafer fallen as manna from heaven, the secret of a wise Jewish astronomer named Flegetanis, who knew of the mysteries of the alchemy of the eastern Mediterranean.

The *Visions* of the Hellenistic scientist Zosimos first spelt out the chemical processes of alchemy. In the beginning was the composition of the sulphurous waters, then their condensation, followed by the separation of the acids from the base metals, and ending with the corrosion of the lead and copper, which became brass and 'gold'. The opening of the *Visions* seemed to describe a dream of achieving the Grail:

I saw a sacrificing priest standing before me at the top of an altar in the form of a bowl. This altar had fifteen steps leading up to it. Then the priest stood up and I heard a voice from above saying to me, 'I have accomplished the descent of the fifteen steps of darkness and the ascent of the steps of light and it is he who sacrifices, that renews me, casting away the coarseness of the body; and being consecrated priest by necessity, I become a spirit.' And having heard the voice of him who stood on the bowl-shaped altar, I questioned him, wishing to find out who he was. He answered me in a weak voice, saying, 'I am Ion, the priest of the sanctuary, and I have survived intolerable violence. For one came headlong in the morning, dismembering me with a sword, and tearing me asunder according to the rigour of harmony. And flaying my head with the sword which he held fast, he mingled my bones with my flesh and burned them in the fire of the treatment, until I learnt by the transformation of the body to become a spirit.'

Zosimos was probably referring to the *krater* in the alchemical text *Corpus Hermeticum*, the holy bowl where each individual soul mixed with the universal mind and the Word of God. In his fifth vision of the priest at the sacred altar celebrating the fearful mysteries, he was told that the holy man wished to put blood into the many bodies in the bowl, 'to make clear the eyes, and to raise up the dead'. This process of regeneration was paralleled not only in other

Hermetic texts, but in Nordic and Celtic rites, as depicted on the first century Danish sacrificial Gunderstrup Cauldron. In the medieval romances, such heresies, particularly the Pelagian and the Gnostic, would play a major role along with alchemy in the quest for the Grail, which was the direct search for the divine. The three great sins of Gnosticism – the separation of the Creator from God the Father, the denial of the divinity of Christ on earth, and the hatred of flesh and matter as the source of all evil – were derived from the teaching of the Jewish philosopher Philo of Alexandria, as well as from Zoroaster, the Persian sage.

In the time of the early Christian Church, the alchemist Simon Magus claimed to be the direct representative of the supreme power of God, a rival Messiah to Christ. His wisdom was the immediate Word of the Lord. 'He was the first to declare,' wrote Saint Irenaeus, 'that he himself was the God who is over all things, and that the world was made by his angels.' The divine principle was fire, which emanated in six elements: heaven and earth, the sun and the moon, air and water – a doctrine which also derived from the Persian fire and sun worshippers who followed Zoroaster. By hearsay and magic, Simon Magus had himself raised in Rome towards heaven as the Anti-Christ in a demonic chariot of fire, only to be brought down by the prayers of Saints Peter and Paul. In his fall, Magus broke both of his legs. Another Christian Father had the heretic buried alive, announcing that he would rise on the third day as Christ had. He was never to appear again.

Among the Gnostic sects, the Nassenes believed in a Cup of Anacreon, which represented the world. In it, God mixed the four elements of earth and air, fire and water, in order to create the world of forms. A contemporary Persian legend told of a Cup of Jamshid, in which all the mysteries of nature could be discerned. In the Hermetic tradition, a vessel filled with *νǒus*, or consciousness, had been sent down from heaven to bathe mankind in divine understanding. As Jung wrote of these three legends in his *Alchemical Studies*, they were early fonts 'in which the immersion takes place and transformation into a spiritual being is effected . . . the uterus of spiritual renewal or rebirth'. Even in the most Christian Grail romance of Robert de Boron, Jesus gave esoteric teaching to Joseph of Arimathea, who established the mysteries of the Grail under the guardianship of its hereditary knights. Classical and Eastern mysticism and alchemy would always be elements in the signs and wonders which would meet the seekers of the true way.

The Hero and the Grail

The idea of the hero making the earth green and reaching the other world and the divine was as old as epic poetry. As the Sumerian poet wrote of the original divine ruler of Mesopotamia:

> *The great prince Enki*
> *Opened the holy furrows*
> *Made grain grow in the perennial field.*

The Epic of Gilgamesh told of the temple builder of Uruk, who fought evil in the person of a forest giant and journeyed to the underworld, only to discover that death was the fate of all men, before his return to his own end, back in his city. This quest for a divine answer to life would inspire the later epics of rites of passage from the *Odyssey* of Homer to the Arthurian cycle of poems about the Knights of the Round Table in search of the Grail.

Homer's Ulysses represented the archetype of the European hero on his mission towards the unknown. His account of his visit to Hades was praised by the royal Alcinous, who said that the form of the story was as a singer would do. With Gilgamesh, Ulysses was the ceaseless wanderer between the living and the dead. Boccaccio was to praise his curiosity, which made him trespass 'because of his desire to see beyond the sign from which no one has ever been able to return'. And with Oedipus, he was the chief of heroes. With words and intelligence, both of them put off their destiny in order to discover the secrets of knowledge on their journey through life.

Greek historical legends may have informed the first Grail romance, the *Perceval* of Chrétien de Troyes, who said it was based on a book donated by his patron, Philip of Flanders. The rulers of the Grail Castle may have represented the House of Atreus, with the Fisher King modelled on Menelaus. The hall of the castle might be derived from the prehistoric palaces of Mycenae and Tiryns. The Holy Lance could be the royal staff given by Zeus to Hermes and finally to Agamemnon. 'This sceptre they worship, naming it a spear,' Pausanias had written. 'The man who acts as priest keeps the sceptre in his house for the year; and sacrifices are offered it daily, and a table is set beside it covered with all kinds of flesh and cakes.' This was a later property of the Grail, the giving of food in abundance. The silver Cup of Atreus, which depicted a golden lamb and signified the possession of the kingdom, was also claimed as an early Grail.

The courts of Charlemagne and the Norman kings could read in Latin translation some of the old Greek romances about the career of Alexander the Great. By the twelfth century, particularly in the *Alexandreis* of Walter of Châtillon, the deeds of the Greek hero rivalled the tales of Troy as sources for parts of the Grail romances. Alexander was legendary as a universal ruler in the Near East long before the crusaders arrived, and his empire was presented as superior to the Roman one. He had wished to be worshipped as divine, and the stories about him made him appear both a warrior and a god.

As a matter of fact, when Alexander had died in Babylon, his embalmed body was placed in a temple on wheels to be dragged back to Greece. His divine remains were diverted to Alexandria, where a mausoleum was built to house them. He had expressed the wish to be buried at the Oracle of Siwa, where another meteorite – as in the Ka'aba at Mecca – was the stone of prophecy. This one was beset with local emeralds, exactly as the green *lapis exilis* fallen from heaven would be represented as the Grail in Wolfram von Eschenbach's *Parzival*. When the Alexandria mausoleum was burned, the holy corpse was said to have been spirited away to Siwa, where the oracle had prophesied that the Greek general would become a god. In one Islamic miniature, Alexander was depicted as worshipping at the black stone in the Ka'aba. He fascinated the Islamic world and was identified with the Two-horned One in the Koran, who was 'given power on earth, and made his way to the furthest west and furthest east; and in response to an appeal from an oppressed people built a wall or rampart of iron and brass against the incursions of Gog and Magog'.

Certainly, the legend of Alexander would join those of Arthur and Charlemagne to represent the three paladins of medieval chivalry. And another common source, the fall of Troy, was accessible in the *Aeneid* of Virgil, who had taken some of his poem from Homer's *Iliad* and *Odyssey* as well as the exploits of Alexander. His Latin epic dealt less with the trials of the soul than with a particular quest in order to fulfil a divine purpose. Although Aeneas also reached the Land of the Dead, he discovered there the answer to his life's work, the creation of the Roman Empire. So fable was turned into the forecast of history. It would serve as an inspiration for the later Holy Roman Empire and the unity of Christendom.

At her feast for Aeneas, Queen Dido of Carthage produced 'a golden bowl, that shone with gems divine'. Filled with wine, it was used by all the priestly rulers of her country. Jupiter and Bacchus were invoked by its presence. In John Dryden's words about the ceremony:

> *The goblet then she took, with nectar crowned*
> *(Sprinkling the first libations on the ground),*
> *And raised it to her mouth with sober grace,*
> *Then, sipping, offered to the next in place.*

This cup of worship and peace was passed round all the guests in a form of communion, and was later used by Dido to pour wine in marriage vows to Aeneas before Juno, Bacchus and Ceres, holding a horn of plenty in her hand. Deserted by Aeneas on his mission towards Rome, Dido committed suicide, only to encounter her lost lover again in Hades, which he had penetrated by nipping off a golden bough of mistletoe in a sacred oak grove, led there by two doves. All these later symbols of the Grail culminated in the curing of the wound of Aeneas, who had been pierced by a dart, at the touch of the goddess mother Venus. She had brought dittany from Crete and brewed it with ambrosia:

> *Unseen she stands,*
> *Tempering the mixture with her heavenly hands,*
> *And pours it in a bowl, already crowned.*

The holy and healing cups and bowls of Virgil derived from the Greek mysteries, as did so many of the Latin gods. Some of the central myths of the Norse gods also seemed to originate from Greece, as well as the most ancient universal cults of an earth goddess. In the accounts of Valhalla, the *Prose Edda* of the Icelander Snorri Sturluson told of a steaming cauldron named Eldhrímnir, which always served the pork of the everlasting boar Sæhrímnir with his renewable flesh, while the eternal goat Heiórún gave bubbling mead from her teats for the drinking horns of the gods at their perpetual feast. When Thor, the mighty thunder god, was challenged to a drinking bout by the underworld Loki, he could not drain his horn because its end was in the ocean; but he created the tides and the foreshore by his swallowings. The mead cauldron of Ymir inspired strength and wisdom in all who drank from it. These legends of gargantuan bounty were supported by earlier charms to the northern goddess of fertility:

> *Erce, Erce, Erce, Mother of Earth . . .*
> *Hail to thee, Earth, mother of men!*
> *Be fruitful in God's embrace,*
> *Filled with food for the use of men.*

Although the Nordic Frigg, or Freya, was not more powerful than Odin, the ruler of the gods, she was similar to Ceres as the goddess of birth and the seasons. And the northern Adonis, the god Balder, loved by Freyja, had strange affinities with the crucified Christ and the legend of the Fisher King. All things were asked never to harm him, but the blind Hodhr threw a shaft of mistletoe at him and pierced him, so that he died until he was resurrected at the End of the World.

In the tenth-century poem of the *Dream of the Rood*, Christ was seen on a jewelled cross brilliant with light. He was being killed by many men piercing Him with shafts until His blood flowed. His body was raised by His followers and encased in gold and silver, as His blood would be in a multitude of reliquaries. Earlier runes on the Ruthwell Cross quoted the *Dream of the Rood* in reference to the killing of Balder by missiles thrown into his body. The confusion between the myth of Balder bleeding from the shaft sent by the blind Hodhr, and the gospel account of Christ pierced in his side by the Holy Lance of the blind centurion, later called Saint Longinus, was remarkable. And so was the myth of the bleeding wound of the Fisher King, that was made by a lance and incurable except by the right answer of a Knight of the Grail. Such Nordic beliefs may well have derived from the teaching of the Druids or from the older cult of an earth goddess, as shown in the obese figurine of the Aurignacian Venus of Willendorf.

Certainly, Celtic beliefs were developed from Druid worship and influenced the sagas of the Arthurian court, which would in turn have their effect on the later Norse sagas. Blessed vessels were created by the metalwork expertise of the Celtic smiths. The Cimbri sent to the Emperor Augustus as a gift 'the most sacred cauldron in their country'. As part of a series of Belgic pit burials in Kent at the time of Caesar's invasion of Britain, the ornamental Aylesford Bucket was used in the ceremonies of death and rebirth. And the famous silver-plated bowl of the first century, the Gunderstrup Cauldron, was embossed with a Druidic scene of sacrifice and regeneration. Dead warriors from an underworld formed a queue to be given life by a mediatory god, who was plunging a prisoner head first into a vessel shaped like the female pudenda. Contemporary Roman writers told of Celtic human sacrifices, who were suffocated in a tub of blood over which others had their heads severed; but the Gunderstrup scene may only represent a ritual baptism for the resurrection of the departed.

The most ancient sacrificial stones of all, such as the Knowth Stone in County Meath dating from 2500 BC, were used for the ritual slaughter of beasts and people, as they were in classical antiquity. The Irish Druids believed that the soul resided in the brain, an organ so venerated in early myth that the wounded Bran the Blessed asked his companions to sever his head and bury it in Britain to act as a talking oracle – the role of Mimir from his well in Norse legend. And the Dagda, the father of the ancient Irish gods, had a cauldron of plenty named Undri, which fed all the hungry. His gigantic club also had the property of the Holy Lance: it could heal as well as kill.

Other forefathers of the children of Danu, who were said to have populated Ireland from four fabulous cities, were Nuada, or Nodens, and Lug, or Ludd. These legendary settlers brought with them other symbols of the Grail as well as the magic cauldron: Lia Fa'il, or the Stone of Destiny; the Gorian sword which was forged before Excalibur; and the Finian Spear of Victory. Lug, who may have given his name to London, where Bran's head was held to live on Tower Hill, was a sun god such as Mithras. The seizing of his fiery spear by the Irish hero Brian was another prophecy of the Grail legends, for Bran killed the royal owner and took the spear from a boiling cauldron.

The last stand of the Druids took place on Holy Island, off Anglesey, and Irish and Welsh traditions would inform most of the Arthurian legends. The summary of the great authority, Roger Sherman Loomis, defined the Celtic roots of the Grail:

> *It is possible on the Celtic hypothesis to account for the precise form of the vessel, namely a deep platter – its properties of miraculous feeding, of selecting those whom it will feed, of prolongation of youth and life; the bleeding spear and adventures connected with it; the broken sword miraculously mended; the magic ship in which Galahad, Perceval and Bors voyaged; Perceval's sister; the Loathly Damsel; the Siege Perilous; the Maimed King; the visits of Gawain and Perceval to his castle; the question test; Gawain's waking in the open; the names of the Grail Kings and Grail heroes; the introduction of Joseph of Arimathea, and many other details.*

Ancient and pagan beliefs were the sources which filled the Grail in its genesis.

Chapter Two

The Need for the Grail

I have heaped together all that I found from the annals of
the Romans, the writings of the Holy Fathers, and the
traditions of our own old men.

Nennius, *Historia Britonum* (c. 800)

A wise religion adopts the pagan. Old myths can be converted to divine belief. In the Grail legend, the ancient tales
of cauldrons of bounty and horns of plenty were transmuted
in the Middle Ages to Christian cups and platters without end
in their giving of food and drink. Yet the Church of Rome
would never quite swallow the quest for the Grail. For this
search derived from the worst of heresies, which was
preached in the Near East and in Britain before the time of
King Arthur.

The great offence to the Bishop of Rome was the idea of a
direct approach to God without the intercession of the
Church. In the early fifth century, two Celtic monks, Pelagius
and Coelestius, were banished from the Holy City for preaching that through their deeds, human beings could perfect
themselves. There was no original sin, as Saint Augustine
was arguing. Therefore a priest, who might absolve sins, was
unnecessary. The believer could reach heaven by his acts
alone on a sinful earth. 'Everything good, and everything
evil,' Pelagius wrote, 'for which we are either praised or
blamed, is not born with us, but done by us.' This doctrine
was condemned by the Council of Ephesus and was to breed
the first crusade of Europeans against Europeans, when the
perfecti of the Cathars would be destroyed by Simon de

Montfort and the Inquisitors. Pelagius was also the forerunner of Calvin, who would split the Christian world with the doctrines of the Puritan and Protestant faith.

What the Celtic heresy of Pelagius did was to deny the authority of Rome. There had already been British revolts against the Caesars led by the cavalry of Maximus and Constantinus, whose conquests in Gaul foretold the legend of King Arthur's victories on the continent. In 429, Germanus, later called Saint Germain in his bishopric at Auxerre, was sent on the first of two visits to Wales to suppress the Pelagian heresy, which was backed by the paramount ruler Vortigern. Faced with an incursion by the Irish and the Pictish Scots, Germanus used his military knowledge to destroy the invaders near Mold in Flint by a charge of warriors shouting 'Alleluia!' After this victory, Germanus was called Saint Harmon in Wales. He set a precedent for later claims that King Arthur won a battle bearing the image of Jesus Christ or the Virgin Mary on his shield.

Yet Germanus failed to root out Vortigern's resistance to the rule of Rome. The Welsh king invited the raiding Saxons to act as his defenders against the Irish, who had already established a beachhead in Wales, and against the Picts in the north. He ceded land and tribute to the Saxons, who were later followed from the continent by other tribes of Angles and Jutes. The new settlers turned on the natives and destroyed the Romano-British urban civilisation of the south-east of England. In about 540 the Celtic monk Gildas wrote in *The Loss and Conquest of Britain* of 'the general destruction of everything good and the general growth of everything evil throughout the land'. Yet one hero led the resistance, a cavalry commander with a Roman name, Ambrosius Aurelianus. Although he was brave on foot, Gildas wrote, Ambrosius was braver still on horseback.

He first burned Vortigern out of his castle in Flint. He then defeated the Saxons in the north-east, but he could not drive them from their southern territories and downs. The counter-attack ended in the siege of Mons Badonicus. The commander at this battle was not named by Gildas, but in the contemporary Easter Annals, a historical miscellany which still survives in the British Museum, an entry in about 518 reads: 'Battle of Badon, in which Arthur carried the cross of our Lord Jesus Christ on his shoulders for three days and three nights, and the Britons triumphed.'

This was a sustained period of Celtic resistance to Nordic penetration, which would become the stuff of legend. No help had come from Rome, and indeed with the sending by Pope Gregory the Great of a second Saint Augustine to Canterbury, the Saxons would become the spearheads of the Italian version of Christianity in Britain. According to the Venerable Bede, the Pope thought that the Angles should also join the angels in heaven. Certainly, the Anglo-Saxons would confirm the supremacy of the Roman rite in England by the middle of the seventh century, at the Synod of Whitby.

King Arthur, however, was a Celtic war commander and a hero among the native peoples of Cornwall, Wales, Ireland and southern Scotland. A different Byzantine rite had passed from the Mediterranean along the old tin trade routes to these Celtic civilisations. From that Greek learning, the Irish monasteries were becoming the leading lights of what were later miscalled the Dark Ages. They were sending missionaries, pilgrim saints and hermits after the example of the desert Christian Fathers to Wales, the Isle of Man and Scotland. There in the time of King Arthur were concentrated the early Christian gravestones inscribed in the Ogham script, that writing in stone of grooves and notches which may have derived from the Druids. Saint Petroc carried the faith to the west of England and Brittany where Celtic refugees had already fled from the Anglo-Saxons: many churches were named after him. Saint Samson also sailed to Cornwall and Brittany with his Irish chariot: his voyage was commemorated on a stained-glass window in the Cathedral of Dol. Saint Columba brought the Irish Word of God to the west of Scotland and the north of England; Saint Guillermus carried it to what would be called Normandy. Other pilgrim saints reached Galicia in Spain, and Orkney, the Shetlands, the Faroes and even Iceland. And Saint Columbanus took the Irish influence deep into France and Italy itself. His foundation of the original monastery of Saint Etienne in Nevers in about 600 is commemorated there: though it was taken over by Benedictines during the Cluniac reform of the eleventh century, a magnificent Grail window still shows a holy lamp burning above the sun-disc at the back of the head of Christ at the Last Supper, blessing the bread of His body on a golden platter, and a bowl of wine.

The most ancient church in England, the wattle building at Glastonbury, was traditionally founded in 433 by Saint Patrick himself; his supposed bones were placed in a stone pyramid covered with gold and silver by the high altar of the first abbey. Other Celtic saints followed him there – notably Columba, Brigit and Benignus – and Glastonbury, or 'the glassy isle', became a mirror for the faith of pilgrims crossing the Irish Sea. The influence of the Greek rite there was proven by the recent excavation of a Byzantine censer on the edge of the abbey precinct; also the presence of Gnostic heresy in the jasper episcopal ring carved with a serpent god, belonging to the Abbot Seffrid Pelochin and still on display at Chichester Cathedral. Although Glastonbury gave way to the Roman influence after the Synod of Whitby, its Celtic past made it continually revered. The Chalice Well and the Tor were held by the Welsh to be manifestations of Annwn, the Otherworld, while Saint David was also said to have been a visitor. Certainly, the *Anglo-Saxon Chronicle* reported that the Pope sent a piece of the True Cross to King Alfred, who then reputedly presented it to the abbey. Its relics would make it, in William of Malmesbury's words, a 'heavenly sanctuary on earth'. Among them would be manna and parts of the rods of Moses and Aaron; the bones of Saint John the Baptist and the milk of the Virgin Mary; and many sacred remains of the Passion, including a nail from the Cross. There was no Grail in early times, however, in spite of the abbey's later identification with Avalon, and the death of

King Arthur and the coming of Joseph of Arimathea to Britain.

An old Cornish legend asserted that Joseph of Arimathea arrived there with his relative, the boy Jesus, and taught him how to extract tin and purge it of its wolfram. According to Herodotus and Diodorus Siculus, the tin trade did exist between Phoenicia and Cornwall in those times. Certainly, the guild of the Cornish tinners used to shout after the metal was flashed: 'Joseph was in the trade.' In Somerset the story was that Christ and Joseph came by ship to Tarshish and stayed in Summerland, another name for the county, and in a place called Paradise. The people of Priddy on the top of the Mendip Hills, the centre of ancient copper and lead mining, also believed that the two holy men spent time in the village. And there was the enduring creed at Glastonbury of the final visit of Joseph of Arimathea with the Grail containing Christ's blood, which he is meant to have dropped into the prehistoric Chalice Well. Joseph's grave was discovered there in medieval times, as were the tombs of King Arthur and Guinevere. Over the Arimathean's bones was an inscription: I CAME TO THE BRITONS AFTER I BURIED CHRIST. I TAUGHT. I REST.

To this faith was added the legend of another visit by Joseph with the young Jesus. Saint Augustine believed the story well enough to write to Pope Gregory that on 'a royal island' to the west, the first missionaries from Rome found a wattle church 'constructed by no human art, but by the hands of Christ Himself, for the salvation of His people'. Allegedly, Joseph had been granted twelve hides of land by the local pagan king, Arviragus, to build his church. This grant appeared to be confirmed by folios from the Norman Domesday Book: 'The Home of God, in the great Monastery of Glastonbury, called the Secret of The Lord. This Glastonbury church possesses in its own Villa XII hides of land which have never paid tax.' The route of Joseph and Jesus to the west of England was held to be from the French Mont Saint-Michel to the English one – the Arthurian voyage of Tristan with La Belle Isoud to King Mark. They then rounded Land's End making for the Jesus Well near Padstow; next on to the Paradise area on the Brue River marked on old Ordnance Survey maps; then by waterway to Godney, the port of Glastonbury, the reputed Isle of Avalon; and back over the Mendip crests to mining Priddy and down the Axe to Uphill on the Bristol Channel for the return voyage to Phoenicia.

The Celtic religious renaissance of the sixth and seventh centuries was based on the Atlantic sea routes, and was set against the authority of Mediterranean Rome. It was spread by holy pilgrims and hermits, the apostles of the later Grail romances. It spoke in resistance to the Nordic, Germanic and later Arabic assaults on the Celtic folk. It demanded a political hero who would defend his people and their independent faith from their enemies. It chose Arthur, the *dux bellorum* or war leader mentioned in the mid-eighth century by the Welsh monk Nennius as the victor of twelve battles, ending in a final defeat in 539 described in the Easter Annals: 'The Battle of Camlann, in which Arthur and Medraut [Mordred] perished. And there was a plague in Britain and Ireland.'

Ignored in centuries of Grail studies has been the actual process of Christian belief in Arthur's Britain. If he carried the image of Jesus on his banner at the siege of Badon, what might the Son of God say to him? If he were a Pelagian like Vortigern, if he rode with the contemporary Celts for their independence against the Anglo-Saxons who were being converted to Rome, then he might have followed the words from the Sermon of the Mount in the Gospel of Saint Matthew: 'Be ye therefore perfect, even as your Father which is in heaven is perfect.'

For the heresy of salvation through good works was the inspiration of the Knights on the quest for the Grail. By his virtue, each member of the Round Table might reach the light of God and the Holy Spirit without the need of a priest to absolve his sins. These wandering mailed horsemen were advised on their way to the Grail Castle by holy men,

modelled on the travelling Celtic preachers who were
spreading their independent faith over the northern Atlantic
seaboard. In the first Grail romance by Chrétien de Troyes,
Perceval was put on the right path for his return to the Grail
Castle by his hermit uncle, who told him that the wounded
Fisher King lived only on the communion host, which
reached him directly from heaven and the Holy Spirit, not
through the Church of Rome. The legends of Arthur and the
Grail were to enshrine the resistance of many peoples to the
authority of the Holy See. That is why they would prove so
popular in their spread across Europe and further, until by the
twelfth century, the Prior of Tewkesbury could state that the
praise of Arthur had reached every place, even Italy.

He is only a little less known to the people of Asia than
to the Britons, as we are informed by the pilgrims who
return from the Eastern lands. The peoples of the East
speak of him, as they do in the West . . . Rome, queen of
cities, sings of his acts, while his wars are known in its
former rival Carthage. Antioch, Armenia and Palestine
celebrate his deeds.

Rome was to try and take over the legend of King Arthur and
the Grail, although it was heretical. This was because the
stories of Camelot and chivalry would inspire the crusaders
to the Levant. Pope Gregory the Great had been happy to
substitute the pagan for the Christian in England. As he wrote
to his envoy Abbot Mellitus:

I have come to the conclusion that the temples of the
idols in England should not on any account be
destroyed. Augustine must smash the idols, but the
temples themselves should be sprinkled with holy water
and altars set up in them in which relics are to be
enclosed. For we ought to take advantage of well-built
temples by purifying them from devil-worship and
dedicating them to the service of the true God. In this

way, I hope the people (seeing their temples are not destroyed) will leave their idolatry and yet continue to frequent the places as formerly, so coming to know and revere the true God.

Perhaps the Great Bowl of the silver Mildenhall Treasure, now in the British Museum, exemplifies the papal wisdom. Among its fourth-century praise of Dionysus and Pan and the demigods and nymphs pouring pitchers of plenty or opening the lids of vases of bounty, Christian fish symbols already burst from the beard and locks of the central sun god Mithras. The one religion used the other to infiltrate the new faith.

Yet in the later case of the Grail, the attempt of Rome to sanctify the legends would be half-hearted. Arthur and the Knights of the Round Table would not be ingested as were other cults of protest. At the time of the historical Arthur, his stance as the Celtic leader in war and faith was clear. He stood against the authority of imperial Rome, which had abandoned its dominions to the ravages of the pagans, although these might later be converted by Christian Rome. To all the emperors and kings who would need to resist the Holy See, Arthur would become the symbol of that opposition.

Where Was Camelot?

The twelve battles in which, according to Nennius, Arthur was the victor can only be surmised as being somewhere on the mainland of Britain. They have variously been sited in Lincolnshire, Northumberland, Cheshire, Strathclyde, Somerset, Wiltshire, Berkshire and East Anglia. Certainly, a defence against the Anglo-Saxon incursion would have involved fighting on a shifting frontier drawn from Devon along the Welsh borders to the Firth of Forth, while the Irish pushing into Pembroke and Argyll implied separate battles on the western shores. These were usually cavalry actions against footsoldiers, for Arthur probably took over the tactics of Ambrosius. In the twelfth-century Black Book of Carmarthen, a collection of early Welsh manuscripts, Arthur's heroes were described in a battle near Southampton as riding swift chargers with long legs, 'red, swooping as milk-white eagles'. And in the late-sixth-century *Gododdin*, Arthur was said to be supreme at slaughter and glutting black ravens.

Keeping a force of hundreds of mailed knights in the field involved sophisticated planning and a wandering court. Recent excavations at Cadbury Castle and other Iron Age hill forts have shown that Celtic warlords returned to these ancient strongholds behind their ditches and earth walls, adding stone and wooden ramparts along with gate towers and halls. Fodder for the horses was easily found on the hill slopes, although not for long. Surprise attack was unlikely over open ground. The feudal system was not yet in place as in the Grail romances. So the court could not be supported by the local country people for much more than a month. King Arthur and his fighters had to ride from place to place to maintain themselves. Even in the late Middle Ages, the royal court was a moveable feast. In Arthur's day, Camelot was on the hoof all over Britain. That palace of later dreams went where the next campaign was.

The probable sites of Arthur's travelling Camelot were these: the Roman city of Colchester, or Camelodunum, where he would have fought the Saxons in East Anglia; Cadbury Castle, where he might resist any advance into the West Country, with Tintagel as a last bastion; Carleon-on-Usk, where he would have struck against the Irish colony in South Wales; Dinas Bran, near Llangollen, which was called after the Celtic god of the speaking head and was given the name of the Grail Castle Corbenic in medieval times; Carlisle, where he would have contained the Danish invaders; Arthur's Seat in Edinburgh, where he would have opposed the Picts from the north, and from the west the Irish, then called the Scotti. The necessity of feeding the cavalry would have kept Arthur in the saddle, as it did the original

Celts of the Russian steppes, who had fought another legendary hero, Alexander the Great.

Tactics insist on movement. That was why the ancient chronicles and Grail romances altered places and names so frequently. And as these sagas and accounts were usually sung or spoken by many voices before they were set down in writing, the variations in spelling and in translation eddied as banners in the wind. What is certain is that the truth of Arthur was taken up by the Celtic bards to create the legend of a conquering hero, who would reflect his fame on to his people. Already by the seventh century, four British royal families had given a son the name of Arthur. He became the Matter of Britain, as opposed to the Matter of France which glorified Charlemagne the supreme Emperor. And there was also the Matter of the classical age of Homer and Virgil, the heroes of Troy and Rome, and of Alexander the Great. These bardic tales would provide the synthesis of the European romances of the Middle Ages, where the Mediterranean traditions met the British, French and German to create the stories of the personal search for the divine.

The actual Celtic Grails which existed from Arthur's time were hanging bowls, not communion chalices in the hands of priests. These round bronze pendants, ornamented with enamel and scrollwork, have been discovered in Warwickshire and Lincolnshire; also three at the sumptuous ship burial at Sutton Hoo, made by a master smith for the East Anglian court. On one bowl, there are six red enamel medallions on the sides, while on the lid appears an emblem of early Christianity – the fish, a Greek acronym of the name Jesus Christ. Simpler metal vessels, which hung over hearths and fires, had held the daily food of hunting and gathering people for dozens of centuries. Pieces of game and roots were added to the top of the stockpot, which, if replenished, provided an inexhaustible supply of soup and stew. This was the material origin of the Celtic Grails, which would feed all who came to them. Perhaps the last vestige of that tradition of a flowing bowl is the stirrup cup, still passed round from saddle to saddle at a modern hunt.

In the early Welsh legends of Arthur, however, the King led his knights on a raid to seize the Spoils of Annwn, including a magic cauldron of rebirth. This lay in another world, or Faerie Fortress; as the Grail Castle would. The rim of the cauldron was ornamented in the style of contemporary hanging bowls with dark-blue enamel and pearls. As *Culhwch and Olwen*, a bardic poem of the time, declared, the cauldron could provide meat and drink for everybody. Yet in this version, Arthur filled it with the treasures of Ireland and took it back from that country to his own. And in the Taliesin poems, another cauldron, that of Ceridwen, gave him divine inspiration and wisdom when he licked three drops of the boiling mixture in the iron vessel off his fingers.

Evidence of the Roman Church's growing suspicion of the legend of Arthur was evident in later Welsh tales about him, in which he was presented as a trickster and a thief. And in various Lives of the Saints, he was shown to be evil. Before the writing of Geoffrey of Monmouth's favourable *History of the Kings of Britain*, Arthur was described in *The Life of Cadog* as full of lust and perversity, while *The Life of Padarn* turned him into a mean and despotic ruler. The Holy See continued to view Arthur as a rebel against its claims to supremacy.

The Words About Arthur

The few who could read in the age of Arthur and in the centuries to follow were priests, and the language was Latin. Most people were illiterate. They heard what they thought, and they thought that was what they knew. Homer, and the bards who succeeded him at the courts of the later warlords of Europe, sang of the exploits of heroes. They also spelled out the genealogies of their patrons, connecting these families to the superhumans of past legend.

A strange legitimacy was conferred by Homer in *The Iliad* on the later dynasties of the Greek cities, connecting them to the gods as well as the myths. Virgil in his *Aeneid* performed the same sleight of birth for the Roman emperors. These revered epics persuaded the Greeks and the Romans that their rulers were blessed and came from the right holy blood. Such was the task of Geoffrey of Monmouth when he wrote in 1135 the sourcebook of King Arthur and the Matter of Britain. He was providing proof that the Norman conquest had inherited the myths of blood and soil of the defeated North Sea islanders. The Normans were the true heirs of the Celts. Both peoples had resisted the Germanic tribes and the power of Rome.

In diplomacy, a country usually allies itself with the enemy of its own immediate enemy. With the manuscript, *The History of the Kings of Britain*, the Welsh or Breton Geoffrey of Monmouth could build up the legend of Arthur to illustrate the fact that the Celts and the Normans had defeated the Anglo-Saxon incursion into England. He went much further and left out much more. The Normans were actually Vikings who had invaded France and taken over Normandy and Brittany in the tenth century. Before that, they had destroyed and colonised Orkney, the Shetlands, northern Scotland, the Western Isles and parts of Ireland, as well as pillaging the monasteries and cities of much of northern Britain. The victory of William the Conqueror in England was only the prelude to the spread of Norman rule to the south-west of France, Sicily and southern Italy, where they became the adversaries of Islam, then spreading its faith across Africa and the Mediterranean to the north of Spain. This clash between Christians and Muslims led to the crusades. Jerusalem had already fallen to Frankish kings when Geoffrey of Monmouth concocted a European empire for King Arthur as large as the true one of Charlemagne.

From the syntheses of the epics to date, Geoffrey created the propaganda for the Norman Empire. By his invention, the mythological Brutus of Troy colonised Britain and released it from a race of giants led by Gogmagog. Telling many more tall stories, two of which Shakespeare used in *King Lear* and

Cymbeline, Geoffrey took his fabulous story on to Arthur. Inspired by the magician Merlin, who was confused with Ambrosius Aurelianus, this legendary emperor spread his dominion to Norway, where the Vikings had originated, and on to the Rhine in a mastery of France. He defeated Flollo, then the Roman tribune of Gaul, in a brilliant contemporary joust. Arthur felled his enemy from his horse and was laid low himself. Covered with blood from a head wound, the British Emperor struck the Roman with his sword Caliburn, or Excalibur, and so sent him to the ground and his soul to the winds. Normandy was given to his cupbearer Sir Belvedere, and Anjou to his seneschal Sir Kay. Thus the Normans were confirmed as the heirs of the Celts and the Vikings, and as the opponents of Rome, which was only saved from Arthur's advance by his death at Camlann and burial on the Isle of Avalon.

Geoffrey of Monmouth insisted that the deeds of Arthur lay in the memories and traditions of many people as surely as if they had been written down. He claimed to have read them in an ancient book given to him by Walter, the Archdeacon of Oxford. Most of the troubadours and chroniclers of the Grail romances would claim ancient sources for their endeavours. William of Malmesbury, who had created his own *Deeds of the Kings of England* ten years before Geoffrey's *History*, declared that his rival invented everything about Arthur and his successors 'from an excessive love of lying, or for the sake of pleasing the Britons.' But William also asserted that Arthur should be commemorated in true histories and not only in Breton fables, because of his long resistance and restoration of Celtic morale.

In later colonial empires, trade would follow the flag. But in the twelfth century, song followed the sword. In the French and British fiefdoms of the Normans, the Welsh and Breton bards and troubadours were predominant. They were like Widsith in the early English poem of the Far Traveller, who claimed to have sung all over Europe and the Near East. He glorified his peers:

29

*Thus wandering, the minstrels travel as chance will
have it through the lands of many different peoples.
Always they are bound to come across, in the north or
the south, some person who is touched by their song and
is generous with his gifts, who will increase his reputation in front of his henchmen showing his nobility of
spirit before worldly things pass away, the light and the
life. He who works for his own good name will be
rewarded on earth by a strong and steady fame.*

After the Dark Ages, Celtic minstrels were moving through
the Atlantic areas, spreading the legends of Arthur and his
companions. Transcendent among them at the court of
Poitou was the Welshman Bleheris. He was the 'fabulous
translator' of Arthurian legend into Norman French, and he
was commemorated by two rivals as someone who knew the
history of all the counts and all the kings of Britain, and 'all
the stories of the Grail'.

The term troubadour derived from the Provençal word *tro-
bar*, to compose, to seek and to find. In that sense, the lays of
the minstrels were quests for the Grail put to words and
music. Certainly, their art was influenced by oriental singers
from Spain as much as by Celtic bards or classical legends.
Arabesques, with their tantalising sadness, became part of
their technique, and the pilgrims and knights setting out to
Palestine repeated the refrains. The wandering minstrels
were the entertainers and reporters of their age, which could
not always distinguish between fancy and fact.

The pilgrim Celtic saints had converted the Atlantic
seaboard to the Greek rite. Now the Welsh and Breton troubadours spread the word of King Arthur, his exploits and his
empire from the ocean through the continent by word of
mouth. A written French text, derived from Geoffrey of
Monmouth's Latin *History*, was set down by Wace of Jersey
in the Channel Islands. He dedicated his creative translation
of the Matter of Britain, *Roman de Brut*, to Eleanor of
Aquitaine, the wife of Henry II of England and Normandy.

With her possessions, the king could claim an Anglo-French empire almost the size of that of Arthur in *The History of the Kings of Britain*. Wace added to the story the legend of the Round Table, which he had heard from other Celtic sources, and ended his account with the hope of the undying King Arthur, ready to be resurrected when his people might need him.

These two seminal texts were copied out hundreds of times in the next centuries before the coming of printing. But in this illiterate era, it was the wandering minstrels who spread the word of Arthur, using Geoffrey of Monmouth and Wace as cue sheets. Since Homer, flattering bards had been the chief entertainers of the courts and the counts. From Poitou and Aquitaine, the fame of Arthur reached Italy, probably with the Breton contingent assembling at Bari for the First Crusade. The early-twelfth-century arch over the north door of Modena Cathedral portrays Arthur of Britain, called Artus, and his knights as they rode to deliver the Queen of Camelot from the Dolorous Tower. In 1165, a mosaic was laid in the cathedral of Otranto, near Bari, showing Arturus Rex carrying a sceptre and riding a goat. This mocking description of the Celtic hero as a kind of devil on a playful pavement satirised the suspicion of the Roman Catholic Church in regard to British and Norman resistance. At the end of the century, Gervase of Tilbury visited the Norman court in Sicily and reported that King Arthur had been sighted living in the fiery crater of Mount Etna, that natural cauldron of Annwn. Again, the Normans of the time were struggling with the papacy for control of southern Italy, and the myth of Arthur's return suited their aggressive diplomacy.

The spreading of the stories of Arthur and his Knights over Europe and the Near East was the seedbed of the Grail. The age of the crusades yearned for a holy mission as well as a justification for taking over new lands in the Mediterranean. Papal blessing for the counterattack on Islam and the capture of the Kingdom of Jerusalem was not enough. For the

Norman, Frankish and German emperors, kings, dukes and counts were often opposed to the political aims of the papacy, which strove to assert its authority over all secular powers. What the chivalry of Europe demanded was a sacred quest which sanctified individual bloody actions without the need for absolution from the Catholic Church, which might withhold the shriving of sins for the benefit of its wily diplomacy. For Rome denied the giving of communion to lay people in the thirteenth century. The Body and Blood of Christ, the host and the chalice were reserved for the priest. Now the Grail could answer the prayer of the knight alone on his way ahead.

Chapter Three

The Knights of the Grail

> There has been a succession of attempts to force the Grail
> to yield a monolithic meaning, to determine for it a precise
> synonym. To some it is the chalice of the Eucharist, to
> others a misinterpretation of the horn of plenty of Celtic
> mythology, and to still others a phallic symbol when taken
> in conjunction with the Lance . . . Was its content the
> Trinity, the Eucharist, or the *manna* of the Hebrews?
>
> Frederick W. Locke, *The Quest for the Holy Grail*

An invention has components. Yet these bits do not cohere
before the assembly. They are merely sources without a
stream, shreds without a shape. Chrétien de Troyes created
the story of the Grail in his *Perceval*, putting it together from
many ancient and contemporary tales, as well as from his
own imagination. His was a synthesis of genius, making
molten many myths to forge for the chivalry of his time a
justification for the search for glory and for God.

For his trade, Chrétien was fortunate in his birth and
career. He was probably born about 1135 at Troyes in
Champagne in France. The city was a crossroads of Eastern
beliefs returning with the crusaders to jostle with the
Christian faith; also a frontier where the Matter of Britain and
Arthur met the Matter of France and Charlemagne. Chrétien
was trained in Latin to be a priest, but became instead a translator of Ovid, particularly the *Art of Love* and *Remedy for
Love*, and two stories from the *Metamorphoses*, the changing
of men and women into beasts and birds. He is believed to

have composed *Erec and Enide*, a tale of Camelot, and he also wrote three more romances for the cultivated Marie, Countess of Champagne, the daughter of the French King Louis VII and Eleanor of Aquitaine, who later married the English King Henry II. His next manuscript was called *Cligès* and dealt with Tristan, although Chrétien set it in Greek Byzantium. The adultery of Queen Guinevere was recounted in *Lancelot* or *The Knight in the Cart*, while *Yvain* or *The Knight with the Lion* was penned in praise of noble love and marriage.

Countess Marie and her mother, indeed, were said to have presided at a Court of Love, which insisted – as did King Arthur's Round Table – on a knightly code of chaste behaviour to women. Marie made Champagne the vineyard of the culture of courtesy and chivalry, but when her husband, Count Henry, went away to the Holy Land and died a week after his return to Troyes, she left public life, refusing to marry the new patron of her poet Chrétien. This was the widowed Philip of Alsace, Count of Flanders and a temporary Regent of France. He died of the plague on the Third Crusade without recapturing Jerusalem, now lost to the Muslim armies of Saladin. In one sense, the invention of the quest for the Grail would symbolise other crusades to regain the Holy City in Palestine.

Chrétien dedicated his last unfinished romance, *Perceval* or *The Story of the Grail*, to this Count of Flanders, whose father, Thierry of Alsace, had even bequeathed a Chapel of the Holy Blood of Christ – the sacred relic was his reward from the King of Jerusalem for valour shown on the Second Crusade and on three other expeditions against the forces of Islam. In a great procession in 1150, he had donated the precious fluid to the city of Bruges. The chapel built to house the relic still exists; round dark brick arches lead to a shadowy altar, over which a golden pelican now settles. The bird was a symbol of the Redeemer, as it was meant to feed its young with its own blood, as shown on the mosaic in Charlemagne's chapel at Aachen; it also represented a distilling vessel for the process of alchemy. Two black Grail tombstones on the floor, however, badly worn from innumerable feet, recall the containers which once held Christ's Blood.

In the neighbouring Gothic church of Our Lady, where the only Michelangelo Madonna and Child outside Italy sits serenely on a side altar, there are early tomb frescoes of the Virgin Mary seated with the Christ child on an oblong Ark of the Covenant, with the twin candles and pillars of the Temple beside them. Moreover, in *Our Lady of the Seven Seas*, the admirable painting by the Renaissance master Adriaan Isenbrandt, the overlay of the early cult of the Magdalene by the Virgin Mary was made evident. The Mother of Christ not only washes the Holy Blood off His body taken from the Cross, but is also the first to see Him out of the Tomb with the kneeling Mary Magdalene wearing the red of her sins. None of the Gospels declare that the Virgin was there at all.

Influenced by the mass faith in the Holy Blood and the fierce stance against heresy taken by Philip of Flanders, Chrétien de Troyes turned the Celtic Grail myths of pagan cauldrons into Christian symbols. In fact, he claimed that he had merely put into verse a lost book loaned to him by his patron.

> *He tried and tried time after time*
> *The best tale ever told to rhyme*
> *The royal courts recount the tale:*
> *It is the story of the Grail.*

Count Philip had fallen out with the King of France before going to the Holy Land. Chrétien also presented Perceval as a rebel against authority. A simple Welsh youth with a lethal proficiency with javelins, he badgered passing knights to find out what they did, and then deserted his mother to make his way to the court of Arthur. There he discovered that a Red Knight had insulted the King and had stolen a gold cup. He pursued the knight and killed him with a javelin through his eye, taking his armour and his horse. He also had the gold cup returned to Arthur. Untaught, Perceval went on his way towards the Grail Castle.

This ingenious opening prophesied the mysteries of the mission. Perceval was then too simple to see the quest for the Holy Grail as more than a fight to recover a stolen precious object. And so he was unaware when he met the crippled King of the Grail Castle fishing in a boat nearby. Directed to that place, Perceval found himself in the finest fortress this side of Beirut in the Near East. There he was given a sword of Arabian, Grecian and Venetian work. The following procession of the Grail was also associated with the East and the crusaders, such as Philip, Count of Flanders. It was led by a squire carrying a white lance with a tip that bled drops of crimson blood.

The discovery of the Holy Lance below the cathedral of Antioch had saved the First Crusade from disaster. This relic was held to be the iron point which the blind Centurion Longinus had put into the side of Christ, only to have his sight restored by the blood and water of the Saviour running down into his eyes. That sacred flow was also said to have been collected by Joseph of Arimathea in the cup used at the Last Supper, a vessel which was to become the chief symbol of the Grail. Yet Perceval in Chrétien's Grail Castle next saw two squires bearing candle-holders, each with ten lights, as if in a Byzantine or Jewish ceremony. These also represented the ever-burning twin golden chandeliers which shone above the tomb of the Prophet Muhammad at Medina. In other romances, *The Song of Antioch* and *The Conquest of Jerusalem*, the champion of the First Crusade, Godfrey de Bouillon, swore that he would seize these two candelabra and place them in their rightful place by the Tomb of Christ. Then a maiden appeared with a jewelled Grail, shining with brilliant light as in the Holy Fire ceremony at Easter in the Church of the Holy Sepulchre. She was followed by another maiden with a silver platter, who passed by the bed of the maimed Fisher King.

This blessed vision of Perceval was nearer to pantheism than to the doctrine of the Roman Catholic Church. Although the bleeding lance was associated with the death of Christ, it also had a parallel in the magic spear of Welsh and Irish literature. This belonged to the god Lug, and was both lethal and life-giving. It could kill as well as make the desert green. It could destroy all the royal enemies, but also a whole kingdom. Its prick could ravage as well as regenerate. The harm of its point could only be blunted in a cauldron or bowl of boiling blood and water: the male principle creating birth from the female. Otherwise, its wounds might lay waste to the land of the Fisher King, who was incurably maimed by its thrust between his thighs.

Chrétien de Troyes went further by combining the Celtic and Nordic cauldron and horn of plenty with the communion chalice. He was not, however, the first to use the word 'Grail'. Meaning a 'dish', *graal* had occurred previously in a romance about Alexander the Great, and earlier as *gradalis*, or a bowl to serve delicacies. In *Perceval*, the vessel appeared to have a lid, which was removed before it served its inexhaustible food for the needs of all present. Platter or closed bowl, it was a giver of plenty, as was the Welsh *dysgl*, one of the legendary Thirteen Treasures of Great Britain. Yet it also contained the host or Body of Christ, the sole food of the Fisher King. And it was carried by a young woman.

This was anathema to the Church of Rome. The communion cup could only be borne by a male priest. The Elevation of the Host to the congregation remained a sacred mystery, which would not be unveiled. Yet to Chrétien, all those in search of perfection might see the Grail themselves. He was associating the giving by Christ of His Body and Blood with pagan goddesses of fertility, the chalice representing the womb. He was also alluding to the Gnostic heresies from the Near East that were spreading across Flanders, Brittany, Champagne, Provence and Italy. These spoke of a *Sophia*, who embodied divine wisdom. The Grail in her hands was the Word and the Light of God, which blazed like the sun on the darkness of this earth, where Satan was fighting for mastery of the flesh.

For the Gnostics, the most significant of Biblical texts came from Saint John the Evangelist: *God is Light, and in Him is no darkness at all*. Their preachers saw themselves as John the Baptist in the Gospel of Saint John: *He was not that Light, but was sent to bear witness of that Light. That was the true Light, which lighteth every man that cometh into the world*. That was the Light that shone from Chrétien's Grail, carried in the female hands of wisdom and rebirth. The Gospel also contained the stories of Nicodemus and Joseph of Arimathea, so significant in the medieval romances about King Arthur and his Knights.

The host within the Grail seen by Perceval was not the communion wafer of Catholic absolution, but rather the blessed bread distributed among all believers at the feasts of the early Christian communities and later the Cathar heretics. It did not so much represent the Body of Christ as the miracle of the loaves and the fishes, where Jesus fed the multitude – the fish was a Greek sign of Christianity, while the Fisher King symbolised the search for salvation within his Castle. In *Perceval*, the maiden carrying the covered bowl of the Grail was followed by another young woman with a silver platter. They were serving sacred food to the Knights of the Grail, but it was not the Eucharist. And Perceval saw no priest, altar or cross inside the castle walls.

Although Chrétien de Troyes was a French-speaking cleric and poet, his influence came from Britain, Rome, Byzantium and the Jerusalem of the crusades. He might have visited the first two places; he knew of the history and creeds of all four. In the sacred objects of the Grail procession, he combined the Celtic and the Nordic with the Christian, the Cabbala and Islam. The bleeding white lance derived from the castle of the god Lug, as well as the hand of Saint Longinus, who let out the blood of Christ with it. The candelabra borne by two young men suggested ancient Jewish and Byzantine ceremonies as well as the tomb of the Prophet Muhammad. There was, indeed, a famous school of the Cabbala at Troyes in Chrétien's time, led by the renowned Rashi. The golden Grail set with gems was a Celtic cornucopia and a Christian chalice. The silver platter represented a cauldron of plenty and the dish on which was once set both the head of John the Baptist and the lamb of the Last Supper. The Grail held many sources and had many shapes. That was only to be expected from a poet who had translated Ovid's *Metamorphoses*. Stirring and blending was natural to the chef of *Perceval*.

Chrétien's last romance contributed to the spiritual awakening of Western Christendom at the time. There were discoveries or rediscoveries in science, mathematics and philosophy; the founding of convents, monasteries and military orders; the flowering of chivalry and courtly love; the making of the Gothic cathedrals; and the arrival of the crusades in Jerusalem, there to build a holy and heavenly city on earth. The quest of the crusaders fed on the quest for the Grail. Both were martial pilgrimages in search of the place of the Holy Spirit; also of peace and plenty on earth before a vision of heaven.

When King Richard the Lionheart came within sight of Jerusalem, he hid his eyes under his shield and turned his crusading army away, as Lancelot did before the Grail. He did not feel fit to achieve his desire. For only a knight without sin could reach the Grail, which ministered to the needs of its guardians in a castle on the Mount of Salvation. The way to the Grail was by trial and test. A knight had to survive sitting at a Last Supper in the empty Judas seat, the Siege Perilous. If he was a sinner, he was swallowed up. If he was stainless, he might search for the divine Light – in fact as well as in fiction.

The Church and the Knight

Perceval invented the bardic quest for the Grail. Yet Saint Bernard, the son of a nobleman from Burgundy, created the real Knights of the Grail. With his brothers and friends in the early twelfth century, he built a monastery at Citeaux and an abbey at Clairvaux, which would become the spiritual beacons of the Europe of the crusades. The genius of Bernard was to put together the Church with chivalry. To defend his Cistercian Order of white monks, he had sanctified the Order of the Knights of the Temple of Solomon, with their black-and-white banner, *Le Beauséant*, of light and dark.

The Cistercian monks and the Knights Templar were always to be linked by place and sympathy, but not by history. For when the Templars were proscribed as heretics and lost their thousands of Commanderies, the white monks kept their distance and their monasteries. Bernard himself was always a disciple of Rome. He could not foresee the consequences of his diplomacy with the Vatican in securing papal blessing for the armoured guardians of pilgrims visiting the holy places in Jerusalem, where the Templars had their base. His bones and his portrait still grace the Treasury of the Cathedral of Saint Peter and Saint Paul at Troyes.

In 1146 Saint Bernard, indeed, preached the Second Crusade to King Louis of France and many nobles at Vézelay. His fervency and tongue of quicksilver, praising the remission of grievous crimes for all who took up the cross, provoked a gale of acceptance. His hearers cried out for the favours of Christ. Before too long, all the prepared red strips of cloth were finished. Saint Bernard had to give up his red robe to be cut into pieces for those who would go east. His helpers became tailors and stitched the pledges of the holy pilgrimage on to the faithful. An orgy of commitment promised another holy war. After preaching later to the people of France, Bernard was able to write to the Pope, 'The Crusaders have multiplied to infinity. Villages and towns are now deserted. You will scarcely find one man for every seven women.'

Saint Bernard's sermons were almost impossible for a Christian knight to resist. The promise of absolution was paramount. In his letter to the English, he emphasised his message:

*What are you doing, you mighty men of valour? What
are you doing, you servants of the cross? Will you throw
to the dogs that which is most holy? Will you cast pearls
before swine? O mighty soldier, O man of war, you now
have a cause for which you can fight without endanger-
ing your soul; a cause in which to win is glorious and
for which to die is but gain . . .*

*Take the sign of the cross. At once you will have
indulgence for all the sins which you confess with a con-
trite heart. It does not cost you much to buy, and if you
wear it with humility, you will find that it is the Kingdom
of Heaven.*

This was a sermon to knights in search of the Grail, if the
finding of the Grail also dealt with the defence of
Jerusalem. Saint Bernard was not preaching a personal
quest for the divine, but the remission of the sins of the crusaders through the Church of Rome, which also wished to
assert its authority over the warlords of Europe. The refrain
of a popular crusading song offered the same benefit: *He
who leaves with Louis need not worry about Hell/His soul
will go to Paradise with Our Lord's angels as well.* Bernard
also persuaded the Pope to consecrate the future Knights of
the Grail, the Templars, founded in Jerusalem in 1118 by
Hugh de Payens and eight companions from Champagne
and Provence. Their duty was to guard the pilgrims to the
Holy Land, where they were masons as well as monks with
a sword. Their strongholds and chapels would become
models for many Grail castles, while their service to
God would make them examples to all chivalry before they
were condemned as traitors to orthodoxy. In his day,
Bernard of Clairvaux compared them to the early saints and
pilgrims:

*They come and go at a sign from their commander; they
wear the clothes which he gives them, seeking neither
other garments nor other food. They are wary of all*

excess in food or clothing, desiring only what is needful.
They live all together, without women or children . . .
Insolent words, vain acts, immoderate laughter, com-
plaints and murmurs, when they are perceived, do not
go unpunished . . . They crop their hair close because
the Gospels tell them it is a shame for a man to tend his
hair. They are never seen combed and rarely washed,
their beards are matted, they reek of dust and bear the
stains of the heat and their harness.

This way of life was modelled on the questing knights of the
Round Table as well as on the early Christian saints. Here the
standards of chivalry met the ordinances of the Church. But
these directives could not bridge the deepening chasm
between Templar wisdom and the Holy See. The knights of
that order were a permanent standing army in Palestine, a
few hundred horsemen holding the Holy City and a broken
necklace of castles across the waste. They were particularly
influenced by the rival Isma'ili warrior sect of the Assassins,
who held fortresses and territories in the mountains near the
Caspian Sea and in Syria. Their founder and first Grand
Master, Hassan Ibn al-Sabbah, was a poet and a scientist and
the inventor of modern terrorism – the *fedayeen* are the
descendants of his fanatical killers for the faith. Marco Polo
on his travels described the stronghold and garden of delights
of this Old Man of the Mountains, where he trained his political murderers. With the tales of the returning crusaders, this
account would provide some of the material for the medieval
stories of a paradise on earth and a Grail Castle of the Fisher
King.

There had been two recognised 'Grails' in Jerusalem. One
of them, described by Albert of Aix, was the golden urn
hanging from the centre of the Dome of the Rock, that marvellous Muslim shrine mistaken by Christian pilgrims for the
Temple of Solomon. That precious vessel was believed to
hold manna from heaven and the Holy Blood of Christ. And
there was the True Cross, recovered from the Orthodox

Syrians in 1099, a golden and jewelled reliquary containing a little of the wood from the torture of Jesus. The rest of the Holy Cross had been taken to Constantinople, but this relic was carried into battle by the crusading knights until it was lost to Saladin at his victory at the Horns of Hattin. It was either sold to the Byzantine Emperor by Saladin's brother and successor, or it disappeared in the Islamic wars after the capture of the Kingdom of Jerusalem.

The loss of the Holy City put an end to the main purpose of the Knights Templar, who were the protectors of pilgrims to the Christian holy places, now in Muslim hands. Although they were to survive for another 120 years as a military order, the Templars had to find a new role. They fell back to the sea and built fortresses there, preparing for another crusade to take back Jerusalem. More and more, the Templars became merchants, bankers and administrators of their estates rather than seekers after the divine.

Their fate was foreshadowed by another crusade, now directed by Rome against its brother Christians in France. The victims – the *cathari*, or pure ones – were called heretics, as the Templars were to be in their turn. Since their foundation by Hugh de Payens, the Templars had been closely connected with the Court of Champagne, Provence and the Langue d'Oc. The patrons of the culture of the south of France, certainly the richest and most civilised in Europe in the twelfth century, supported the crusades and died while serving upon them. But the kings of France coveted these independent principalities, and the popes distrusted the increasing power of the Cathar priests, called *perfecti*, who wanted to reform the faith by preaching a personal contact with the Light of God.

Both the Cathars and the Templars were influenced by Manichean, Sufi and Islamic doctrines, as well as by early Christianity and the Cabbala. They believed the flesh was corrupt and life was an ascension to the spiritual, rather like the quest for the Grail. In the Merovingian crypt of the basilica of Saint-Victor at Marseilles, carvings of a descending serpent of wisdom and a Tree of Life and the Knowledge of Good and Evil with its roots exposed adorn one column in evidence of the enduring heresies of the Langue d'Oc. For the Cathars were convinced that Lucifer, or the devil, had brought about the creation of man. Plato, in the *Gorgias*, was right when he quoted Euripides: 'Who knows, if life be death, and if death be life?' Also right was the Grail king in the romance *Diû Krône*: 'We only seem to be alive, in reality we are dead.' In that German text, the Grail was a casket containing a piece of bread, a third of which was presented to the Grail king. Beside it was a beaker holding three drops of the Holy Blood. Through the mystical feast, known as the *manisola*, and the *consolamentum*, the chaste kiss of reception into the faith, the *perfecti* took their initiates into the path of the Spirit. This religion was certainly more pure and personal than Catholicism at the time, for an individual was made responsible for his or her own soul by an ascetic way of life. Cathar influences were evident in the quest for the Grail and in the early crusading zeal to reach the holy city of Jerusalem. The Albigensian Crusade was turned into a tragedy against a source of the previous crusades to the east.

Saint Bernard, too, incited this perversion of a holy war. He considered the people of the south of France to be little better than heathens:

> *The churches are empty, the people have no priests; the priests are not shown the respect which is their due. The Christians deny Christ and their temples resemble synagogues. The sacred character of God's sanctuaries is ignored, and the sacraments are not accounted holy. Feast days are not observed with due solemnity. Men die in their sins and their souls are carried off, alas, before the awesome Judgement Seat without their being reconciled with the Lord and provided with the holy sacraments. Children do not learn to know Christ and the grace of baptism is not conferred on them.*

White and black monks preached the conversion of Provence to the orthodox faith. They denounced the direct contact with God so attractive to the south of France with its wandering knights and minstrels. The concept of the quest for self-perfection through trial, hope and fear was thought an oriental and mystic heresy, even if its philosophy had wide popular appeal in the Grail romances and the poems and love songs of the troubadours. The ruthless and ambitious Simon de Montfort was given the task of suppressing the heresy by fire and slaughter. When he was finally killed at the siege of Toulouse by a stone on his head, a Cathar poet wrote an ironical vindication of his crusade:

> *If, to kill men and splatter their blood,*
> *To lose their souls and connive in murder,*
> *To believe in perverse advice, to light up burnings,*
> *To destroy the barons and dishonour their rank,*
> *To seize lands and support Arrogance,*
> *To swell evil and suppress the good,*
> *To massacre women and kill their children,*
> *Or if, for all that, a man may,*
> *In this world, so conquer Jesus Christ,*
> *Then that one has the right to the crown*
> *And to shine in glory in the sky.*

The lands and cities of the Langue d'Oc were as thoroughly ravaged as the Waste Land of the Fisher King. Predictably, Montségur, one of the last Cathar castles to hold out, was held to be the Grail Castle, where spiritual food and life were available to the *perfecti*. The Catholic besiegers called it the 'Synagogue of Satan', the term which the Cathars used for the Church of Rome. There may have been a form of Mithraic worship at a temple of the sun at Montségur, which was the heart of the heresy. A chalice and other treasures used at the *manisola* were said to have been smuggled out of the stronghold by four refugees before its fall and to be buried still – another real Grail – in the caves near that

45

fortress or at Usson. Although some of the Templars joined in the Albigensian Crusade, most of the Cathar knights who escaped the slaughter were to be received into the Military Order of the Temple of Solomon, which was itself permeated with oriental influences.

The Grail epics were always an irritant to the Catholic Church, which was prepared to order the massacre of Christians seeking a direct approach to the divine Word and Light. In both *Perceval* and the later *Parzival* of Wolfram von Eschenbach, the way to the Grail was suggested by a holy lay hermit. Such a revelation might be reached in a castle not of this world. The priests of Rome had little to do with the transmission of the grace of God to humanity through a jewelled cup or a dove of the Holy Spirit. The premier romances of the Grail diminished the role of the Church as the mediator between heaven and earth. Even if the Knights of the Grail went to Mass regularly and the Holy Spirit came to them at Camelot during the feast of Pentecost, their trials along the many ways to the Castle of the Fisher King made them able to experience or pass by the grace of God. By their deeds, not by the Latin of the Vulgate, they were chosen to view the divine.

The Real Grails

Once the quest for the Grail had been described by Chrétien de Troyes, many actual Grails were identified within the Christian faith. Although that sacred vessel had ancient and pagan sources, it was declared to lie within the bowls, dishes, weapons and instruments that the Gospels associated with the Last Supper and the Crucifixion. Anything that was believed to have contained or touched the blood of Jesus Christ was considered to be a kind of Grail. In the ecstatic confusion of the real and the visionary which was the inspiration of the Crusades and the early Middle Ages, sacred relics were venerated and became the advertisements of the abbeys and cathedrals which were spreading the worship of

God across Europe. If the ceremony of the Mass changed bread and wine into the Body and Blood of the Son of God, His actual image, drops from His veins, or evidence of His martyrdom in Jerusalem were the literal proofs of a dominant faith. Holy relics were the medieval verdict of history on the Bible. What was believed, had taken place.

The most precious Grails of the twelfth century were the Holy Lance and the Holy Shroud, the Holy Veil given to Saint Veronica, the True Cross, the Crown of Thorns and the cup of Joseph of Arimathea. All were surrounded by jewelled reliquaries of precious metal. As early as the sixth century, Antonius Placentinus had reported that the Holy Lance and the Chalice of the Last Supper were on show in the Church of Sion and the Basilica of the Holy Sepulchre. Although these vanished with the Arab conquest of Palestine, pieces of the True Cross emerged again in Byzantium, or Constantinople, along with the Crown of Thorns, the Holy Shroud and the Holy Veil, ransomed from the Muslims at the siege of Edessa and returned to Greek Christian ceremonies.

Three years before the Fourth Crusade seized Constantinople in 1204, the treasurer of the Pharos Chapel, Nicolas Mesarites, warned the enemies of the Byzantine Emperor not to attack the place: 'In this chapel, Christ rises again, and the Shroud with the burial linens is the clear proof . . . They still smell of myrrh and are indestructible since they once enshrouded the dead body, anointed and naked, of the Almighty after his Passion.' But a crusader, Robert de Clari, saw the Holy Shroud in the Church of Saint Mary Blachernae. Here 'was kept the Shroud in which Our Lord has been wrapped, which stood up straight every Good Friday, so that the features of Our Lord could be plainly seen there.'

After Jerusalem, Constantinople was considered Christendom's second repository of holy relics. Along with the golden *capsula* containing the veil of Saint Veronica, and the jewelled holder of the Holy Shroud, there were a host of others. Mesarites stopped a mob seeking the blessed relics by telling them of three other instruments of the Passion which he also held in the palace. The first was 'the holy Crown of Thorns, which remained intact because it took on incorruptibility from touching the sacred head of Jesus'. The second was the last 'Holy Nail preserved just as it was when it penetrated the most holy and merciful Flesh'. The third was the *flagellum*, the whip with the thongs that still bore the blood of Christ. These five remains of the Passion were among the holy treasures of Constantinople which remained for the looting.

There were so many other sacred valuables. As early as the fourth century, the bodies of Saints Andrew, Luke and Timothy had been disinterred for reburial in the Sancta Sophia. Most of these relics were now plundered by the Venetians and the crusaders. By a long and elaborate process of international bribes, saintly King Louis IX of France arranged for the Byzantine Crown of Thorns in its Grail casket to be redeemed from Venice and enshrined in Paris within the miracle of the building of the Sainte Chapelle. Even when the Treasury of the Basilica of San Marco was gutted by fire in 1231, the most holy of the looted remains were providentially spared by the flames – the wood of the True Cross, the flask of the Blood of Jesus Christ, and the head of Saint John the Baptist. Fire forged faith; it did not destroy it. Until the French Revolution scattered the relics in the Sainte Chapelle, these were venerated for their profusion.

When Robert de Clari found his most precious relic – the Holy Shroud or Veil – in Constantinople, he added a description of another Grail. For the image of Christ was on a cloth imbued with the Water and Blood of Jesus, soaked with the fluids from His Body. In the Church of Saint Mary, the cloth with His features was contained in a rich vessel 'of gold hanging in the middle of the chapel by heavy silver chains'. To the Knights Templar that container of His Blood and the image of His head signified a Grail, for the Holy Shroud certainly came into their possession after the sack of Constantinople. When their Grand Master, Jacques de

Molay, was to be executed in 1314, he was burned alive with another Templar, Geoffrey de Charny, Preceptor of Normandy. One generation later, another Geoffrey de Charny emerged as the possessor of the Shroud, for which he built a shrine at Liray near Troyes in Champagne. This was apt, given that Chrétien de Troyes had written the first story of the Grail. The Shroud's new guardian, however, was killed at the Battle of Poitiers, where he lost the sacred Oriflamme of Saint Denis to the English.

The mania for parading and viewing evidence of the Crucifixion and the bones of the saints was part of a faith which believed in the resurrection of the body. More than a pagan cult of the dead hero, orthodox Christianity continued to venerate the flesh as the home of the Holy Spirit. Saint Augustine himself had complained of travelling salesmen dressed as monks who sold pieces of martyrs; but he had praised the carrying of the remains of Saint Stephen to Tibilis, where these worked miracles. Although this traffic was outlawed, ambitious abbots and bishops went on buying sacred bits and housing them in precious boxes to attract contributions from massed congregations. Pope Gregory the Great had refused to donate the head of Saint Paul to the Byzantine Empress Constantina, yet his condemnation of cutting up the bodies of the martyrs and distributing them for profit was ineffective.

So many relics of Christ found their way to the West that miracles were needed to explain the host of them. Paulinus declared that the True Cross at Jerusalem renewed itself, however many slivers were cut from it. As a profound study of medieval faith and fable found, the belief in

> *the power and fragments of the cross to multiply themselves was constant in the Middle Ages, and was compared to that of the body of Christ in the Eucharist. The nails of the cross had the same power of reproducing themselves, though many nails perhaps contained only filings of the originals. The crown of thorns, spear,*

sponge, and reed, the seamless coat, the pillar to which our Lord was bound, the stone of the sepulchre, earth from that or from the Holy Land, even our Lord's footprints, were known from the fourth century.

There were dozens of authenticated examples of napkins with the sweat of Jesus, of boards from the Bethlehem manger, and of the Holy Coat that the Empress Helena was said to have given originally to Trèves. Christ's tooth and even the foreskin from His circumcision were encased in gold and blazed with gems.

These lesser Grails of Europe multiplied in His name. In his abbey, Angilbert described parts of the True Cross and the manger, the sandals and vestment of Jesus, the vinegar sponge of the Crucifixion and water from the Jordan river, a hair from the beard of Saint Peter and milk from the Virgin Mary. There were two attested heads of John the Baptist and three bodies of Mary Magdalene. Of the eight hundred monasteries and ten thousand churches in Germany in the twelfth century, many claimed to possess more than five hundred sacred objects. As in the story of the Grail, all remains of the suffering of Christ and of the saints were held to retain the grace of God and to give out the Light of the Spirit. They could perform miracles and were talismans against danger.

The power of sacred relics was unique to medieval Christianity. It was based on the articles of the faith. At the Last Supper, Jesus had broken bread and given it to His disciples, saying that it was His Body. He had offered them wine, saying that it was His Blood. At the ceremony of Communion, the crusaders literally believed that the consecrated bread and wine was changed into the Body and Blood of Christ. Christians also believed that their own bodies would be resurrected at the Second Coming. No such corporeal faith lay in the Jewish or Muslim religions. But it allowed the Christians of the Middle Ages to become obsessed with bones and vials of blood and objects that were said to derive from the tombs of the saints and martyrs. These even sanctified the weapons of war. In Roland's lament at his death for his blade, Durandal, he recalled the sacred treasures in his sword:

> *Ah, Durandal, you are holy and fair*
> *Many are the relics in your gilded hilt:*
> *Saint Peter's tooth, some of Saint Basil's blood,*
> *Hairs from the head of lordly Saint Denis.*
> *Part of a robe that blessed Mary wore.*
> *It would be wrong for infidels to hold you:*
> *To wield you is for Christian men alone.*

What Arthur had been to the history of the kings of Britain, Charlemagne was to a Europe that did not yet know its name. He had formed the Holy Roman Empire, recalling the majesty of the past and the holy city on the Tiber that preached a united Christendom. He had built his own new Jerusalem at Aachen, with its sacred octagonal chapel where later emperors would be crowned, and filled it with holy relics. The Treasury of the Dom still houses many reliquaries; three of the Bohemian ones show through rock crystal some holy things: the belt of the Virgin Mary, the belt of Jesus and the rope used to whip Him. A great pilgrimage still takes place every seven years around the Virgin's dress which she wore at His birth, His swaddling clothes and loin-cloth, and the shroud of John the Baptist. The thigh bone of Charlemagne himself is displayed in a triple-spired reliquary, along with a piece of a nail driven through the feet of Christ, a splinter of the True Cross and a fragment of the Crown of Thorns. Most striking is a horn, said to be Charlemagne's, but dating from the tenth century; it is made from an elephant's tusk and serves as a reminder of the Roman cornucopia; also of Roland's last bugle call from Roncesvalles before his death.

The octagonal marble chapel of the emperor in the Dom is the fount of the Matter of France. Influenced by the Baptisteries at Byzantine Ravenna and the original Church of

51

the Holy Sepulchre in Jerusalem, the mosaics and marble patterns predict the symbols of the Grail legend. Over the entrance, a mosaic displays the Heavenly Jerusalem, surrounded within its circular walls by four men in white robes pouring from Greek jars the four sacred rivers of Eden. The Temple of Solomon with its two pillars and quartet of arches looks classical, but is surmounted by a cross, while below are curtains hiding the Ark and a hanging lamp. Beside the windows are chalice patterns made of coloured marble; over a door is an eight-pointed cross with a round stone or cosmos dropping from it. Yet most prophetic is the mosaic over the golden altar, which shows the Holy Spirit as a dove descending with rays of fire, some in the shape of the Cross, and holding in its beak the Word of God to lay on the empty throne of Charlemagne. This allegory of the divine emperor bringing revelation to his people as King David did in Israel is confirmed by a Latin inscription declaring that God gave Charlemagne the right to build his Temple because he ruled so well.

These forecasts of the Grail legend are confirmed by the masterpiece of the Aachen Passion Altar, which was painted in about 1520, when the Reformation had already begun the destruction of Christian unity and the cult of the Grail was in decline. The right-hand panel is of the Deposition from the Cross. A sensual Mary Magdalene wipes the blood from Christ's wounded feet with her long red hair, open-mouthed in misery as she kneels in her red robe. The Crown of Thorns has fallen beside her. Saint John and the Virgin Mary are praying with sunbursts behind their heads, while Nicodemus and Joseph of Arimathea remove Christ's Body from the Tomb in the background, then stand by His corpse, ready to prepare it for burial. In the centrepiece, Joseph carries the Grail bucket, which now contains the vinegar given to the nailed Christ on a sponge, while the Magdalene again reaches up to His bleeding feet with her hand.

The chapel and Treasury at Aachen were to become the inspiration for the architecture and the collection of holy relics across all Europe. Although Charlemagne's empire at his death was split into three parts, and these into many more duchies and countries, the mystery of that blessed *imperium* continued to haunt the imagination of the medieval troubadours, particularly the legend of Roland and his end. Versions of *The Song of Roland*, indeed, were being sung at the time of the First Crusade, and gave the best contemporary insight into the barbaric, fearful and proud temperament of the European knight. Recalling a defeat by Charlemagne in his campaign against the Ummayads in Spain, the destruction of his rearguard in a Basque ambush at Roncesvalles was translated into a heroic slaughter of the Muslim hordes and the sacrifice of a hero and martyr through betrayal. This legendary epic was shot through with the silk and blood of the period. It was a declaration of a holy war against Islam, in which chivalry was restricted to the knights on both sides, while there was no mercy for the rest of humanity. Those who died in Charlemagne's cause would enter the gates of paradise, as the sanguinary Archbishop Turpin promised. 'Infidels are wrong and Christians are in the right,' proclaimed Count Roland. 'I will set no bad example.' Killing a few hundred infidels with Durandal – which could split rock like the Shamir that built the Temple of Solomon, and King Arthur's Excalibur – Roland thought a good example, even though he condemned himself and his twenty thousand men to death by refusing to summon help from Charlemagne with his horn. The sacred relics in the hilt of Durandal made it more murderous, while the count's arrogance and the butchery of the enemy turned strategic folly into sacred romance.

The Song of Roland presaged the disaster that would befall the later Christian Kingdom of Jerusalem, which was born in the confused ideal of a crusade, and condemned by the pride and treachery of the actual rulers of the expeditionary force that was to occupy Palestine. In *The Song of Roland*, the Franks were the Chosen People of God, and their enemies were doomed to hell or the sword unless they accepted conversion. When Charlemagne took Córdoba and razed its walls, the poet took it as a matter of course that 'all infidels in the city had been slain/Or else converted to the Christian faith.' The Holy Roman Emperor himself held court in the great garden or paradise there, created by the Moorish king, 'the foe of God, who served Muhammad and to Apollyon prayed.' The massacre of the unbelievers who resisted a forced conversion to Christianity was advocated as a habitual strategy in the counterattack of Europe on Islam. To die in such a holy war would be to enter the heavenly gates with warrior angels as a guide. When Count Roland prayed with his dying words for remission of his sins, he offered up to God the mailed glove on his right fist, and Saint Gabriel took it from his hand. And so he died:

> *To him God sent angels and Cherubim*
> *Along with Saint Michael of the Peril;*
> *And with them came down Saint Gabriel*
> *To carry the Count's soul up to paradise.*

The master of the School of Charlemagne, the British monk Alcuin, might advise the Emperor that it was better to copy the example of the saints than to carry around their bones. Yet with the prevailing mania for relics, his counsel went unheeded, certainly in the case of Roland and Durandal. And after the crusades and the fall of Constantinople, multitudes of sanctified things – blood and bones, wood and linen, hair and nails – were brought back from the Near East to become the blessed treasures of the West. The success of the story of the Grail invested these precious pieces with even more mystery and veneration. And yet, however infinitely the Light of God might manifest itself to pilgrims everywhere through religious things, the Knights of the Round Table only sought one source of the Grail. In the diversity of all these widespread relics, certain traditions and legends began to predominate in Germany, France and Britain about particularly sacred vessels. Already by 1204, in the chronicle of Helinandus, a French monk, the Grail was designated as the bowl that Jesus had used at the Last Supper with His disciples. It had appeared in a vision to a British hermit five hundred years before. And one particular Viking and Norman family joined the Knights Templar in being seen and seeing themselves as keepers of the Grail and other religious treasures.

The Family of the Holy Light

If the Light of God was seen in relics in the Middle Ages, the Word of God was heard in names. A child was baptised and given a Christian name from the Gospels. Churches and cathedrals were called after the disciples and the holy fathers. War banners were named after heroes and martyrs to the faith such as Saint George, and war leaders were ennobled under the titles of saints. There was a mighty significance in a chosen name.

Members of a Viking family which later elected the name of St Clair had first settled in Orkney and the Shetlands, bringing with them their old Nordic beliefs in Odin, who searched for wisdom from the gods by hanging himself from the World Tree that kept heaven from hell. They were also Christians and produced a Saint Magnus, who was killed by a blow to the temple, in the manner of the Master Mason Hiram Abiff, the builder of the Temple of Jerusalem. Although no Grail was yet imagined, they knew of the sacred cup which Jesus had passed round the disciples at the Last Supper; also of the vessel in which Joseph of Arimathea had caught Christ's blood from the Cross.

Recruited by the warband of Rolf the Ganger, and related to his brother Einar, these Norsemen from Orkney joined in the attack on France. By 911, they had taken the French name of St Clair, for that was the name of the treaty between Rolf and the French king which ceded the north-west of France to the Vikings. To defend these new 'Normans', the St Clairs were made the border barons against any attack from Paris, and they built a castle on the river l'Epte. Although their name derived from the Latin *clarus* – clarity or truth – and there were to be nine beatified Clares in all, this particular saint was Guillermus, a pilgrim Scot of the seventh century. His name, written in Latin as Sancto Claro, gave his adopted Norse family the reputation of seekers after the Holy Light or the Grail Quest. The surviving statue of Guillermus at the holy well by the Epte shows him carrying his severed head in his hands like John the Baptist, another martyr to the lust of a local Salome.

There was only one other holy name more popular in the naming of the villages of Normandy, and that was Saint Fraimbault, who later was associated with Lancelot of the Lake. First the Breton troubadours had sung of the Arthurian legends, and then Wace had turned Geoffrey of Monmouth into French verse, serving the same cause as the Welsh poet. He wrote propaganda for the Norman cause. His *Roman de Rou* (or Rolf) was a little *Iliad*: the exploits of the Viking Ganger changed him into a second Arthur. One episode in Wace told of Hugh of Mortimer with three other knights, one of them a St Clair, on a charge against 'a body of the Angles who had fallen back on a rising ground, and they slew many'. So Arthur's defence of England was equated with the Norman conquest of this island. Nine of the St Clairs had fought with Duke William at Hastings, and they had been richly rewarded with fiefs and honours as far as Wales.

A dozen villages and castles named St Clair also attested to the growing power of that family across France. Their name made them appear as seekers for the Holy Light, if not descendants of Lancelot himself, now thought to be the popular Saint Fraimbault. The similarities between the two have been well documented. Both of their names signified the lance of the lake. Both were the sons of kings or chiefs who lived in the sixth century. Both were carried away to live by water in the Pays d'Erne in Normandy. Both had adventures in carts and ended as hermits. And both sought for the Grail or Holy Light, the name of their neighbours the St Clairs, who seemed to link themselves more with Perceval than the erring Lancelot.

Modern research has also suggested that Lancelot was a Scottish chief, as the St Clairs would become. Geoffrey of Monmouth called that supreme knight *Anguselus*, while Chrétien de Troyes called him *rois d'Escoce* or king of Scotland, and Wace made him *Angusel*. Tradition identified him as the head of the clan Angus, which had the same Viking-Norman ancestry as the St Clairs, who had also progressed to Scotland with Princess Margaret Atheling from her exile in Hungary. She brought with her another Grail, a golden cruciform casket containing a piece of the True Cross. Her cupbearer and protector was another St Clair, who delivered her and the Black Rood to her husband, King Malcolm III. For the next seven hundred years, the St Clairs would remain the keepers of the sacred regalia of the northern dynasty.

The family was closely associated with the Templars, particularly in Scotland, where the St Clair castle and chapel at Rosslyn were near the Templar headquarters and the Cistercian abbey of Melrose. As in Normandy at the Epte castle, Rosslyn defended the Scots kingdom and Edinburgh from any English attack down the Esk. To their heritage of Nordic Christianity, the crusading St Clairs began to add Templar knowledge, particularly gained from the Manicheans and Gnostics of the Near East, who believed in the struggle between God and Satan for control of this earth, and in the wise serpent, who gave the human race the knowledge of Good and Evil.

In the Near East, the Templars could not maintain their coastal castles. After the fall of the Kingdom of Acre, they were forced to escape with their treasures and archives. The more precious objects would reach the Temple in Paris. But when later the military order was proscribed, much of the treasure was to be spirited away to the safe keeping of the Grail family recognised by the Templars, the Sancto Claros or St Clairs of Rosslyn. Already appointed as the guardians of the sacred things of Scotland, they became the Perpetual Masters of the Guilds, Crafts and Masons there. Their duty would be to build a Grail chapel to house these secret treasures along the lines of Templar wisdom and architecture.

The Story of the Grail was the romance of its age. Its creation by Chrétien de Troyes provided a leading light for the crusades, although it was written at the time of the fall of Jerusalem. Near the city of his birth, the Knights Templar built a series of their Commanderies on a chain of lakes surrounded by woods, which were called Grand Orient, Little Orient and Temple Forest. There Perceval was meant to have discovered his Grail Castle again, and there Templar treasures including the Grails from Constantinople are still said to be buried. A legend of an Asian prince Pérille even claimed that he had established an Arthurian military order named 'The Templists' to protect the Grail in its French castle. Certainly, the real military knights and their associated Norman families brought back from the East a special wisdom. The literature of the Grail would enshrine their esoteric quest towards good and evil, the sun and the night.

Chapter Four

The Joseph Grail

'I will tell you,' the hermit said to Lancelot, 'the right of
the matter.'

Anon, *The Quest of the Holy Grail*

Joseph at Avalon and Sarras

The Grail romances became so popular with the crusaders
that the French demanded a Christian and a Norman purpose.
Robert de Boron added the biblical legend of Joseph of
Arimathea, who brought the Grail from Jerusalem to Britain
and France, and who provided the lineage of the Fisher King
and the heroic knights. Two particular prose stories, *The
Quest of the Holy Grail* and *The History of the Grail*, confirmed the links between the white Cistercian monks and the
Templars of the red cross, giving the conquests of chivalry
the sanction of the chalice. Yet in these professions of
Christian faith, paganism, heresy and alchemy were never
quite transmuted into the true faith.

The Celtic sources of the Grail were anathema to Robert
de Boron, although he may have added corroboration to the
claims of the monks of Glastonbury Abbey, who declared at
the end of the twelfth century that they had unearthed the
bones of King Arthur and his Queen. The Abbey had been
burned down in 1184, and King Henry II had died five years
later. Abbot Henry de Sully needed a miracle to raise funds
and restore the holy place. As his contemporary Gerald of
Wales recorded, he read the leaden cross found by the graves,

59

which was inscribed in Latin: HERE IN THE ISLE OF AVALON LIES BURIED THE RENOWNED KING ARTHUR, WITH GUINEVERE, HIS SECOND WIFE. As for the discovery:

> The body was reduced to dust, but it was lifted up into the fresh air from the depths of the grave and carried with the [huge] bones to a more proper place of burial. In the same grave was found a tress of woman's hair, yellow and lovely to see, plaited and coiled with exquisite art, and belonging no doubt to Arthur's wife.

These relics provided for the rebuilding of Glastonbury. Under the inspired leadership of Henry of Blois, the nephew of the English King Henry I, the abbey went through a Cluniac reform before it fell into the hands of the Cistercians, the white monks established by Saint Bernard. A mystical 'sapphire' altar, probably of porphyry, was installed, covered with gold and silver and gemstones. The cult of King Arthur and the Round Table was encouraged, although the only surviving carvings of knights in armour in the ruined abbey are over the north doorway of the Lady Chapel in a sequence depicting the Massacre of the Innocents. One of the murderous warriors even bears a shield with a flowering cross upon it. The bones of King Arthur and his Queen were housed in a black marble mausoleum with two pairs of lions at their heads and their feet.

The family of Abbot Henry de Sully would claim a similar miracle to secure the future of the Norman Abbey of Fécamp. There the Holy Blood collected by Joseph of Arimathea was meant to have been washed up, concealed in two lead caskets within a fig-tree trunk. Both events had to do with the bringing of the Grail by Joseph of Arimathea to Sarras in France and Avalon in Britain. This was the subject of the Burgundian poet, Robert de Boron, who may himself have served time in a Saracen gaol in the Holy Land. Although he claimed that his source was an original Latin text, he appeared to borrow from the *Perceval* of Chrétien de Troyes, as well as from its later prologues, one of which told how the kingdom of Logres became the Waste Land. The *First Continuation* by Gautier de Doulens recited the adventures of Gawain at the Grail Castle, where he was nourished by the heavenly vessel but failed to put together the broken sword that had destroyed the realm of the Fisher King. Yet Gawain did ask the question about the bleeding lance, and so restored the barren to the bountiful. Another continuation by Manassier told of Perceval making the shattered sword into one and himself becoming the Grail King.

In *Joseph of Arimathea* by Robert de Boron, Joseph was a knight in the service of Pontius Pilate, who gave him the vessel which had caught the Blood of Christ on the Cross, and also permission to bury His Body. With Nicodemus, Joseph prepared the corpse, beginning the tradition of the Grail as a stone on which the dead Jesus bled.

> *While they were washing it, the wounds began to bleed, which made them very afraid, for they remembered the stone at the foot of the Cross that was split open by the falling blood. Then Joseph thought of his vessel and decided that the drops would be better preserved there than in any other place. So he took it and collected the blood from the wounds. He wrapped the body in a fine cloth and laid it in a stone sarcophagus which he had long possessed, meaning to be buried in it himself one day. He concealed the sarcophagus with a large flat rock so that Christ's disciples might not be able to steal the body. But he took the vessel with the blood home with him.*

Imprisoned by the Jews, Joseph was visited by Christ, who gave him back the vessel holding most of the Holy Blood that had fallen from His Body at the funeral preparations. 'You shall have it and preserve it,' Christ said, 'and all they into whose charge you shall commit it . . . Whoever knows about it will be better loved in this world, and the company of those who have news of it and write books about it will be more sought after than other people.' When Joseph asked why the Grail had been given to him, Christ answered:

You did take Me down from the Cross and lay Me in your sepulchre, after I had sat by Simon Peter at the meal and said that I would be betrayed. Because this happened at table, tables will be set up in the future, so that I may be sacrificed. The table signifies the Cross; the vessels in which the sacrifice and consecration will be made signify the grave where you laid Me. This is the cup in which My Body will be consecrated in the form of the Host. The paten that will be put upon it signifies the stone with which you closed the mouth of the tomb, the cloth that will be spread over it signifies the linen that you wound round My Body. Thus the meaning of your action will be known to Christendom for all time, until the end of the world.

For Robert de Boron, the Grail was a 'vase' which contained the Holy Blood of Jesus. It was the vessel and the dish for the bread and the paschal lamb at the Last Supper; also for catching the fluid from the wounds of Christ on the Cross. So it was a giver of sacred food and drink as well as a container of suffering and judgement. When Joseph was later imprisoned, the Grail kept him alive for forty years. Only when he gave it to Bron, another version of the Celtic god Bran, could he depart from the earth, while Bron took this talisman of immortality to the West.

Bron later caught a fish and laid it beside the Grail. So he became the Rich Fisher of the Grail Castle of Corbenic. This Christian symbolism was also a signal of bounty and life. *IXθEUS* or *FISH* was the Greek acronym for *JESUS CHRIST GOD*. It represented the miracles of food for all – the loaves and the fishes – and of living in the great waters of birth. De Boron even compared the joy of those who saw the Grail to a fish escaping from a guddling hand:

> *It is like the ease of the fish*
> *Which a man holds in his hand*
> *And from that hand it swims free . . .*

Joseph and Bron took the Grail to Sarras and Avalon. It was kept on a table beside a cup and a book, which was the Word of God in the New Testament. It had become the allegory of the conversion of France and England to the Roman Catholic faith. The Grail Castle was located at Glastonbury, thus joining Christianity to the bones of the legendary British Arthur. De Boron's poem confirmed a precious legend in the apocryphal *Evangelium Nicodemi*, but it added that Joseph of Arimathea brought the Grail to the most ancient Christian abbey in the south-west of England. And for all of its elevation of the Passion and the Eucharist, it still upheld the Celtic myth of the magic cauldron of plenty and of judgement.

The Quest of the Holy Grail

The enduring version of the Grail story, which was the original part of the prose *Lancelot* cycle, was probably written by a Cistercian monk. In the account of another member of that order, Cesarius of Heisterbach, the subject was more stimulating than the Good Book. He told a tale of the Abbot Gevardur who, faced with a dozen sleepy monks, awoke them with another version of 'In the beginning was the Word': 'Listen, brothers, listen! I have something new and wonderful to tell you. Once upon a time was a King. His name was Arthur . . .'

The order of the white monks was always associated with the Knights Templar. Galahad was now preferred to Perceval as the man without sin who could find the Grail. Significantly, he had to prove his descent from King Solomon to take up the mystic sword of David which would achieve his quest – the Templars were the Knights of the

Temple of Solomon in Jerusalem. As Emma Jung wrote in *The Grail Legend*, 'In the *Quest*, many motifs, such as the legend of Solomon, which stem from Oriental fables are to be found side by side with Celtic motifs.' The Grail itself was a dish of plenty when it came to King Arthur's court at Whitsuntide. There the Round Table of the universe of the knights was said to be the third most important table in the world, the first being the square table of the Last Supper, the second the square Grail table of Joseph of Arimathea. There was a clap of thunder and a brilliant ray of light, as if all were illuminated 'by the grace of the Holy Ghost'. The Grail then appeared, covered with white samite, floating free. 'The hall was filled with a pleasant fragrance, as though all the spices of the earth were spilled there. When the Grail went round the table, each person was served with the food he desired.'

The Grail appeared at Arthur's court for the first time since it had dispensed manna from heaven to the Israelites and the paschal lamb at the Last Supper, only because Galahad, the son of Lancelot by the daughter of the Fisher King and the descendant of King David and Joseph, had sat in the Siege Perilous at the Round Table, the Judas seat which tipped any imperfect knight into hell. He had also pulled the sword from the floating stone to prove his saintliness. The twelve best knights, matching the apostles, left on the quest for the Grail, after hearing Mass. The first stop of Galahad himself was at an abbey of white monks, where he earned by jousting a sacred white shield bearing a red cross traced from the blood of Joseph – the sign of the Templars, who were the mailed fist of the Cistercians.

The Grail next appeared to Galahad's father Lancelot, who was too sinful to receive its grace because of his love for Queen Guinevere. Looking through an iron grille into an ancient chapel, he saw a silver table covered by a silken altar-cloth lit by the six-branched silver candlestick that signified the six days of the Creation. In a waking dream, he saw the table, the candlestick and the Grail issue from the chapel to where a wounded knight lay beneath a stone cross. The knight was healed and took Lancelot's arms, the holy objects returned to the chapel, while Lancelot himself never stirred, either from exhaustion or from the weight of sin. A heavenly voice then reproached him for daring to approach the Grail when he was 'harder than stone, more bitter than wood, more barren and bare than the fig tree'.

Perceval then rode to the chapel of his aunt, who was once called the Queen of the Waste Land. He learned more of his family history, including the bringing of the Grail to Britain. The other knights on the quest, particularly Gawain and Bors, went through their trials and temptations in a sort of chivalric *Pilgrim's Progress*. But while Bors was justifying himself by his works like a Protestant before his time, Galahad was justifying himself by his faith. The pair of them, together with Perceval, reached the Ship of Solomon, so rich in biblical allusions to the Ark of Noah and the Ark of the Temple with its tabernacle of the holy of holies. On board they found a bed like that of Ulysses, hewn from a living tree representing the Tree of Life in the Garden of Eden; the blood of Abel, killed by his brother Cain; and the True Cross. Its three posts were a natural white, red and emerald green, the colours of alchemy comprehended by Solomon, who was 'wise with the knowledge that would be grasped by human understanding; he knew the powers of every precious stone, the virtues of all herbs, and had a more perfect knowledge of the course of the firmament and of the stars than any except for God Himself.'

On the bed lay the sword of King David made by Solomon, with a stone pommel combining all the colours found on earth, each with its own virtue in magic and science. The hilt of the sword had two ribs, one made from the salamander or serpent of wisdom, the other from a Euphrates fish, which induced forgetfulness and purpose. Celtic and Gnostic in shape, it was like the sword of Arthur in the *Dream of Rhonabwy*, with two serpents inscribed upon it in gold. When drawn, 'two flames of fire burst out of the jaws of the two serpents, and so wonderful was the sword, it was hard for anyone to gaze at it'. The Ship of Solomon had been launched by a man descending from heaven, who blessed it with water sprinkled from a silver pail and told its builder that the last knight of his line would lie on the bed and be told about him. Galahad took up the Sword of David and lay on his forefather's bed.

Later, Lancelot replaced Galahad on the Ship of Solomon to search for the Grail Castle on the sea. Finding a fortress guarded by two lions, he came to a chamber so bright that all the candles on earth might be burning there. He observed the Holy Vessel, now covered with red samite, on its silver table. Angels swung silver censers or held candlesticks and crosses. An old man raised the host to a Trinity of three men. One of them was given to him in the place of the host, and he staggered under the weight of the divine body. As Lancelot went to his aid, he was struck down. As he was recovering in the sea castle, the Grail appeared at table to feed all with their desires. Although Lancelot might not reach the Holy Vessel, he could benefit from its bounty.

Five years later, Galahad, Perceval and Bors reached the Castle of Corbenic of the maimed Fisher King. There Galahad put together the two pieces of the broken sword which had wounded Joseph of Arimathea in the thigh. Then a man from heaven in the robes of a bishop, carried on a throne by four angels, appeared as Joseph, the first Christian bishop consecrated by the Lord God in Sarras, the Heavenly City in France from where the Grail had been carried on to Britain. Joseph was set down beside the Holy Vessel on its silver table near the Fisher King. The four angles now bore candles, a cloth of red samite and the bleeding Holy Lance. The candles were placed on the table, the red cloth was laid beside the Grail, while the drops of blood from the raised lance fell into the sacred cup, which was then covered with the cloth. In the vision of the knights, Joseph performed the miracle of transubstantiation in which a burning child replaced the host, before disappearing. Then the bleeding naked Christ appeared from the Holy Vessel and gave the sacrament from it to the kneeling knights, who found the blessed food 'so honied and delectable it was as if the essence of all sweetness was housed within their bodies'. And the vision of Jesus identified the Grail:

It is the platter in which Christ partook of the paschal lamb with His disciples. It is the platter which has shown itself agreeable to those whom I have found my faithful servants, they whose sight has ever stricken the faithless. And because it has shown itself agreeable to all my people, it is called most properly the Holy Grail.

The vision of Christ commanded Galahad to remove the sacred dish from the British castle of Corbenic to the heavenly city of Sarras. Yet first he must heal the wounds of the Fisher King with drops of blood from the Holy Lance. Once the King was healed, the Waste Land turned green, and he entered a monastery of the white monks. So the Cistercians rejoined the story of the quest, while the Arthurian knights of the red cross of the Templars were compared by the spirit of Jesus to the apostles. 'For as they ate with me at the Last Supper, even so did you eat with me now at the table of the Holy Grail.'

Bors, Perceval and Galahad now returned to the Ship of Solomon, where they found the Grail resting on its silver table on the bed of the Tree of Life and the Cross. After a voyage, Galahad carried the great weight of the table into Sarras, where the knights were imprisoned until Galahad was chosen as king. He had made an ark of gold and precious stones, a huge reliquary to house the Grail on its silver table, and praying before it with Bors and Perceval, Galahad saw Joseph of Arimathea, who released his spirit from his body to reach heaven.

A great marvel followed immediately on Galahad's death. The two remaining companions saw quite plainly a hand come down from heaven, but not the body it

*belonged to. It proceeded straight to the Holy Vessel
and took both it and the lance, and carried them up to
heaven, to the end that no man since has ever dared to
say he saw the Holy Grail.*

Many distinguished French critics saw *The Quest of the
Holy Grail* as a Christian allegory, imbued with the mysticism of Saint Bernard's doctrine of grace and mystical union
with God. Although the Grail was never described, it represented the dish at the Last Supper, the vessel in which Joseph
of Arimathea caught the blood of Jesus on the Cross, and the
chalice at the Eucharist. It was the grace and bounty of God.
And while it might appear and be given to all, only the pure
in heart could receive it. Yet in the *Quest*, Celtic and heretic
doctrines survived. Knights might see the Grail during their
trials and tribulations without benefit of the Church. And as
one supporter of the Christian emphasis of the *Quest*
admitted:

*At the very heart of the Grail legend there lies a grave
ambivalence in that the relics of the Last Supper and the
Passion are made to appear responsible for the malefic
enchantments and perils afflicting King Arthur's kingdom, while the sacred lance and the miraculous sword
of King David, the 'sword of the spirit', appear at times
in the light of weapons of vengeance and Nemesis.
Underlying the Christian symbolism there flows a
primitive current that occasionally threatens to perturb
the smooth and limpid surface of the stream.*

The History of the Grail

The whole of the prose Lancelot cycle, which culminated in
the writing in about 1230 of *The History of the Grail*, was
probably designed by one author from Champagne. He could
well have attended Saint Bernard's school at Clairvaux, near
the Troyes of the Chrétien who composed the original

Perceval. Certainly the cycle was French in bias, concentrating on the exploits of Lancelot, appropriated by the Normans as their knight from the Ban de Benoic, and stressing the return of the Grail from Avalon at Glastonbury to Sarras in the south of France. The works of the cycle – particularly the lengthy *Lancelot*, in which the Grail cured the knight of his madness – made cross-references to the other texts in the series, while the *Mort d'Artu* followed Wace in using the conquests of Arthur and Lancelot to prefigure the Norman empire in France and Britain.

The author of *The History of the Grail* claimed to have received the Word of God in 717, more than five hundred years before the French text was written. He declared that he was an anonymous hermit who found himself in the wild part of a heathen land on Good Friday night, and fell asleep. A voice from heaven called to him four times, and told him to wake and learn of three things in one, and one in three. He saw a man of surpassing beauty who represented the Trinity. He could not stand the blazing brightness of this vision, so the man blew light into his eyes, gave him the gift of tongues and put a torch in his mouth. He said he was the Fountain of Wisdom and the Perfect Master, identified by Nicodemus, who brought Joseph of Arimathea the myrrh and aloes to embalm the body of Jesus.

The man took the hermit's hand and gave him a book no larger than his palm. The man declared that he had written the marvels in the book, then he disappeared in thunder, earthquake and blinding sunburst. The hermit fell to the ground after his mystic vision, but he woke to find the book and read its beginning:

> Here is the book of Thy Descent,
> Here is the Book of the Sangreal,
> Here begin the terrors,
> Here begin the miracles.

The hermit hid the book in a cabinet by his altar, only to

find it gone the next day, in the manner that Christ had risen from His tomb. He was told to walk on a path to the Stone and the Valley of the Dead, or the underworld, and the Cross of the Seven Roads. On the altar of a forest chapel, he discovered again the divine book and was ordered by Christ to make a copy. This was *The History of the Grail*. As the author said, he would not have dared to write it if it had not been revealed to him.

So the *History* was the first description of the Grail as the literal Word of God. It gave the authority of the Almighty to the legend of Joseph of Arimathea, as well as creating a myth of the conversion of Britain to Christianity. In the romance, Joseph collected the Blood of Christ on the Cross in the *escuele*, or dish, used at the Last Supper. He was put in prison for forty-three years by the Jews, but fed by manna from the Grail. Freed by the Roman emperor Vespasian, he was baptised and sailed as a missionary from the Holy Land with his wife and virgin son on the Ship of Solomon. The sacred dish was enshrined in a precious ark. Reaching the port of Sarras in the south of France, then governed by Saracens, Joseph converted the infidel rulers. An initiate of the mysteries of the Grail within the Ark, he was consecrated by Christ Himself as the first bishop of western Europe. Briefly a sinner, he was pierced in the thigh by the lance of an angel, foretelling the fate of the Fisher King. But his piety cured his wound without the need of the intervention of a Knight of the Round Table.

From Sarras, Joseph proceeded on his mission to Britain. The Grail worked its wonders; it was now the symbol of Christ's miracle, multiplying the loaves and fishes to feed thousands of the faithful. Alain, the nephew of Joseph and twelfth son of his brother-in-law Bron, had caught the original fish and became the first Fisher King, building the castle of Corbenic to house the Grail and wait for the coming of Galahad, here born by divine intervention to the aged Joseph and his wife as Galaad, so similar to the Gilead of the Bible.

The Grail of the *History* was not a chalice, but a dish or

platter of plenty. Britain was said to be converted to the Greek rite directly from Jerusalem and Constantinople, as was happening from Ireland in the time of King Arthur, who was said to have as an ancestor the Empress Helena, the discoverer of the True Cross in Jerusalem. The Gospel according to Saint John had put the stamp of the New Testament on Nicodemus, Joseph of Arimathea, the Bread of Life and the Holy Blood. Seeming almost a Gnostic, Jesus declared to Nicodemus, 'a ruler of the Jews', in that text:

> *And as Moses lifted up the serpent in the wilderness,*
> *even so must the Son of Man be lifted up:*
> *That whosoever believeth may in Him have eternal*
> *life.*
> *For God so loved the world, that He gave his only*
> *begotten Son . . .*

It was Jesus who told the Jews of Himself as the bountiful Grail.

> *I am the bread of life.*
> *Your fathers did eat the manna in the wilderness, and*
> *they died.*
> *This is the bread which cometh down out of heaven,*
> *that a man may eat thereof, and not die . . .*
> *Verily, verily, I say unto you, Except ye eat the flesh*
> *of the Son of Man and drink His blood, ye have not life*
> *in yourselves.*

Moreover, Jesus chose Judas in his fatal betrayal of his Master, giving him the sop at the Last Supper by telling him, 'That thou doest, do quickly,' and so creating the Siege Perilous that would kill the unworthy at the Round Table.

> *It was Joseph of Arimathea and Nicodemus who pre-*
> *pared Christ for his tomb.*
> *So they took the body of Jesus and bound it in linen*

cloths with the spices, as the custom of the Jews is to bury.

Now in the place where he was crucified there was a garden; and in the garden a new tomb wherein was never man yet laid.

And it was the risen Christ who stood on the shore of Lake Tiberias and watched the disciples as they fished.

Jesus therefore saith unto them, Children, have ye aught to eat? They answered Him, No.

And he said unto them, Cast the net on the right side of the boat, and ye shall find. They cast, therefore, and now they were not able to draw it for the multitude of fishes . . .

So when they got out upon the land, they see a fire of coals there, and fish laid thereon, and bread . . .

Jesus saith unto them, Come and break your fast. And none of the disciples durst inquire of Him, Who art Thou? knowing that it was the Lord.

Such passages from the Gospel according to Saint John were used by the author of *The History of the Grail* to give further authenticity to his claim that his text was copied from a book actually written by Jesus. That the Gospel was Gnostic and heretical as much as Catholic and orthodox did not trouble an inspired writer, who used of his knights the dangerous word *perfecti*, the name of the leaders of the Cathars. He was already mixing the pagan and the Christian elements in Robert de Boron's version of *Joseph of Arimathea*. The prose *Lancelot* cycle became famous for its amalgam of myth and faith. Some hundred manuscripts still survive. In the words of a leading French critic, the series was 'the best propagator of the conception which represented chivalry as an ideal of moral nobility, far removed from the reality in the brutal society of the Middle Ages.' As on the hilt of Roland's sword, the Holy Cross stood above the bloody blade.

Chapter Five

The Celtic Grail

Hear ye the history of the most holy vessel that is called
the Grail, in which the precious blood of Jesus was
received on the day that He was put on the Cross.

Anon, *Perlesvaus*

The Templar Knights were also named as the keepers of the
Grail in the anonymous romance *Perlesvaus*, but now they
were crusaders against pagan Islam. The Grail was the vessel which caught Christ's blood collected by Joseph of
Arimathea. There was no peace or compromise with Muslim
chivalry or faith in the *Perlesvaus*. Its unknown French
author claimed that it was based on a Latin book written by a
monk of Glastonbury, and it was propaganda for King
Arthur's burial there. Yet its detailed accounts of weapons,
armour and military strategy, as well as its praise of the
Knights of the Grail protecting their sacred secret in their
mantles embroidered with red crosses, suggested that the
writer was a sympathiser of the Templar Order. The Grail
was described as the Eucharistic chalice of the Last Supper
brought over to Britain by Joseph of Arimathea; but that was
its final and fifth form as seen by King Arthur after attending
a sacrament given by hermits. The bleeding lance was also
the Holy Lance of Longinus, which pierced Christ's side on
the Cross and was rediscovered by the crusaders at Antioch.
Also visible was the bloody sword that had cut off the head
of Saint John the Baptist, revered by the monastic knights.
And the Grail Castle was put into transcendental terms, full
of sweet scents and aromatic spices. It was called Eden, the

Castle of Joy and the Castle of Souls, while the river around the walls came from the Earthly Paradise. And all who died within were assured of reaching paradise in heaven.

There was a strong Celtic influence in the legends of the Grail, particularly about an otherworld to which the dying heroes went – Arthur to Avalon, Bran to the blessed isles of the west rather than to the Munsalvaesche or Mount of Salvation, on which the Grail Castle was built. All the marvels of that castle of the Fisher King were further to be found in the castle of the divine Lug, which had held the treasures of the Celtic gods, including a bleeding lance – this was also possessed by the Welsh Grail knight Peredur – a bottomless drinking vessel, a cauldron that could feed an army, an unconquerable sword, and a stone fallen from heaven as in *Parzival* – a Stone of Destiny, or Scone, on which the Irish and Scots kings were crowned until the English took it away for their coronations of the kings of Great Britain in Westminster. After seven hundred years, its formal return to Scotland was finally granted.

The Grail of the *Perlesvaus*

In the *Perlesvaus*, Joseph of Arimathea was said to be the author of the romance through the voice of an angel. The text mentioned both him and Saint Longinus, who honoured the body of Christ, burying it in the Holy Sepulchre with the Holy Lance which had pierced His side, and the Grail used by Joseph to drain His Blood. Descended from King David, Joseph was the progenitor of the Grail lineage until the time of King Arthur. Perceval, the perfect knight, had failed to ask the right question of the Fisher King, allowing Arthur's kingdom to be changed into a Waste Land. The king had become slothful; his best knights had left the Round Table. To redeem himself, Arthur went to Saint Austin's chapel in Wales, where he saw a vision of Christ as child and Redeemer. Returning to his court at Cardeuil, he met Perceval's sister, who healed him of a wound with blood from the severed head of a Black Knight. She told him of Perceval's youth in Wales, where he had lost his inheritance to the Lord of the Moors. She reproached Arthur for bearing the name of so evil a king; she did not know that he had begun to reform.

Holding court at Penzance, Arthur was drinking from his golden cup when three maidens entered the hall. They were surrounded by scents and covered with jewels; but the first was bald. She had lost her hair because of Perceval's failure at the Grail Castle, but she brought the shield of Joseph for him – azure and silver with a red cross. Again with the Celtic stress on severed heads and gory relics, she carried with her in a cart drawn by three harts the heads of one hundred and fifty knights sealed in caskets of gold, silver and lead. Leaving the court, the maidens met Gawain, who took up the quest. After various adventures, he asked a hermit how to attain the Grail.

> '*Sir,*' *Gawain said,* '*by what way can a man reach this castle?*'
> '*Sir,*' *the hermit said,* '*none may teach you except for the Will of God. And would you reach it?*'
> '*Sir,*' *Gawain said,* '*it is my great desire.*'

Seeking the Grail Castle, Gawain found himself in meadows near a forest. High walls and battlements enclosed the great halls of Camelot; its dead lord Alain was descended from Joseph of Arimathea. His widow was beset by the Lord of the Moors, whom Gawain defeated in combat, so freeing the castle. Riding through further trials to the Land of the Fisher King, Gawain reached the Grail Castle, but was refused entrance until he returned with a sacred Templar relic, the sword which had beheaded Saint John the Baptist. 'If you bring that sword,' a priest told Gawain, 'you may freely come into the castle, and everywhere in the realm of the Fisher King, you will be made most welcome.'

Gawain won the relic from the cannibal Gurguran, who

ruled Scotland and was now converted to Christianity – a memory of the first Irish missions to the pagan Picts. Now the knight was conducted by angels and rode over the perilous bridges into the Grail Castle; they were flaming with the fire of the Holy Ghost, and the castle was ablaze with brightness. He gave the Biblical sword to the maimed Fisher King, who was reclining on an ivory bed before a cross of gold containing a piece of the True Cross. Then Gawain met with a group of initiates, who had a red cross on their breasts, and two masters. After a feast with twelve of the knights, however, he repeated the mistake of Perceval in failing to ask the right question of the diseased Fisher King. He was struck dumb by the sight of the Grail and the three drops of blood falling from the Holy Lance, held in the hands of two maidens. He was not the perfect knight. He could not heal the King's wounds. Yet he had a vision of two angels bearing golden candlesticks and of the Grail as flesh 'with a king crowned, nailed on a Cross, and a spear fast in his side'.

Lancelot now took up the quest. The brutality of the period intruded on his mission. Martyrdom was presented to Lancelot in the guise of mutilation. He sat with the lady of a castle:

> *The first course was brought in by knights in chains who had their noses cut off. The second by knights in chains who had their eyes put out, so that squires led them. The third course was brought in by knights with one hand and chained. After that, other knights with one foot brought in the fourth course. And with the fifth course came tall and fair knights, each with a naked sword used to cut off their heads, now given to the lady.*

Lancelot disliked such sacrifice, and refused to be the lord of the castle. He was accused of loving Queen Guinevere too much, and so set off after the Grail, which he could never reach because of his mortal sin. Arriving at the Castle of the Fisher King, he was richly fed at an ivory table with the other knights, from vessels of gold and silver, but the Grail did not appear. He was not worthy of it.

Perceval again took up the quest, carrying the shield of azure and silver with the red cross of Joseph of Arimathea. A curious encounter with another red cross in the forest left him watching a white hart torn apart by hounds. A knight and a maiden appeared, collected the bloody pieces in golden vessels and kissed the cross. When Perceval kissed it, he smelled all the scents of paradise. Two priests then came on the scene and sent him away. They kissed and whipped the cross with a rod, then they wept. When Perceval protested, one of the priests told him that it was no concern of his what they did. The mystery of their Christian act or heresy was theirs alone.

Ignoring the treacherous killing of the son of King Arthur, Perceval rode to his mother's aid at Camelot. He met his sister, who told him of the death of the Fisher King and the disappearance of the Grail. His castle had been seized by the King of Chastel Mortel, who upheld the Old Laws and not the New Testament. Meanwhile, the Lord of the Moors had again taken Camelot from Perceval's mother. In delivering his mother's castle from Islam, Perceval proved himself the pagan Celtic knight rather than the crusader. His killing of the Muslim chief and his warriors was exactly the scene of ritual slaughter depicted on the ancient Gunderstrup Cauldron of Druid sacrifices:

> *'Our Lord God commanded in both the Old Law and the New,' Perceval said, 'that justice should be done to mass-killers and traitors, and justice will be done upon you so that His Law is not transgressed.' He had a great vat made ready in the middle of the court, and ordered the eleven Moorish captive knights to be brought out. He had their heads severed into the vat with all the blood drained from their bodies, then he had the flesh taken out so there was only the blood in the vat. After that, he disarmed the Lord of the Moors and took him before the vessel filled with blood. Perceval had the*

*Lord's hands and feet bound fast, and after that he said:
'You were never satisfied with the blood of the knights
of my lady mother, now I will satisfy you with the blood
of your own knights.' So he had the Lord of the Moors
hanged by the feet in the vat with his head in the blood
as far as his shoulders, until he was drowned and
quenched. After that, Perceval had all the twelve bodies
and heads dumped in an ancient burial pit beside an old
chapel in the forest, while the vat of blood was cast into
the river, so that the waters were all red.*

If any act in the Grail romances identified the Grail with the
Celtic sacrificial cauldron of death and rebirth, it was this
bloodiness of the perfect knight Perceval on the way to the
Grail Castle in the rescue of his family from the evil deeds of
the Muslims. While the vat of slaughter was not identified
with the Grail, it was a necessary rite of passage for Perceval
to achieve the Grail, which was finally to be seen by King
Arthur in five different forms. Destroying the Castle of
Copper, where metal men made by alchemy worshipped a
brazen bull, Perceval reached the land of the Grail, riding on
a white mule and carrying the shield with the red cross. He
crossed more bridges of peril, forcing the King of Chastel
Mortel – the Cain of his brother, the good Fisher King – to
commit suicide from fear. Now Perceval saw, in the castle
chapel, the Grail appear again, and the bleeding Holy Lance,
and the sword which had beheaded Saint John the Baptist,
and many other holy relics. These now included the Holy
Shroud obtained by his sister, and the body of his ancestor
Joseph of Arimathea. 'For Our Lord God much loved the
place.' Perceval buried the Fisher King in a tabernacle loaded
with precious stones, illuminated by a divine light that did
not come from candles. The New Law or Testament was
preached, and Perceval killed those who did not follow it.
'The evil belief was done away in her kingdom, and all were
assured again in the New Law by the courage of the Good
Knight.'

King Arthur was now summoned back from Cardeuil to the quest by an angelic voice and two suns in the sky. His son's head, smelling of sweet spices, was brought back to him in a casket. Rebellion was brewing in Brittany from his seneschal, Kay, and Brian of the Isles. Passing through Tintagel on his mission, Arthur heard of the death of Queen Guinevere from grief at the loss of their son, and of an invasion by Brian of the Isles. Lancelot left him to bury the Queen and repel the attack, while Arthur pursued his vow. Reaching the Grail Castle and the river from the Earthly Paradise and the Valley of Plenty, Arthur had a vision of his quest:

> *The Grail appeared at the ceremony of the mass, in five different forms that none ought to tell. For the secret things of the sacrament should not be told openly, except by him given by God to tell them. King Arthur beheld all the changes; the last of them was a change into a chalice.*

In none of the Grail romances was there a vision of its holiness that so confirmed its infinite metamorphoses. It appeared in many shapes; it altered its substance and its essence; it was all things to all knights, yet it gave all that was needed – divine food, drink and grace. The hermit who had held the Mass found a writ under the Host which declared that 'Our Lord God would that His Body be sacrificed in such a vessel, and that this should be set on record.' And he told Arthur that the bell which he carried was one of three cast by Solomon for the Saviour, Mary Magdalene and the Saints, and sent by Pope Gregory the Great to Britain. So Arthur was to institute in his realm the chalice and the peal of bells to announce the celebration of the Mass.

Civil war broke out in the kingdom of Arthur, who even wrongly imprisoned Lancelot for treachery. Perceval was carried over the sea to the Castle of the Four Horns, where he found a company of white monks with a red cross on their breasts. They led him to a glass casket entombing an armed knight. They washed at a great gold basin and dined gloriously. Perceval was given a white shield and was directed to a Plenteous Island to redeem the knights' heads sealed in the gold, silver and lead caskets in the cart of the maidens, as well as the head of the local king and queen. He took back all the severed heads and was given a golden cup of healing for his chivalry and pains.

Finally, Perceval returned to the Grail Castle, where he found his widowed mother and his sister, who led with him a religious life there until their deaths. A voice from heaven told him that the Holy Grail would no longer manifest itself. He must take it elsewhere. He distributed the holy relics to the churches and abbeys of Britain, where they remained as evidence of the Grail. He himself waited for the coming of the blessed Templar ship with its white sail and red cross. The bodies of his mother and the Fisher King were buried in the richest coffins of gold and silver that had ever been seen. And Perceval departed on the Ship of Solomon to another world, taking with him the body of Joseph of Arimathea, while the Grail Castle fell into slow ruin.

Here ends the story of the most Holy Grail. Joseph placed it on record and gives the blessing of Our Lord to all who hear and honour it. The Latin text which inspired the Romance was taken in the Isle of Avalon, in a holy house of religion that stands at the head of the Adventurous Moors, where King Arthur and Queen Guinevere lie, according to the witness of the religious good men there.

So the author of the *Perlesvaus* ended his book, giving the credit to his patron, Jean de Nesle, who had served on the Fourth Crusade that took Constantinople rather than Jerusalem. Certainly, he was a propagandist of the white monks at Glastonbury as well as of the Templars, who had come into possession of two 'Grails' at the fall of

Constantinople: the jewelled vessels containing the Holy Shroud and the Holy Veil of Saint Veronica. And yet the *Perlesvaus* was more significant for its Celtic relish in severed heads like those of the divine Bran, and in sacrificial cauldrons of blood, while the Grail itself was translated into mystical as well as actual shapes. This was a sanguinary Christianity, well suited to the chivalry and slaughter of the crusades.

The Grail of *Peredur*

Another Welsh tale of the Grail in the ancient collection of Celtic texts, the *Mabinogion*, named the Good Knight as Peredur, a popular name in Celtic literature. A Peredur with steel arms was slain with his companions at the Battle of Cattraeth at the beginning of the sixth century. In his *History* and *Vita Merlini*, Geoffrey of Monmouth recorded two kings called Peredur and a knight of the Round Table of the same name. The *Dream of Rhonabwy* dealt with a Peredur of the Long Lance, while *pryderi*, or 'anxiety', was the attribute given to the mythological princes of Dyved, who ruled in South Wales, one of the probable realms of King Arthur.

The romance of *Peredur* may even have antedated the *Perceval* of Chrétien de Troyes. They were both written at much the same time and probably from the same sources. Certainly, its primitive content referred to a Welsh knight as the heir of King Arthur, with a kingdom extending from Scotland and the north of England to the West Country and Wales proper. The motive of Peredur was revenge on the killers of his father and his six or eleven brothers. He was summoned by his uncle Arthur to Caerleon in order that he might become the last king of the Grail Castle. At the stronghold of a second uncle, he passed the test of the sword, cutting an iron column in two with his blade. Then a horrific Grail procession took place. Two youths entered the hall carrying 'a spear of huge size, and three streams of blood running along it from the socket to the floor'. All who were there cried out in grief. And then 'two maidens came in hold-ing a great platter between them, with a man's head on the platter bathed in blood'.

This version of the Grail procession was a Celtic blood ritual, referring to the sacred head of Bran, as well as a gory reminder of the death of Saint John the Baptist. Later in the story, Peredur heard of the truth of the spear and the platter. The head was that of Peredur's cousin, who had been killed by the Caerloyw Witches, and Peredur must avenge him. Yet in a Grail romance, it also symbolised the Holy Lance of Saint Longinus and the Holy Vessel of the Last Supper and the Crucifixion. This startling confusion between pagan and Christian was paralleled in the *Perlesvaus*, when a maiden brought to the hero in an ivory vessel his cousin's remains, along with all the other severed heads of the knights of that text. And Wolfram von Eschenbach, in his *Parzival*, would echo the general mourning of the court at the sight of the youth with the bleeding spear.

More Celtic mysteries were revealed when Peredur went to the court of the Witches to improve his military skills; a tradition of women warriors that stretched back as far as the Amazons. He then fell into an ecstatic trance before a her-mit's cell, a necessary preliminary for so many knights on the Quest of the Grail. He looked out at dawn on a fall of fresh snow. A female hawk was feasting on the bloody body of a wild duck. Disturbed by the stamping of Peredur's horse, it flew off, to be replaced by a carrion raven. The combination of red spots, black feathers and white snow reminded the demented knight of his beloved Blanchefleur, with her crim-son cheeks, raven curls and alabaster skin. Madly, Peredur struck dozens of Arthur's knights to the ground, before his uncle restored him to his senses.

Peredur's adventures became more mythical. He had to kill a Black Worm with a magical stone in its tail; also a mon-ster named Addanc, which lived under a dark lake and killed other knights with its stone spear. Eventually he reached Constantinople, as the crusaders would. There he became the husband of a beautiful empress, whose foremother Helena was meant to be a progenitor of King Arthur. She gave him a prehistoric stone talisman with magical powers, similar to the Stone of Scone, the Grail in *Parzival* or the sapphire pendant of Charlemagne. And Peredur was the sire of the Swan Knight Lohengrin in this genealogy of the Fisher Kings. Returning to the Grail Castle, he was initiated as its ruler, becoming celibate until his death. His last act of vengeance was to kill his mentors, the Witches, with the help of King Arthur. For they had maimed the previous Fisher King as well as severing the head of his cousin, which had appeared on the bloody platter of the Grail.

This most Celtic of romances stressed the roots of the legends of the Grail in Welsh mythology. Its leading scholar identified six prototypes: the pearl-rimmed cauldron of the Head of Annwn; the Cauldron of Britain always guarded by Manawyd; a similar cauldron of Bran; the Cup of Truth of Manannan; the cup of sovereignty in the palace of Lug; and the Cauldron of Blathnat. All these sacred vessels shared characteristics of the Grail, with its many properties. They could heal wounds and madness with sweet spices. They could provide endless supplies of food and drink in the manner of the Cornucopia of the classical age. As was said of the unearthly palace of Labraid in the Irish poem of the *Sickbed of Cuchulinn*:

> *There is a vat there with joyous mead,*
> *Which is distributed to the household.*
> *It continues ever – enduring is the custom –*
> *So that it is always constantly full.*

Another shared property of the Celtic and Christian Grails was their refusal to sustain the unworthy. In Robert de Boron's *Joseph*, when the Blessed Jew from Arimathea fed the multitude with the Grail, one part of the crowd was filled with sweetness and its heart's desire, while the other part felt nothing. The Cup of Truth of Manannan shattered if three lies were told, and combined its pieces if three truths were said. And in the Cauldron of Britain, the meat of a coward would never boil, while the meat of a hero was instantly cooked.

An interpretation of the Grail Castle of Corbenic equated it with the Greek and Celtic horn of plenty. In Old French, it was *li Chastel del Cor Benit*, or the Castle of the Blessed Horn, the name of one of the Cathar fortresses. In the *Livre de Caradoc*, a horn that tested the virtue of the drinker was described as ivory, studded with precious stones, and *beneis*, or blessed. This ancient version of a Grail of plenty, allied with the fiery and bleeding spear of Lug, and with the trial of the Good Knight in welding together his broken sword as in the Sword of Gurgulain, were all reminders of the Celtic origins of the legend.

The mysteries of the Grail confirmed their Gnostic doctrines. Only Master Blihis could reveal them in the *Elucidation* that preceded *The History of the Grail*. In the *Continuation* by Gautier de Doulens, the maiden on the white mule said that these were matters too sacred for anybody not in the holy life to tell. Robert de Boron declared in his *Joseph* that he did not dare to describe his story, unless he had the great book in which were written the secrets called the Grail. And in the *Didot Perceval*, the Voice of God said to Bron: 'Our Lord commands you to teach to Perceval those secret words which he taught Joseph in prison, when he delivered the Grail to you.'

Peredur and *Perceval* drew from a similar tradition and material, yet they did not correspond except in the guiding myth of the Grail. Both were probably inspired by the Irish *Baile in Scáil*, an account of Conn's visit to the palace of the god Lug, who appeared as a pale horseman. Conn arrived to find a princess on a crystal throne, who gave him magic food and wine from a golden drinking cup. With each draught, Lug named the descendants of Conn who would reign in Tara. The place and the figures disappeared, leaving Conn with two Grails in the shape of a golden vessel and a silver vat.

Conn's posterity and power were confirmed in the Irish myth, while Peredur and Perceval failed in their first attempts to replace the Fisher King at the Grail Castle. When Peredur saw the maiden bearing the Grail platter, he did not realise that she was the empress whom he would later marry and so achieve power and his inheritance. And in *Peredur*, unlike in *Perceval*, the author was conscious that the Welsh peoples were being invaded and conquered by the Normans, who had taken over England. The huge and bleeding spear that preceded this platter was a symbol of a wasted Wales with its wounds and sufferings. His hero had to inspire his countrymen to resistance before he could rule again in the Celtic castle of the Grail.

The Fisher King himself was usually called Bron after the Celtic god Bran, and his characteristics were confused remarkably with those of the legendary Joseph of Arimathea in the quest romances. The head of Bran was kept alive by spiritual food, as was Joseph in prison. Both had access to magic vessels which dispensed life. Bran, indeed, was also wounded in the leg by a poisoned lance, and was connected with the sea, a fisher of men; so was Joseph with his miracles. And as the leading Welsh commentator on *Peredur* has pronounced, the melting pot between Celtic and Christian sources in the tales of the Arthurian knights was striking:

The story of the Grail is the story of a symbol which is transferred from one religion to another, retaining most of its original significance. The Celtic god who possessed the marvellous vessel was the god of the sun, lord of the Otherworld, creator of mankind. The maiden who carried the cup and 'married' the hero was Sovereignty, the goddess who represented the kingdom. The union between hero and goddess symbolised the possession of his kingdom by the hero. In the sovereignty tales the hero is given food, and in the Grail castle the events occur during, or shortly after, a meal.

The symbolism was easily fused with already existing

*Christian symbolism. The ceremony is still connected
with food and drink of a kind easily recognized by men,
but endowed with ritual significance. The Last Supper
was a meal on which was based the sacrament of Holy
Communion . . . The Grail's power to produce food may
be traced to the marvellous vessels possessed by the
gods and Otherworld beings in Celtic mythology. The
power to move of itself comes from the same source.
Both characteristics were easily adapted to the
demands of Christianity by attributing them to the
power of God.*

Ancient and Celtic and Christian was the Grail. And yet in
Germany, other resonances would be added to its grace,
which would become the mythological music and vision of
the late nineteenth century.

Chapter Six

The Grail of Germany

Then Kyot my master read the tale Flegetanis told,
And he searched in old books of Latin for the name of the
    people,
Who God accounted worthy of keeping the wonderful Grail,
Who were true and pure in their acts and in their humble
    hearts.

Wolfram von Eschenbach, *Parzival*

If the Celtic bards dwelt on a Grail of blood and sacrifice and
the French troubadours elected a Grail of bounty and love,
the German poets of the time preferred a Grail of chivalry
and of stone. The Arthurian romances passed over to the
Hohenstaufen renaissance in Germany with the works of
Hartmann von Aue. Almost as obscure as the other authors
of the Round Table, he was probably a knight himself in
imperial service, from the canton of Zurich in Switzerland. In
the last two decades of the twelfth century, he wrote epics in
verse, including an *Erec* and an *Iwein*, adapted from Chrétien
de Troyes and the Welsh *Owein* in the *Mabinogion*. These
Arthurian adventures concentrated more on his contemporary society of serving knights than on any search for the
divine. He praised chivalry as a social and moral duty. His
heroes were limited in their use of force by a code, not by the
intervention of grace or angels. Both of his German successors in Arthurian romances, the rivals Wolfram von
Eschenbach and Gottfried von Strassburg, praised his
genius: 'How he adorns his stories inside and out with words

and wisdom!' Whoever could appreciate fine language had to grant von Aue 'the crown and the laurels'.

Gottfried von Strassburg could not extend such admiration to the greatest of his fellow poets, Wolfram von Eschenbach. His own *Tristan* was a polished piece in praise of courtly love, but in the middle of his work he denounced the author of *Parzival* as 'the friend of the hare', fanciful and inclined to alchemy and nonsense. He totally misunderstood Wolfram's subtlety and fervency in pursuing the secrets of the Grail. For Gottfried, that quest from Camelot for the source of divine plenty and grace was merely the consuming passion found by Tristan and Isolde in the Cave of Lovers – no hermit's retreat with a bare altar.

> *Their high feast was Love, who gilded all their joys; she brought them King Arthur's Round Table as homage and all its company a thousand times a day. What better food could they have for body or soul? Man was there with Woman, Woman there with Man. What else should they be needing? They had what they were meant to have, they had reached the goal of their desire.*

This praise of ecstasy in human want was secondary to the author of *Parzival*. Like Hartmann von Aue, Wolfram was probably a poor and unfree knight in imperial service, from Upper Franconia in Bavaria. He reached the court of the Landgrave Hermann of Thuringia, who had also welcomed the great *minnesinger* Walther von der Vogelweide. A claim to illiteracy – 'I haven't a letter to my name' – may well have been proof of his sense of irony. If he said that he could neither read nor write, in company with so many of the troubadours, yet he knew in depth much of contemporary German and French literature, as well as oriental tales. In the Grail romances, his *Parzival* and *Titurel* would translate their messages to Wagner's operas, so that we may still hear and see some of those lost splendours and mysteries.

Parzival and the East

In giving the source of his *Parzival*, Wolfram von Eschenbach claimed that Chrétien de Troyes had wronged the tale, which actually derived from a Provençal cleric named Kyot, probably Guiot de Provins, a supporter of the Knights Templar, who visited Mayence in 1184 when the Holy Roman Emperor Frederick Barbarossa conferred knighthood on his sons at Pentecost. But Wolfram further claimed that the true source of the Grail was oriental. A Jewish astrologer named Flegetanis had recorded the story in a foreign language, most likely Arabic, in Toledo under the Moors.

> *And the heathen Flegetanis could read in the high*
> *heavens*
> *How the stars roll on their courses, how they circle the*
> *silent sky,*
> *And the time when the wandering ends, and the life and*
> *the fate of men*
> *He read in the stars, and he saw strange secrets . . .*

Watching the heavens, Flegetanis discerned the mystery of the Grail, which was written in a cluster of stars. Angels had left it on earth to be guarded by the best of the knights, as *Parzival* would relate. It was identified as a green stone fallen from heaven after the battle of Lucifer with the Trinity. Furthermore, it had close affinities with the source of the sacred Islamic black stone at the centre of Mecca, a meteorite also believed to have fallen from heaven and to be a means of communication with God. The Koran stated that it was given by the Angel Gabriel at the time of the building of the cubic shrine, the Ka'aba, where it was kept. The Muslim commentator, Ibn Malik, also told of a vision of the Prophet Muhammad, in which He ascended to the skies and saw a green goblet 'of such penetrating brightness that all the seven heavens are illuminated by it . . .' A voice declared, 'O Muhammad, the All Highest God has created this goblet for

Your enlightenment.' Both divine stone and cup remain important in Islamic belief.

For thirteen hundred years, pilgrims on the *hajji* to Mecca have been directed to enter the Ka'aba and kiss the black meteorite embedded in the wall. Once it was stolen by a Shi'ite sect, but it was ransomed and returned. Religious traditions associated the sacred stone with Adam and with Abraham, as well as with Allah, stating that an angel brought it to earth to record the deeds of the faithful, to be examined on the Day of Judgement. Worn smooth by tens of millions of lips, this heavenly blessing was the sole object from the pagan temple which the Prophet Muhammad kept when he converted the idolatrous shrine at Mecca into an Islamic temple. Apparently, a flash of lightning persuaded the Prophet to retain this Muslim Grail. As the poet Ikbal Ali Shah wrote, the Ka'aba was the heart of the body of the world:

> *And the stone that you call the Black Stone was itself a ball of dazzling light. In ages past, the Prophet said, it shone like the crescent moon, until at last the shadows, falling from the sinful hearts of those who gazed on it, turned its surface black. And since this amber gem, that came to earth from Paradise with the Holy Spirit, has received such impressions upon itself, what should be the impressions which our hearts receive? Indeed, whoever shall touch it, being pure of conscience, is like him who has shaken hands with God.*

In *Parzival*, Wolfram von Eschenbach went as far as giving his perfect Christian knight a piebald half-brother, Feirefiz, born in the Levant. The subtext of the long romance was, indeed, the reconciliation of Christians and Muslims, and their respect for one another; also the change of nature of the Grail to a stone fallen from heaven as at Mecca. *Parzival* began by defining lack of faith as dark and the Christian soul as white.

*As one sees the magpie's feathers, which are both black
    and white,
Yet one may win no blessing . . .*

Eschenbach also stressed the hidden significance of his text:
'I tell my story like the bowstring and not like the bow. The
string is here a figure of speech. Now *you* think the bow is
fast, but faster is the arrow sped by the string.'

In *Parzival*, Gamuret Angevin, a knight from the crusading
French family of Fulk of Anjou, which produced the kings of
Jerusalem, took up service with the Muslim Baruch of
Baghdad. Dressed in his surcoat 'green as the emerald vase',
Gamuret defended a black Muslim queen's city, defeating
Scots, Norse and French crusaders. He then married the
queen, returned to Europe and left her with their son Feirefiz,
striped like a humbug, 'dark and light, black and white . . . as
a magpie the hue of his face and hair'. Feirefiz grew up to
become a supreme knight, whose surcoat of precious stones,
asbestos shield and cloak of salamander could defeat the
knights of fire. Back in Europe, Gamuret married Queen
Herzeloyde and then returned to fight for the Baruch at
Alexandria, where he was treacherously killed because the
blood of a he-goat was poured on to his diamond helmet,
which made it soft as a sponge and vulnerable to a spearthrust.
Other crusaders serving their Muslim rulers buried the
Angevin knight under an emerald cross presented by the
Baruch, while Parzival was born to Gamuret's abandoned
queen.

As in the romance of Chrétien de Troyes, Parzival began
his career in chivalry as a fool, a rapist and a robber. So when
the Fisher King, with his incurable wound, whose 'life was
but dying', directed him to the Grail Castle, he was tongue-
tied at the wonders that he saw. A squire carried the bleeding
Holy Lance through the great hall in front of the assembled
knights of the Holy Grail, while the Grail Queen bore the
Grail stone on a cushion of green silk:

Root and blossom of Paradise garden, that thing that
    men call 'The Grail',
The crown of all earthly wishes, fair fullness that never
    shall fail.

Unknown to Parzival, the Grail Queen was his aunt. She laid the Grail on a pillar of jacinth, and its horn of plenty nourished all the knights and maidens in the castle.

It was the Grail that fed them, who before the Grail
    did stand.
For the food and drink each was desiring, each might
    stretch out his hand . . .
Food warm or cold, or dishes that known or unknown
    can be,
Food wild or tame – Such riches you never on earth
    shall find . . .
For the Grail was the crown of blessing, the bounty of
    the earth's delight.

Parzival was given a mystical sword, its hilt carved from a ruby. But he did not question the mystery of the bleeding lance, the abundant Grail or the incurable wound of the Fisher King. Simpleton that he was, he woke in the morning in a deserted castle and rode away to King Arthur's camp, where he was blamed by the sorceress Cundrie for not asking the Fisher King the question that would heal him. He was even told that his Muslim half-brother Feirefiz would marry the Grail Princess on Munsalvaesche, the Mount of Salvation. Parzival left again on the quest for the Grail, and killed a knight who was defending the Grail Castle. He was bitter against God, who had made a fool of him. But he met a hermit, Trevrizent, who had a green shrine or reliquary, and who revealed to him the origin of the Grail and the nature of its later defenders.

Here *Parzival* specifically identified the Knights of the Grail as *Templeise*, wearing white surcoats with red crosses as the Templar Knights did. The Templars, of course, had many contacts with their Muslim equivalents, the Sufis, and some of their secret practices – particularly a belief in self-less obedience and purity – derived from oriental mysticism. The German romance preached religious toleration between Christianity and Islam, especially when a crusader might rule over a Muslim land or a Muslim over Christian believers. When Parzival finally asked the Fisher King the right question and healed him, and himself became the Grail King, Feirefiz was baptised from a ruby font standing on a round pillar of jasper: this was filled with holy water by the Grail. Feirefiz now married the princess of the castle, who would give birth to the Christian African emperor Prester John. The black-and-white colour of his skin could now be seen as the Templar battle-flag, *Beauséant*. At his baptism, these words appeared carved on the Grail, a prophecy of the fate of Lohengrin, the son of Parzival:

> *The Templar whom God to a strange folk should send*
> *   as head,*
> *Must ban all word or question of his country or home*
> *   or race,*
> *If his subjects want their rights from him and would in*
> *   his sight find grace,*
> *They must not ask his origin, for he must leave them*
> *   straightaway.*

This concept of semi-divine rule on earth by a companionship of mysterious monastic Knights Templar confirmed the links between the concept of the Grail, the crusades and the military orders, which were influenced by Islam because of a mutual respect bred by long diplomacy and frequent wars over the Holy Land and Jerusalem. The Knights of the Grail were the heirs of classical, oriental, Celtic and Christian tradition. They were called to their duty individually by God. Their family names appeared by a miracle on the Grail itself. Only they might benefit from its blessedness.

And, most significantly, Wolfram von Eschenbach wrote of the Knights of the Grail:

> *By a stone they live,*
> *And that stone is both pure and precious – Its name*
> *   you have never heard?*
> *Men call it Lapis Exilis –*
>
> *If you daily look at that stone*
> *(If a man you are, or a maiden) for a hundred years,*
> *If you look on its power, your hair will not grow grey,*
> *   your face appears*
> *The same as when you first saw it, your flesh and your*
> *   bone will not fail*
> *But young you will live for ever – And this stone all*
> *   men call the Grail.*

Wolfram von Eschenbach developed this description of the Grail as a stone taken down from heaven by angels, who then returned on high because of the sins of mankind. On Good Friday, a dove flew down with the white host to lay on the stone – the Body and Blood of Christ.

> *The stone from the Host receives all good that on earth*
> *   may be*
> *Of food or drink, which the earth bears as the bounty*
> *   of Paradise.*
> *All things in wood or water and all that fly beneath the*
> *   skies.*

This fallen stone, which was all fruitfulness and gave eternal youth, was also called *lapis exilis* by the alchemist Arnold of Villanova. He identified it as the Philosopher's Stone, not as the Grail. It was not made from green emerald, but was unremarkable in appearance. Such a correspondence made commentators look for alchemy in *Parzival* and presume that the author meant *lapis elixir*, the life-giving or Philosopher's Stone. Certainly Wolfram von Eschenbach was influenced by oriental and Cathar beliefs. The Jewish philosopher Flegetanis, whom he declared to be the discoverer of the Grail and of the bloodline of King Solomon, was thought to be Thabit ben Qorah, who lived in Baghdad at the end of the ninth century and translated Greek texts into Arabic from the legendary emerald tablet of Hermes Trismegistus, the semi-mythical founder of alchemy. Moreover, Wolfram's authority, Kyot or Guiot de Provins, was said to have lived in Jerusalem and at the court of Frederick Barbarossa, as well as being an initiate of the Templar mysteries, including their association with the Gnostics and the Assassins, the Islamic sect founded by the Old Man of the Mountains, almost as important in eastern myth as King Solomon. The Templars were believed to be the guardians both of the Grail and of the Temple of Solomon. It was perhaps significant that Solomon's Temple stood upon a rock, *lapis*, at the centre of the world, and it contained the Ark of the Covenant, the fount of the Christian faith. The cornerstone 'which the builders refused' in the Psalms was another symbol of Christ. And it was also upon this *lapis* or rock that the Christian Church was founded.

In the Book of Revelation of Saint John the Divine, the Holy Spirit as a stone and a green gem, or fire and crystal, was also emphasised. As the holy man saw in his vision:

> *Straightaway I was in the Spirit: and, behold, there was a throne set in heaven, and one sitting upon the throne. And he that sat was to look upon like a jasper stone and a sardius; and there was a rainbow round the throne, like an emerald to look upon . . . There were seven lamps of fire burning before the throne, which are the seven Spirits of God. And before the throne there was a sea of glass like unto crystal . . .*

The visions of the legendary Knights of the Grail of *Parzival* also depicted the Holy Vessel as a sacred stone.

Indeed, a blessed stone was the foundation of the faith, as

Bishop William Durand de Mende made clear in his thirteenth-century manual for understanding the symbolic significance of cathedrals and churches. Repeating from the words of Christ, 'I will liken him unto a wise man, which built his house upon a rock,' the bishop or the priest who had permission to conduct the ceremony should sprinkle holy water to chase from that place ghosts and demons. Then he should put on the foundations the first stone, on which would have been engraved the sign of the Cross. Onyx should adorn the sanctuary, while the church should be the replica of the human body of Christ, facing to the east.

As for the chalices in the church, Bishop de Mende admitted that they were first carved from simple wood, then made of glass, but at the Council of Reims, Pope Urban had said that the ceremony of the Mass must use vessels of gold or silver; brass might serve in poor churches.

> *The chalice must not then be of glass, because of its fragility and the danger of spilling the Blood of Christ, nor of wood, because it is porous and like a sponge, and absorbs the Blood of Our Lord, nor of tin or copper, because the force of the poison produced by these metals provokes bile and vomiting.*

Quoting from the Bible that many chalices were made in gold, the Bishop declared that we should offer the Lord what was most precious to us to vanquish our avarice, even if He preferred plain holders of His Body and Blood.

Another source for *Parzival* was a legendary treasure of Solomon, which was taken to Rome after the fall of Jerusalem, then seized by the Visigoths. When Muslim armies captured Toledo, they asked after Solomon's Table, which was meant to be able to feed all who sat down to eat and to be made from a gigantic emerald, the sacred green stone of the alchemists. The Table was said to be hidden away in a Grail Castle in the mountains of Spain. Charlemagne was also said to have copied the Table of

Solomon by having the universe made as three circles in jewels and precious metals, then set on legs of gold as another version of King Arthur's Round Table, for himself and twelve knights. The Koran itself referred to a table brought down from Heaven by Jesus to feed Him and the Apostles, but this divine gift disappeared again because of the sins of mankind.

Significantly, in *Parzival*, when the oriental sorceress Cundrie came to the court of King Arthur, she listed seven planets by their Arabic names. She was not referring to the cosmic disc of silk spread on the grass as a knightly table; but she was conferring a blessing on Parzival, prophesying that he would become the Fisher King and the father of the perfect Swan Knight Lohengrin, who would be his heir. He was fated to succeed by the courses of the heavens, although when he would be asked about his origins, he would have to abandon his family and retire into the obscurity of his arrival.

Listen, Parzival! The highest planet Zwal [Saturn]
And swift Almustri [Jupiter], Almaret [Mars] and
*   bright Samsi [the Sun],*
They declare your fortune. The fifth is called Alligufir
*   [Venus],*
And the sixth Alkiter [Mercury], and the nearest one
*   Alkamer [the Moon].*
I do not speak as in a dream. These are the stayers in
*   the firmament.*
Their whirling speed controls their opposing paths.
Care is gone now. All the circuit of these stars
*   encompasses,*
All they illuminate is in your reach to be attained and
*   won.*

There had been little oriental alchemy in the *Perlesvaus*, which also named the crusading Templars as the keepers of the Grail. But they were hardly given Muslim blood brothers as Parzival was Feirefiz. They were presented as brutal killers against pagan Islam. The Grail was the chalice of Christ's blood, not a mystic stone which might also signify *vas Hermetis* or the Philosopher's Stone of the alchemists, capable of transmuting all to spiritual harmony. Cruder and uncompromising, the Celtic texts lacked the sympathetic synthesis of the mysticism of the Near East, which was the history of the Grail as given in *Parzival*, according to the hermit Trevrizent, who made the hero repent and reach for his goal at last.

Parzival was told that when Lucifer rebelled against the Lord God, some of the angels took neither side. They were sent down to earth to look after the Grail. Wavering between good and evil like Parzival in the sinful and dual world of the Cathars, they were recalled to heaven, leaving their charge with the family of Titurel. He was lamed in his old age, although kept alive by the Grail, while his successor and son Frimutel was killed, to be replaced by his son King Anfortas. Trevrizent was the brother of the Grail King, while the mother of Parzival, Herzeloyde, was his sister. Another sister had died giving birth to a daughter, Sigune, while the third sister, Repanse de Schoye, was still unmarried and led the twenty-four maidens who carried the Grail in procession.

Another source of the Grail in *Parzival* was most likely a version of the *Alexanderlied*. In this Latin book of the exploits of the Greek conqueror, Alexander went to the Earthly Paradise, which some poets declared was, or was near to, the Grail Castle. He was presented with a stone which gave youth to the old. This *lapis exilis* was like a human eye, but brilliant and rare in its colours. An ancient Jew told Alexander that it would tip the scales, heavier than any sack of gold, yet a feather would weigh more if any dirt stained the holy stone. While human greed was insatiable, even the eye of the conqueror would be stopped by dust. 'This stone came before you, master of the world. It warns you and rebukes you. This small talisman restrains you from desire and base ambition.'

So Alexander was deterred from making the whole earth

into his empire. This tale of the stone from paradise was an admirable metaphor for Wolfram's version of the Grail. It was also the fountain of life, restoring youth to the aged. Although Wolfram wrote that his stone was given its powers by a dove descending from heaven on Good Friday with a bountiful wafer in its beak, its provenance was Greek and Jewish and Islamic mythology and belief. The Host brought by the Holy Spirit was the gilt on the pagan rock.

While he was composing his *Parzival*, Wolfram was living in the forest castle of Wildenberc, probably near Amorbach in the Odenwald. In describing the Grail Castle of Munsalvaesche, he correctly put together the Mount of Salvation with the Wild Mountain, derived from the Latin *silvaticus* or 'wooded' as much as *salvationis* or 'redemption'. The Grail itself was kept in a temple, allowing its keepers to be called *Templeise* or Templars. Uniquely, the bleeding spear which was lamented by the Knights of the Grail had a poisoned head, occasionally thrust into the stinking wound of King Anfortas to relieve his pain with another one, if the planets stood against him.

The pair of silver knives in the Grail procession had been made by the mystic smith Trebuchet to cut off the hard ice round the tip of the piercing and healing spear. They may be connected with the knives used by Nicodemus to scrape off the dried blood of Christ. These were discarded when Anfortas was cured of the sinful sore in his genitals, and Parzival himself became the Grail King, with Repanse de Schoye, as the goddess of plenty, bearing the Grail. Lay people performed all the ceremonies of the Grail, and a priest was only brought into Munsalvaesche to baptise the pagan Feirefiz – even then, the font was filled with holy water by the power of the Grail, which was the direct grace of God brought to the elect without the intervention of the Catholic Church.

Moreover, the Grail was given the power of restoring youth. After his recovery, Anfortas was declared to look more beautiful than Parzival himself. The mythical phoenix, which rose reborn from the flame and the ashes, was uniquely associated by Wolfram with the Grail, suggesting its powers of resurrection before the Millennium. The comparison also recalled the Fourth of the Twelve Keys of the alchemist Basilius Valentinus:

> *When ashes and sand are thoroughly baked for just the right amount of time, the master makes a glass out of them which henceforth will always resist the fire and resembles in colour a transparent stone and can no longer be recognised as ash. To the ignorant that is a great mysterious art, but not to the wise, for by knowledge and repeated experience it becomes a handicraft . . . At the Last Judgement the world will be judged by fire – fire that has been created by the Master out of nothing – the world must again become ashes through fire; out of these ashes will the Phoenix at last bring forth again her young.*

Wolfram gave his holy stone the further power of creating a paradise on earth around Munsalvaesche and granting a life approaching the eternal to its dedicated servants. In this way, the Wild or Wooded Mountain became the true one of salvation, and the Waste Land was turned into a Garden of Eden.

Parzival made the Knights of the Grail a higher order than those of the Round Table. While they might move from the Court of King Arthur to Munsalvaesche, nobody could join the elect without being named on the Grail, the judge of his knightly service. The military orders of the crusades, particularly the Templars and the Teutonic Knights, inspired Wolfram into grading such cavaliers dedicated to God above the run of the *ritter* in imperial service. Yet their duty was mortal combat. Parzival could not conceive of any way of finding the Grail without jousting, if necessary to the death. He was, indeed, only saved from killing his half-brother Feirefiz by the breaking of his sword through the will of God. As he told Trevrizent:

If one can win fame in this world and paradise
In the next, through the use of shield and lance,
Then knightly fighting was my only wish.
I fought where I could find a combat.
So I have acquired some fame. If God is wise in battle,
He ought to summon me there [to the Grail Castle]
So they will know me: I will turn down no fight.

Knightly devotion and loyalty, or *triuwe*, to a feudal lord was linked to devotion to the Lord God Almighty. Parzival began his adventures hardly knowing the difference, but Trevrizent instructed him to be true without wavering, 'since God himself is devotion'. In return for the love of Christ, the knight should serve His representatives on earth, the good rulers and the holy men, as well as save priests and women.

Four levels of existence in the works of Wolfram were complemented by four of time. There was the romantic world of King Arthur in the past. There were the real exploits of the House of Anjou exemplified by Gamuret, the father of Parzival, in Europe and the Near East. There were the adventures of Gawain, who rode between legend and fact, and served Wolfram as a vehicle to extol and gently mock the ideals of contemporary German chivalry. A higher dimension called everyone upon the Quest of the Grail. Politically, Wolfram was urging an ordered and disciplined succession to the Grail Castle of the Holy Roman Empire, the octagonal palace chapel of Charlemagne within Aachen Cathedral where his heirs were crowned. Spiritually, he demanded that the high standards of the crusading knights of the military orders be followed by all the imperial servants of Germany. Only through such a mystic sense of duty could a holy reign be reached.

The Perfection of *Titurel*

For his next epic, Wolfram turned back to the legend of Charlemagne in defence of the Holy Roman Empire. Shortly before his death, the Landgrave of Thuringia gave Wolfram a French romance, *Aliscans*, about William of Orange, the first cousin of the Emperor, a great warrior who ended as a Benedictine monk and saint near Montpellier. *Willehalm* was a paean of praise to the virtues of holy soldiers in the military orders. Wolfram combined *Aliscans* with the *Chanson de Roland* and the old German *Rolandslied* to commemorate Charlemagne's defeat at Roncesvalles with his successful conquest of north-eastern Spain, in which the historical William played a large part by a cavalry manoeuvre in the capture of Barcelona. He was eventually canonized as Saint William of Aquitaine.

The enemy was Islam; yet with his respect for Muslim chivalry, Wolfram did not make monsters of the foe. Their leader was King Terramer, a pagan said to worship Mahmet, Apolle, Tervagant and Kahun. His sin was to try and take the crown of the Holy Roman Empire. Rome itself was named nine times in the text, but not as the central city of Christendom, only in relation to Charlemagne at Aachen, where the imperial power lay. Wolfram's inspiration was probably his new patron, the young Landgrave Ludwig, a saintly crusader who had married another saint, the Hungarian Princess Elisabeth. On Ludwig's death from the plague while helping the Emperor Frederick II on a punitive expedition to the Holy Land, Elisabeth put on a Franciscan habit and devoted the rest of her life to the poor and the sick. She was canonised shortly after her death, and would be resurrected in Wagner's *Tannhäuser* as the Landgrave's unmarried niece, as well as in *Willehalm* as Countess Giburc, a 'holy lady'.

The opening of Wolfram's epic was devoutly Christian, with an invocation to the power of God over all things, even the elements important to the Gnostics and the alchemists:

In Thy hand runs the swiftness of the seven stars so they sustain the sky. Air, water, fire, and earth dwell wholly within Thy grandeur. At Thy command stand all things,

*wild and tame, that live. Moreover, Thy divine might
has delimited bright day and dark night and differenti-
ated them by the course of the sun. Never shall be, never
was Thy equal. The virtues of all stones, the odours of
all herbs Thou knowest utterly. Thy Spirit has substan-
tiated style and content of true writing, and my mind
takes note of Thee mightily. Of all that is written in
books I have remained unskilled; I am learned in no
wise but in having skill with which insight endows me.*

Apparently, Wolfram had been stung by the attack on the
heretical parts of *Parzival*, which he now excused as his lack
of skill, while stressing the supremacy of the Christian God
over all. Indeed, he soon mentioned *Parzival*, to say that it
had been praised by many people, but many also 'found fault
with it and adorned their narrative better'. In *Willehalm*, he
would state his own and others' complaints 'that men and
women of loyal nature have made since Jesus for baptism's
sake was plunged into Jordan'. He would now produce a
matchless and worthy story, told with dignity and truth, so
silencing the critics of his honour as a German knight.

Although *Willehalm* was not a Grail romance, it did deal
with the Holy Lance and characters from *Parzival*. The
hero's nephew Vivianz asked for the wafer of the Eucharist
as he lay dying, with the words, 'Yet give me His Body,
Whose Incarnation died of the blind man's spear when
Godhead survived.' In the *Aliscans*, Rainouart, another hero,
had prayed during a lull in a battle, 'By the lance Thou was
wounded deep. Longinus did that, who had good reward, for
where he saw not before, (that by faith it might be known),
Thy blood did pour down upon his hands, and when he
touched his eyes, he had illumination . . .' And as in *Parzival*,
the burning fragrance of aloe wood, which was in the air
when the body and soul of Vivianz were parted, was also
sensed in the Grail Castle when the wound of King Anfortas
was fumigated.

As for the Saracen army under King Terramer, many of

the host were descended from characters in *Parzival*. The King of Morocco came from the Baruch who had buried Parzival's father Gamuret. The Burgrave of Tasmê had inherited the city from Feirefiz, and he carried on his master's banner the animal device that Feirefiz had also used. Azagonc, where all the people were black, now had a Moorish king, although both Gamuret and Feirefiz had ruled there. And the helmet of King Terramer himself had been forged by the son of the legendary smith Trebuchet, the maker of the sword of the Grail King. In his orthodox crusading epic, Wolfram would not drop all the references to his poem of religious tolerance, *Parzival*.

Yet the abiding heritage of the Grail legend depended on the fragments of Wolfram's *Titurel*, later completed by another poet, Albrecht, under his predecessor's name as *Jüngurer Titurel*, 'The Young Titurel'. The theme of *Titurel* had been self-control, or the leash, which kept the knight or the dog on the true quest. Titurel had given the crown of the Grail Castle to his last surviving son, Frimutel, who was soon to die. His abdication was mourned by the Templars, 'whom he had often saved from many a difficult situation when he was defending the Grail with his own hand and with their aid'. Wolfram stressed again the importance of kinship and inheritance, particularly to the succession of the Holy Roman Empire. But his message was the leash on the hound, long and adorned with a green Arabian band and precious stones, emeralds, rubies, diamonds, chrysolites and garnets, held by Schionatulander, who had been on a crusade with Gamuret:

> Let me tell you what else he laid hold of along with the hound: he must experience unflinchingly grief lined with toil and great striving for combat. The hound's leash was indeed for him the source of joyless times.

The young Schionatulander must die while jousting in defence of the lands of Parzival. Inevitably, the love which he felt for the maiden Sigune became a trail of blood which led him to his death. Yet in the *Jüngerer Titurel* of Albrecht, the leash became a kind of Grail. Its pursuit would lead the hero to the Grail Castle. It also had messages written upon it, but they praised the code of the holy knight more than the desire for the divine.

In Albrecht's long story, the Grail Castle was a version of the Heavenly Jerusalem. Many stanzas praised its construction. On the top of its columns flew angels. Its altars were of sapphire beneath velvet canopies. The doves which brought the host of the Grail in *Parzival* were sculptures. God was the source of all the architecture. The dome of the castle was the cosmos and set towards the east. An astronomical clock charted the movements of the heavens. In the small temple in the centre, there was an organ with singing birds, a sculpture of the Last Judgment, bells, gargoyles and all the paraphernalia of Gothic cathedrals.

Believing in unbelief, Albrecht transmitted his Grail Castle to India, a magic realm where it could hardly be visited. This fanciful Temple of Solomon would not have convinced even a credulous medieval audience. Yet Albrecht's tale followed Wolfram's *Parzival* in its concentration on the hero finding his desire through self-discipline. In *Parzival*, the Grail was changed from a cornucopia of bounty to the bond of a way of life shared by an elect. In *Jüngerer Titurel*, the jewelled leash took the place of the Grail. The quest of Schionatulander was to retrieve it for his beloved Sigune, a member of the Grail family. His goal was perfect Christian knighthood, not the vision of God's grace. He proved himself the best of the knights of King Arthur, but not a holy seeker. The leash only brought joy to its possessor, while the Grail brought plenty and release from suffering.

The leash was always material, hardly spiritual. When Sigune read the messages upon it at the court of King Arthur, they were a sermon on knighthood. God and priests should be served; widows and orphans should be protected. Human traits were preferable to those of animals. A sense of shame, generosity and courage were the leading virtues. A Christian and knightly morality replaced the perilous quest for revelation. After the hero's final crusade to the East, he put the flashing leash on his helmet in his last Western combat, where it and he were destroyed. It was only the talisman of a German hero, never the search for the answer of God.

The Grail itself for Albrecht enhanced that of Wolfram. In his temple within the jewelled Grail Castle, a floating stone was the centre of the world. It represented Alexander's oracle at Siwa, the Stone of Destiny of the Celts, the meteoric Ka'aba at Mecca, and the step into heaven of the Prophet under the Dome of the Rock in Jerusalem. Yet Albrecht also took that version of the Grail into alchemy. He wrote that the Grail was a crystal, a compound of fire and water. These two of the four humours of medieval chemistry were capable of birth and resurrection. In that stone was the secret of life.

Chapter Seven

The Prodigal Grail

The scholars who have offered the three chief solutions for
the problem of the Grail have been able to make out an
excellent case. The Grail as Celtic talisman, as fertility
symbol, as Christian relic – each conception is supported by
masses of detailed evidence. The judicious scholar is driven
to admit that the Grail has signified many things to many
men at many times.

Roger Sherman Loomis, *Celtic Myth and Arthurian
Romance*

In the Middle Ages, faith mixed with fact. Miracles were not
confined to the time of Christ. They were still frequent happenings when holy relics were found. Saint Louis of France
said that miracles were only necessary for those who did not
believe. Bishop Hugh of Lincoln declared that those who
took the Eucharist daily did not need to pursue signs and
wonders. Yet the people of that age needed present proofs to
confirm their creed. For these were written in the Old
Testament as well as the New. Before Moses led the
Israelites out of Egypt, he overcame their doubts by changing his rod into the serpent of wisdom and by the transformation of the waters of the Nile into blood. Elijah called
down fire from the Lord to challenge the pagan priests. And
although Jesus refused to perform miracles to prove that He
was the Son of God, He relented by feeding the five thousand, as the Grail would, and by changing water into wine at
the feast at Cana.

Actually, one of the reasons for the spread of the Grail romances was a papal edict through a Lateran Council. In 1215, Innocent III withheld the communion cup from the laity. The dogma of transubstantiation was confirmed. Only the priest might eat and drink the Body and Blood of Christ before the congregation. This ban increased the power of the Church, which now stood between the supplicant and salvation. Yet, equally, it added to the appeal of a legend which told of the personal approach to God directly through a life of trial. When the Grail was also described as a Christian symbol from the Last Supper, the heresy that the religious institution from Rome had little significance in reaching the divine was most attractive.

The doctrine of transubstantiation was a late addition to the Catholic Church. One of its first appearances was in the sixth-century Coptic *Book of the Resurrection*, which told of the Apostles celebrating the sacrament after the Ascension of Christ. The mystical text stated: 'His body was upon the table, which they were all gathered around. And they divided it. They saw the blood of Jesus pouring out as living blood into the cup.' Such visions were also described by Gerald of Wales, when he wrote of the conversion of some of the heretic Paterini to the truth faith. In Ferrara, they saw the Host changed into a Holy Lamb or pieces of flesh and blood. In the ninth book of the *Dialogus Miraculorum* of Caesarius of Heisterbach, many witnesses spoke of the wafer taking the shape of Christ, or the wine changing into blood. Sometimes the Host became a crucified Child, whose blood flowed into the chalice. In the different Grail romances, all of these miraculous visions were variously given to Perceval, Galahad and Gawain, who once saw the Grail as flesh 'with a king crowned, nailed on a Cross, and a spear fast in his side'. These sightings derived from the popular religious culture of the period.

Other Grail stories were told in medieval terms. That holy vessel was given the power of selecting good from evil, the sheep from the goats, the blessed from the sinners. Dissolute priests often found the communion cup empty, while a dove flew off with the wafer. Before he was burned in 1290, a Jew of Billittes was denounced for blasphemy. The accusation declared that he had stabbed a consecrated Host and nailed it to a wall:

> *Blood was shed from it. He cast it into the fire: it flew round the room. Mad with rage, he fixed it on a stake and flogged it. He tried in vain to cut it in pieces. Again he fixed it to the wall and stabbed it, and a river of blood flowed from it. Finally he threw it into a cauldron of boiling water, which became bloody. The Host rose in the air, and the Jew saw Christ on the cross.*

Such metaphors as the bloody cauldron seemed to have their genesis in the Celtic chivalric romances about the Grail. Certainly, Caesarius of Heisterbach affirmed that a knight took the sacrament before a joust to safeguard himself from wounds. When he had won, he declared to his opponent that he had only eaten the Host that day. The reply was, 'If you had eaten the Devil, I would have overcome you.' Albigensian heretics, who were walking on water, were said to have drowned when the consecrated wafer was cast into the river. And when the Italian founder of the Apostolici was burned in 1300, he put out the fire by calling on the help of the fallen angel Asmodeus, only to have it rekindled by the bringing of the Host.

In the bloody romance of the *Perlesvaus*, the Grail was said to appear to King Arthur at the ceremony of the Mass 'in five different forms that none ought to tell'. The reason was that the Catholic Church had now reserved to the priests the mysteries of the sacrament. Only those elected by God should speak of them. 'King Arthur beheld all the changes; the last of them was a change into a chalice.' This communion cup was not now his to receive. It was withheld by the Church because of his regal sins. Yet the Grail was not always so constrained. It remained accessible to any perfect knight, who might reach it by his own endeavours.

The Destruction of the Guardians

The Knights Templar did have a direct approach to the divine without the benefit of the Catholic Church, which they appeared to serve. It was their worst heresy, although they were charged with many others. They shared this spiritual arrogance with their Islamic counterparts, the Sufis. To some, that name came from the Arabic for wool: for others, it derived from *Sophia* or Wisdom, dear to the Gnostics. As with the troubadours, the Sufis wrote poems of mystical love in the style of the Song of Solomon. Their cup of wine was a transcendent chalice, which might be broken at death.

The Sufis – like the Isma'ilis, the Templars and the Cathars – divided their initiates into classes: the Masters, the Prophets and the Saints. The Masters were the everlasting priesthood standing between the human and the divine; the Prophets were the teachers and messengers of the will of God; while the Saints reached the Heavenly Light through their good life on earth. The Templars had their Masters, too, and the Cathars their *perfecti*, with grades beneath them. The point of all these mystical orders and sects was clear. Total enlightenment was only given by God to the elect.

The prophet Muhammad himself was subject to ecstatic visions. He was given some of the text of the Koran in his dreams after visits from the Angel Gabriel, who brought him the command of God.

> *'He came to me,' said the apostle of God, 'while I was asleep, with a coverlet of brocade whereon was some writing, and said, "Read!" I said, "What shall I read?" He pressed me with it so tightly that I thought it was death; then he let me go and said, "Read!" I said, "What shall I read?" He pressed me with it again so that I thought it was death; then he let me go and said "Read!" I said, "What shall I read?" He pressed me with it the third time so that I thought it was death and said, "Read!" I said, "What then shall I read?" – and*

this I said only to deliver myself from him, lest he should do the same to me again. He said:

> *"Read in the name of the Lord who created,*
> *Who created man of blood coagulated.*
> *Read! Thy Lord is the most beneficent,*
> *Who taught by the pen,*
> *Taught that which they knew not unto men."*

'So I read it, and he departed from me. And I awoke from my sleep, and it was as though the words were written on my heart.'

Such were the trances in which the Knights of the Round Table saw the Grail turn into flesh. Such was the vision that the prophet Muhammad had of the green goblet, when he ascended into the seventh heaven from the Dome of the Rock in Jerusalem. Such was the Prophet's decision, when he decided to retain the pagan Ka'aba in Mecca as the holy cornerstone of Islam. As the Koranic verse testified: 'Glory be to Him who made His servant go by night from the Sacred Temple to the farther Temple whose surroundings We have blessed, that We might show him some of Our signs.'

The Sufis also felt, along with the Gnostics, a personal sense of identity with God, which put them at odds with their orthodox churches. They likened their mystical experiences to the prophet Muhammad's *mi'raj* or vision of the divine. Their otherworld, however, was not that of the Celts or the Arthurian Grail Castle. It was not a heaven or a hell, but rather an area in the cosmos where the individual soul met the One Maker of the universe. The prophet Muhammad had spoken in the Koran of the ninety-nine names of God. But for the Sufis, there were infinite names of God, each appropriate to the seeker after His identity. As with the quest for the Grail, it revealed itself in the form appropriate to each searcher after its truth.

The Sufis also stressed self-knowledge as the only way of

progress towards the knowledge of God. This was the lesson of Bernard of Clairvaux, the founder of the Cistercian monks and the supporter of the Knights Templar. It was echoed also in the character of Perceval in the first Grail romance by Chrétien de Troyes. Saint Bernard even dared to write his *Advice to a Pope* on this theme:

> *What does it profit you if you gain the whole world and lose one person – yourself? Even if you were a wise man your wisdom would lack something if it did not benefit you. How much would it lack? Everything, I feel. Although you know every mystery, the width of the earth, the height of the heavens, the depth of the sea, if you do not know yourself, you are like a building without a foundation; you raise not a structure but ruins. Whatever you construct outside yourself will be but a pile of dust blown by the wind. Therefore, he is not wise, whose wisdom is no benefit to himself. The wisdom of a wise man will benefit him and he will be the first to drink from the waters of his own well. Therefore, let your consideration begin and end with yourself . . . You should consider what you are, who you are, and what sort of man you are: what you are in nature, who you are in person, and what sort of man you are in character. What you are, for example, is man. Who you are: Pope and Supreme Pontiff. What sort of man: kind, gentle, and so forth.*

In the original Grail tale, Perceval did not understand his own name, let alone his nature. Even when he was told what he was called, he did not know whether his name was the true one. Ignorance of the death of his mother at his departure, and of himself, made him fail his test at the Grail Castle. Saint Bernard had condemned not knowing oneself as the source of pride and sin. To be unaware was not good enough:

> *Do you suppose it availed the first man, or was it*

allowed that he did not sin willingly, because he pleaded his wife, that is, the weakness of the flesh, in defence? Or will the stoners of the first martyrs, because they stopped their ears, be excusable through ignorance? . . . For God knows what you do not know, and He is the one who judges you.

Self-knowledge and self-control might allow the Sufi or the Knight Templar to achieve the ecstatic vision of the One Creator, whose sign was the Grail. Perceval might have achieved that as Parzival did in his German story, for Chrétien de Troyes left his original masterpiece incomplete. He did describe the Grail as golden and jewelled, but blazing with brilliant light, *tant sainte chose*, or such a sacred thing. It was more than the Christian chalice, it was the giver of spiritual life which by its qualities had also nourished for fifteen years the body of the maimed Fisher King. It was the Holy Light which blazed from the stone Grail in *Parzival*, the Shining Wisdom of the One that united Sufi and Gnostic and Knight Templar in the vision of the unity of the universal.

This was not the heresy for which the Templars would be condemned. They were brought down by the original sins of Perceval: arrogance and ignorance of themselves within the ways of the world. With the loss of their function as the defenders of pilgrims and the Temple of Solomon in Jerusalem, they had become money brokers and guardians of treasure rather than the Grail. They owned some nine thousand manors across Europe, all of which were free of taxes, and they provided security for the storage and transport of bullion. The treasury of the King of France was normally kept in the vaults of the Temple in Paris; the King himself took refuge there when threatened by mobs. The only cash drafts that were readily redeemable were issued by the Templars. They became the bankers of the Levant, and later of most of the courts of Europe. When King Louis VII accepted a large loan from the order, he noted that the money must be repaid quickly, 'lest their House be defamed and destroyed'. Even the Muslims banked with the Templars, in case the fortunes of war should force them to ally themselves with the Christians. Though usury was forbidden to Christians in the Middle Ages, the Templars added to the money they stored or transported by paying back an agreed sum less than the original amount, while a debtor returned more than his debt. The Paris Temple became the centre of the world's money market.

The Templars were so proud that they became the judges of monarchs in the way that the Grail judged sinners. 'So long as you do exercise justice,' the Master of the Temple declared to Henry III of England, 'you will reign, but if you infringe it, you will cease to be King.' The implication was that he might be deposed by the military order.

Pride, or *superbia*, was considered the worst of sins in the Middle Ages. To this, the Templars added secret rituals and diplomacy, which aggravated the envy and hatred of them by the princes and the people. They were seen both as the poor knights of Christendom and as rich conspirators against the state and public welfare. When King Philip IV of France imprisoned more than six hundred of the three thousand Templars in the country in 1307, according to Inquisition records, their interrogation and torture produced confessions which corroborated medieval superstitions, but were the result of applying force and pain. They were not the evidence of truth.

Although the initiation rights of the Templars were secret, there was a Rule of the Temple. Their hidden regulations were to provide the key to their destruction, although they could hardly have existed as a proud and efficient military caste without special ceremonies to distinguish them from other orders such as the Knights Hospitaller of Saint John and the Teutonic Knights. The investitures were secret, being held under cover of darkness in a guarded chapter house. The Rule was clandestine in so far as it was known in its entirety to only the highest officers of the Temple. We know it merely in copies, which describe the constitution of the order, and the duties and ceremonies of each rank. But because of this element of secrecy, and because the original manuscript of the Rule has not survived, opponents of the Templars have always postulated the existence of a separate and secret Rule that would endorse blasphemy and sexual licence.

An unbiased account of their initiation ritual gave the following details. The Master of the Temple asked the assembled knights three times if there was any objection to a particular novice's admission to the order. The novice himself was shown 'the great hardships of the House, and the commandments of charity that existed'. He was also asked if he had a wife or betrothed, debts or hidden disease, other vows or other master. If the novice answered these questions satisfactorily, he knelt in front of the Master and asked to become 'the serf and slave of the House'. The Master replied that many things were required of him and that the Templars' beautiful horses and costume were no more than the 'outer shell' of their life, as was the armour of the knights in the Grail quest. The self-control and service taught by Saint Bernard was their duty.

You do not know the hard commandments that are within; because it is a hard thing for you, who are master of yourself, to make yourself the serf of another. For you will scarcely ever do what you want; if you wish to be on this side of the sea, you will be sent to the other side; or if you wish to be in Acre, you will be sent to the land of Tripoli or Antioch or Armenia, or you will be sent to Apulia or Sicily or Lombardy or France or Burgundy or England or to many other lands where we have Houses and possessions. If you wish to sleep, you will be made to stay awake; and if you sometimes wish to stay awake, you will be ordered to go and rest in your bed.

Guiot de Provins, the contemporary monk and poet who belonged to Holy Orders and condemned his own time as 'vile and filthy', testified to the Templars' integrity, praising them above all other religious orders. He found them dedicated unto death, ascetic knights whom his shrinking flesh could admire and refuse to join.

> *Better far be cowardly and alive,*
> *Than dead, the most famous of them all.*
> *The Order of the Templars, I know well,*
> *Is beautiful and excellent and sure –*
> *But keeping healthy keeps me from war.*

Guiot from Provence had been the most likely source of the *Parzival* of Wolfram von Eschenbach, who certainly shared his opinion of the worthiness of the Knight's Templar, whom he made the Keepers of the Grail. After their destruction, many would join another military order familiar to Wolfram, the Teutonic Knights, then carving out an empire towards Russia. Their new headquarters was in the stronghold of Marienburg in Prussia. Their opportunity lay on the eastern marches, and they did not wish to share in the fate of the Templars in France. They would be protected in Germany as military agents of the states and the bishops on a crusade to dominate and convert the pagan Lithuanians. With its twelve bailiwicks in the Holy Roman Empire stretching from Alsace to Austria and Saxony, and its Baltic conquests as far as Livonia, the order was a temporal power. The inhabitants were converted to Christianity by the sword and the efficient administration of the knights from their fortresses. As the English philosopher and cleric Roger Bacon observed, the brothers of the Teutonic Order who laboured for the conversion of the heathens wanted to reduce them to serfdom. Resistance to the Christian Knights was against 'oppression, not the arguments of a superior religion'.

Particularly significant in the German military order was its cult of the Virgin Mary. Her office was said daily, while a twenty-foot-tall mosaic in gold of Her was inlaid on the church of the great castle of the order at Marienburg. This was a development in northern Europe from the more oriental beliefs of the Templars, although their Rule also declared Our Lady to be the beginning and the end of their religion. Her supreme symbol as Queen of Heaven was the foliate rose, the rose of the centre of the world. She was also the living Grail, for She contained and gave birth to the Body and Blood of Her Son.

Those Templar Knights who managed to escape by sea went to Scotland and to Portugal, where they landed near Nazare and proceeded to their main stronghold at Tomar. There they were particularly well received because of their experience in navigation. They were incorporated into the same order under another title, the Knights of Christ. The ships of the renamed order sailed under the eight-pointed red cross of the Templars. The African explorer Vasco da Gama was a Knight of Christ, and Prince Henry the Navigator was to become a Grand Master.

In other European countries, the Templars merged with the Knights Hospitaller of Saint John, or left the order and went underground. The other seaborne French refugee Templars made their way to Scotland, probably with their treasury and the remaining archives from the Paris Temple. One French Masonic tradition declares that the records and wealth – perhaps including the two precious Grails containing the Holy Blood from the sack of Constantinople – were taken on nine vessels to the Isle of Mey in the Firth of Forth near the St Clair castle of Rosslyn. Some of these vessels also went to Ireland and then to the Western Isles of Scotland. Indeed, a recent inquiry has discovered Templar graves by Kilmartin church, near Loch Awe in Argyll. One tombstone bears the steps of the Temple of Solomon leading up to a foliate cross beside a Crusader sword. At the ruined chapel of Kilneuair to the east of Loch Awe, there are the remains of an ancient circular church, and a gravestone with the Templar *cross patté*, as there is at neighbouring Kilmichael Glassary. And near Castle Sween lies the fallen chapel of

Kilmory, where another Templar cross is carved by a sailing ship, far larger than a war galley, and by a masonic set-square – found only on the early graves of members of that order.

The Keepers of the Grail identified by some of the authors of the romances had been destroyed by the fear of Rome and the avarice of the King of France. They had been condemned for their pride and for their heresy, which was not worship of the Devil, but a sympathy with mystical sects in Islam as well as Christianity. Their darkest sin was paradoxically the doctrine preached by Saint Bernard. Knowledge and control of self allowed a direct vision of the Word and the Light of God. Every knight must go alone on his journey to divine understanding. No Crown or Church should be a barrier. Each soul might reach eternal bliss on its own. To approach the Grail was a personal choice.

Own Grails

As a member of the St Clair family, I had leased Rosslyn Castle for two weeks. I had previously visited the chapel there; but I needed more time to consider its infinite complexities. I was warned of its connections with the Knights Templar and the Grail; but at that time, religious orthodoxy hardly wanted to stress these condemned correspondences. Fortune and a sore foot made me stumble over the first Grail stone in Scotland that had been identified for a century or more. A chalice was carved along the granite slab, which was only three feet in length. Within the cup at the top was an eight-pointed cypher of the Templars, which referred to the Holy Light within Christ's blood in the shape of an 'engrailed' octagon with a rose at its centre. It bore the name of the dead man, carved in Lombard lettering: WILLHM DE SINNCLER. The very name of the chapel was said to derive from the Old Scottish ROS-LIN, or Rosy Stream or Fall, again suggesting the Blood of Christ. The St Clair knights of the Middle Ages had fought with the 'Engrailed Cross' on their shields; these were also carved on the chapel walls. The base of the Grail or chalice formed the pattern of the steps to the Temple of Solomon.

Moreover, the corrupted spelling of the name of the man who had been buried under the stone was included within the steps of the base of the Grail. The last two letters of his name, E R, had been turned up at a right angle in the set-square of the Templars and the Master Masons. E R usually signified in the Middle Ages *ET RELIQUA*, meaning AND HIS REMAINS or RELICS. The battle sword that ran down the other side of the stem of the cup had a hilt that curved down at either end, characteristic of knights' swords in the first part of the fourteenth century, when Lombard lettering was inscribed on tombstones. While the communion cup of the Grail signified the grave of a Scottish Master of the Temple, the stone dated from the early fourteenth century, when the Templars had been dissolved and their leaders had been tortured and burned alive in France.

The Sancto Claro family were already the keepers of the royal treasure and holy relics in Scotland. Their name connected them with the Holy Light and the Grail. The dating of the sword hilt and the Lombard lettering identified this particular Sir William de St Clair on the stone. He had fought with the excommunicated Templars and with Robert the Bruce at Bannockburn, and had died in 1330, while taking Bruce's heart in a silver casket to be buried at Jerusalem. Surrounded by the Moorish cavalry in Spain, he and Sir James Douglas together with two other Scottish knights had flung the casket into the enemy ranks, then had charged the whole Muslim army and been slaughtered. Their courage had so earned the respect of their foes that the Heart of Bruce and the relics of the four knights were returned to the sole Scottish survivor, Sir William Keith, who took them back to their native land. The Heart of Bruce was buried at Melrose Abbey, where it has recently been excavated and verified. Douglas's heart is interred at his family chapel, while the bones of William de St Clair were apparently buried at Rosslyn. The remains of the Templars were often placed in the position of the skull over crossed leg-bones, an important symbol in their ritual and later Masonic ceremonies. If William de St Clair, as a Master of the Temple, was buried in this fashion, it would explain the small size of his tombstone.

I found a second Grail and Templar stone in the Commendator's House of Melrose Abbey. The dark crimson ruins of this Cistercian institution, the first of that order in Scotland, was founded seven years after Hugh de Payens had come to the country in 1129 to initiate the Templar centre at Balantrodoch. It was built on the southernmost tip of a swath of land stretching up to Edinburgh that included two Augustinian hospices on the hills and on the coast, another major Cistercian foundation near Dalkeith at Newbattle, and the St Clair lands around Rosslyn. That family was always intimately connected with the white monks and the military order.

The tombstone at Melrose was even smaller than the St Clair one in Rosslyn Chapel, and its design was different. Inside the cup of the chalice was a small eight-pointed cross fleury within a large eight-pointed foliated cross. An elongated dirk pointed down inside the stem of the cup to the base, again depicted as the steps of Calvary and of the Temple of Solomon. The name of the dead knight was not engraved upon it. Nearby were other fragments from Templar graves, floral crosses contained within a circle or a disc-head, and a boss of the five-petalled rose and the symbol of the Virgin Mary. Another boss was carved with clam shells, the emblem of the pilgrimage route to Compostela in Spain.

My third Grail discovered was found at the church at Corstorphine near Edinburgh. Sir Adam Forrester had founded it fifty years before the St Clair chapel, and his son John built it into a collegiate church at the same time as Rosslyn. John married Jean, the daughter of Prince Henry St Clair, the Earl of Orkney and an early voyager to North America, and still lies beside his wife on a tomb in the church, she in a long dress with stone pleats, her Bible clasped in her hands. On the opposite wall of the church is set a huge

Templar stone with a cross fleury inside a circle and a stem leading down to the steps of Calvary and the Temple of Solomon: a crusader sword is etched by its side. By the Priest's Door another memorial stone is inscribed to a chaplain named Robert Heriot, who died in 1443. Its only ornament is a chalice or Grail, which looks like two triangles set on end with the world as a ball dropping within. It was used as a model for the silver communion cups of later centuries. These are still in use at Corstorphine, emblems of the Grail.

At Currie, south-west of Edinburgh on the Water of Leith, on a bridle-path from Rosslyn over the Pentland Hills, the Templars built an industrial base, using water power to grind flour and crush iron and silver ore from their quarry near Linlithgow. Lying in fragments outside the Georgian church there are broken carved stones, recently unearthed and set as a border to the path. Two of them are Grail and Templar stones, the chalice ending in the steps of the Temple of Solomon. One of them is carved with a strange and beautiful cup, containing two circles with an opening between them, as if Christ's blood were pouring down into the hollow stem of the Grail. On one side a dirk in incised; on the other a knight's sword with rounded pommel and square hilt. The other chalice encloses five circles within a star, the symbol of the Virgin Mary: only one sword is carved on the stone, with a triangular pommel and down-curving hilt. Two other broken tombstones show the Templar octagonal cross within a disc-head, while one is incised with a mallet and divides a compass on either side of the stem of the Grail cup.

After their proscription by the Pope and the King of France, some of the Knights Templar had fled to the Western Isles and Argyll. And there in the ruins of Sadell Abbey, I found another carving of the Grail. This time the chalice was carried by a monk. The stone had been raised so that it was flanked by defending crusaders, still a perfect setting for that close connection between the Cistercians and the Templars, the two orders which Saint Bernard had helped to found and have blessed.

Then in Normandy I found more Templar signs, which seemed to prove the connection between the military order and the Knights of the Round Table. At the twelfth-century church of Saint Fraimbault-de-Lassay, two weathered tombstones are built into the north-east outer wall. Just visible are a mallet set above a chalice, then another chalice with a cross on its stem. More eight-pointed masonic crosses are incised on the walls. Within the church is a statue of Saint Fraimbault, who is believed in Normandy to have been Lancelot of the Lake. He holds a spade and a book: the book is the Word of God, another Grail, while the Templars were known as the Knights of the Sword and the Trowel, the forerunners of the Masonic movements. Cup and Word, building tool and carved stone, Arthurian figure and warrior saint, combined in holy and historical relics. The head of Fraimbault still lies in the church sanctuary, although his body was transferred in the tenth century from his birthplace to the crypt of the Chapelle Royale at Senlis, where his tomb is still venerated, although the chapel was desecrated during the French Revolution and is now restored as the Franz Liszt Auditorium.

Even if the figure of Lancelot was based on Saint Fraimbault, both Geoffrey of Monmouth and Chrétien de Troyes wrote that most of the exploits of the Knights of the Round Table took place in the British realm of King Arthur. The whole cycle, indeed, is still called the Matter of Britain: the romances of the Matter of France are concerned with Charlemagne and Roland, not with Lancelot. There is little justification for claiming a Lancelot circuit in Normandy, with its Fosse d'Arthur and misty lakes from which Excalibur may have been pulled from the floating stone and thrown back to be grasped by the hand of a water maiden. The only visible truth of the connection is at Saint Fraimbault-de-Lassay, where the Knights Templar left behind two of their Grail stones. As they were the guardians of pilgrims and the holy places, and as they were identified as the Knights of the Grail, they indicated that Normandy was another step on the way to the divine vision. With the

Normans now holding the north-west of France and much of Britain, the myth of Arthur easily traversed the Channel.

Yet the ultimate proof was painted above me on the ceiling of the principal Templar Commandery of the County of Comminges and Couserans, founded in 1156 at Monsaunès near Toulouse, on the pilgrim way to Compostela, which the knights of the order were sworn to defend. The romanesque chapel in stone and brick, a great rectangle ended by a choir in a semicircle, houses the confirmation of the Templars as the Keepers of the Grail and the Holy Spirit. On the vault is painted a red octagonal cross *pattée*, which supports a chalice bowl ornamented by the flower with six petals of the builders and masons of the *compagnonnage* of Master James, and by the entwined worms or serpents of Gnostic wisdom. Arrowheads as plumblines and stars with the sun and the moon, triangles and pyramids, and an encompassing cosmic bowl argue for greater mysteries within this medieval military order.

These were my signs and discoveries on the start of my search for the Grail. And as has been done at Corstorphine, later I had made a silver chalice modelled on the Grail tombstone at Rosslyn. If one may never achieve the vision of the Holy Vessel, one may create something from the discovery of a symbol used to show its presence in past lives. I hope that my silver cup will be used in the services in that Scottish chapel, which still blesses the modern Knights Templar, as well as the Christian faithful, in its ceremonies.

What is the Grail?

In one sense, every cup or bowl or reliquary with a sacred purpose is a Grail, an emblem of one of its properties. For it may be present as manna or ambrosia, as blinding light or the Holy Spirit, as bounty or baptism, as the sacrifice of captives or of Jesus Christ, as a heavenly stone or a severed head, as a jewelled chalice or a bleeding lance, as a platter or a book, as a fish or a dove with the host in its beak. Many are the forms of the Grail. After all, the search for its discovery is a personal quest. If that holy presence is sensed, it may appear in a different visioin to each seeker. Any sign of it is equally valid to the seer.

Yet the markers along the way are enigmatic. They are not as clear as the indications on all the roads that lead to Rome. They are variable and often insubstantial. Rather as the Stations of the Cross can only be symbols of the truth of the Passion, so the pointers to the Grail may only suggest a path to a beatific vision of its manifestation. Each finder discovers a unique insight into the divine.

This is not deconstruction. The viewer does not create a picture of the Grail, any more than a reader understands the text of the holy books better than the God who made the Word. The Grail shines to those who are worthy to receive it after long trials of the body and the soul. In the Grail romances, it came to King Arthur and the Knights of the Round Table in a series of altered states, or not at all. The point was that its changing presence was only possible given the experiences and mistakes of its seeker. Divine grace granted a view of the Grail as a reward for the long journey towards perfection. Each sight of it was suited to the individual struggle towards it.

To travel towards the Grail was to take one of the multitudinous and mysterious ways of creation. Through the control of the body and the refining of the spirit, an understanding of self might be followed by a revelation of the divine. To attain the ever-changing Grail was to search deep within and so reach out to a personal path to God.

Chapter Eight

Where Were the Grails?

Heaven is as near to us in Britain as in Palestine.

Saint Jerome

The abbeys and cathedrals of Europe competed with each other to attract pilgrims through their holy relics. The source of these sacred remains was Palestine, which the Byzantine emperor Constantine the Great and his mother Helena had made into the goal of Christian faith. As Gibbon wrote of the Empress, 'she united the credulity of old age with the warm feelings of a recent conversion'. At the age of seventy-nine, she was taken by Bishop Macarios around the sites of the Passion. The three Crosses of Jesus and the two thieves were discovered, marked by Pilate's board identifying the King of the Jews and the four nails driven into His Body. One of these nails calmed a storm in the Adriatic, another became the bit in the mouth of the emperor's warhorse. Most importantly, the Church of the Holy Sepulchre, with its great rotunda, was built over the tomb of Christ, as later the Dome of the Rock would be built over the stepping-stone of the Prophet Muhammad to heaven.

As Dante recognised, the three great places for Christian pilgrimages in the Middle Ages were Jerusalem in the Holy Land, Compostela in the north-west of Spain, and Rome. Yet Jerusalem was the greatest attraction, for it was held to be the Heavenly City, the centre of the earth and even the gateway to Paradise. The pilgrim guide to the city, the *Breviarus* of the sixth century, claimed that the sacred relics there included the True Cross, the Holy Lance, the Crown of

125

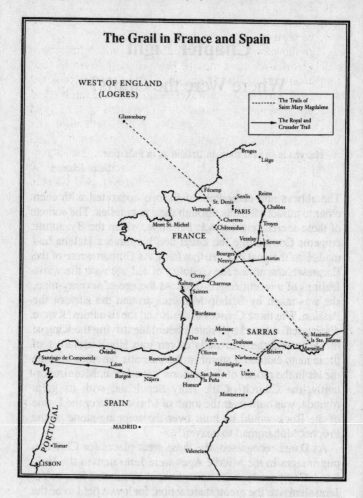

The Grail in France and Spain

WEST OF ENGLAND
(LOGRES)

- - - - The Trails of
Saint Mary Magdalene

→ The Royal and
Crusader Trail

Glastonbury

Bruges · Liège

Fécamp · Senlis · Reims
St. Denis · Chalôns
Verneuil · PARIS
Chartres · Troyes
Mont St. Michel · Châteaudun
FRANCE · Vezelay · Semur
Bourges · Autun
Neuvy

Civray
Aulnay · Charroux
Saintes

Bordeaux

Moissac · SARRAS
Dax · Auch · Toulouse · St. Maximin-
Oloron · Narbonne · la Ste. Baume
Santiago de Compostela · Oviedo · Roncesvalles · Béziers · Marseilles
Léon · Montségur
Burgos · Nájera · Jaca · San Juan de · Usson
Huesca · la Peña
Montserrat

SPAIN

PORTUGAL

MADRID ·

Tomar

Valencia ·

LISBON

Thorns, the column of Christ's flagellation, the stones from
the stoning of Saint Stephen and two later symbols of the
Grail – the horn with the divine oil which had anointed David

as King of Israel, and the platter of blood which had held the severed head of Saint John the Baptist.

With the success of the First Crusade – which had fortunately rediscovered the missing Holy Lance at Antioch – and the establishment of the Kingdom of Jerusalem for a hundred years, pilgrims could now travel there in relative safety. And they could see and even touch the containers of the Blood and Body of Christ, His tomb and the stained remains of His execution. Although the crusaders brought back many fragments of the holy relics to be housed in little Grails all across Europe, enough remained in the Church of the Holy Sepulchre to attract many of the faithful, even after Saladin had recaptured Jerusalem for the Muslim faith. William Wey, a fellow of the Royal College of Eton, travelled once to Compostela and twice to Jerusalem in the middle of the fifteenth century, and left a charming doggerel about the treasures in the Holy City. He had his doubts, particularly over the authenticity of the bloodstains of Christ on the pillar where He was flogged, and the lamp over His sepulchre, which was put out at His death and reappeared at His resurrection. Wey also feared that the stone on which the Body of Christ had been laid was taken away to Constantinople, while the Saviour's footprints preserved on the hard rock seemed to be carved by hand. Yet even so, he was overwhelmed by the sacred relics 'within the temple of Jerusalem':

> *The first place within the door*
> *Is our Lord's holy sepulchre.*
> *The next that is without failing,*
> *Is a chapel of our Lady where friars do sing.*
> *There was Our Lady in her prayer*
> *When Christ was risen from his sepulchre,*
> *And He full lowly, when He come thither,*
> *Said unto her, Hail, holy Mother.*
> *And in that same chapel is*
> *Of the pillar a great piece*

That Christ Jesus was bound unto,
When Pilate him beat, and wrought him woe.
There is in that place a stone also
That a dead man by the cross was raised from.
Without the chapel door,
Right in the chapel floor,
There is a stone, round and plain
Where Jesus as a gardener met with Magdalene.
In that stone by Christ was made
An hold wherein he put his spade.
By yonder, as pilgrims gone,
They find two holes in a stone:
In those holes Christ's legs were put,
And with chains fast knit,
There is by a vault within,
Which is called Christ's prison.

Next to that in our procession
Is a place of great devotion.
There at the dice knights gan play
Who should bear Christ's tunic away.
Beyond there is a pillar also,
Upon which Christ sat naked through;
Where the knights, to his scorn,
Set on his head a crown of thorn.
Beyond is a chapel, it is right low,
Twenty paces down as men it know;
In that chapel under the ground
There was the holy cross found.
There is full remission in that place
To all men that thither go for grace . . .

These blessed objects were only some of the evidence of the Passion available in Palestine. Many had been transported away by the Byzantines and the crusaders. With the cult of relics, which were held to work fashionable miracles, a lucrative trade lay in small pieces of the remains of the

Crucifixion and the Saints. The custom of cutting up the remnants of martyrs and distributing them to new churches and abbeys that bore their sacred names spread from east to west. As Theodoret observed as early as the fifth century:

> *No single tomb covers a martyr's body. Cities and villages, having divided the bodies among themselves, entitle them preservers of their souls and healers, and honour them as guardians of their city and protectors. They employ them as intercessors and obtain divine gifts through them. Though the whole body be divided, the grace is undivided, and the smallest relic has equal power with the whole body of the martyr.*

Each remnant of a martyr or of the Passion was housed in a reliquary, resplendent with jewels, gold and silver. And other symbols of the Last Supper, particularly the chalice, had become parts of love feasts in early Christianity. In his *Confessions*, Saint Augustine had denounced the practice of drinking wine from decorated cups in memory of holy men. Many examples of these vessels incised with the heads of Saint Peter and Saint Paul and resembling Celtic sacrificial bowls have been excavated near Rome, merely a continuation of the pagan practice of pouring libations to the gods and celebrating the dead. Saint Jerome also reproached a friend, who asked him to a feast, with the words, 'We must celebrate the birthday of Peter rather with exaltation of spirit than with abundance of food.' Yet when a broken crystal chalice placed on the altar of Saint Lawrence was miraculously restored as whole, Gregory of Tours reported that the Bishop of Milan had to institute new feasts for the saint to satisfy public demand.

With the sack of Constantinople and the loss of Jerusalem, the attention of Western pilgrims turned to those points near the coasts of the Atlantic and the Mediterranean where the first saints and missionaries were said to have landed, bringing the gospel with them from the Holy Land. The foremost of these places was Santiago de Compostela in the north of Spain, followed by Saint Maximin in the south of France and Fécamp in Normandy. These were the ports of the legendary conversion of mainland Europe. One account of Saint James held that he had landed in Galicia and preached the gospel before returning to Jerusalem where he was beheaded by the Romans. Another declared that his body had arrived in a marble ship, had chased away a devilish snake set on him by a witch, Queen Lupa, and was finally buried in Santiago de Compostela by a knight covered in scallop shells, the badge of pilgrims to the renowned shrine and cathedral.

Certainly, Saint James became the patriotic symbol of the small kingdom of the Asturias and of the Spanish crusades against the Moors. He is shown on the tympanum of his cathedral at Santiago, riding a white horse and killing the infidels at the Battle of Clavijo, after a mysterious reappearance. On the eve of the fall of Coimbra, he was said to have appeared to a doubting Greek bishop in a dream while dressed as a crusader in white, saying, 'God has made me a soldier and a contestant and set me to fight for the Christians against the Saracens and to gain the victory for them.' On his visit to Compostela, William Wey discovered more than the patron saint's remains, confirmed by Beatus's celebrated *Commentaries on the Apocalypse*. There was the tunic of Jesus, remnants of Saints Paul, Stephen and Sylvester, and the incorruptible body of Zebedee the fisherman, the father of Saint James, who was also the nephew of the Virgin Mary and the cousin of Christ. Treasures, indeed, which made the journey worthwhile. The image above the Tree of Jesse in the Portico de la Gloria of Saint James, who had curbed the infidel and driven the pagan from Spain, was even more inspiring than Saint George of the Near East and England, or Saint Andrew of Scotland. And the miracles of healing at his shrine were attested in a sermon attributed to Pope Calixtus II:

From the time it was begun until today, that church dis-
plays the glory of the miracles of Saint James. For the
sick are restored to health, the blind receive their sight,
many tongues that were dumb are loosed, the deaf hear
again, the lame are given the strength to walk, demoni-
acs are set free, and what is even more, the prayers of
the faithful are heard, their vows are fulfilled, and the
chains of their sins are unloosed.

Although the capital of the empire of Charlemagne at
Aachen still houses many blessed relics, those not seized by
Napoleon have mainly been transferred to Vienna. The
Hofburg there now holds the Imperial Crown, the Holy
Lance, the Gothic Sceptre and Charlemagne's Gospel Book,
as well as a large Roman agate dish once thought to be the
Grail, along with a narwhale horn, the Cornucopia of the
ancients. In the Sacred Treasury is Saint Stephen's purse of
the eleventh century, a reliquary containing one of the nails
from the Passion, and a monstrance holding a fragment of the
True Cross. Still in the Dom at Aachen is a golden casket of
Charlemagne, which used to contain some of the Holy
Blood. A portion was later given to Richard, Earl of
Cornwall, who transferred it in a chest to Ashridge and to the
Cistercian abbey built by him at Hailes – he also rebuilt
Tintagel Castle in memory of King Arthur. His gift of sacred
relics to his English abbey became so famous that Chaucer
referred to it in *The Canterbury Tales*:

> *By Goddes precious herte, and by his nails,*
> *And by the blood of Christ that is of Hailes.*

Hailes Abbey was destroyed by Henry VIII at the
Dissolution of the Monasteries. Only the base to its Shrine of
the Holy Blood persists. In *Divers Miracles at Hailes*, a picture of the reliquary shows the doors of the six-sided chalice
opened by angels to display the liquefying and healing blood
behind its crystal glass panels. Destroyed at the Reformation

131

as a forgery, the Blood remained a reminder of miraculous cures, and in the neighbouring twelfth-century parish church, an octagonal stone font recalls Cistercian simplicity. Ashridge was also pillaged and its glories dispersed. Edmund, the son of Richard of Cornwall, was its founder, while its monks were Bonhommes with connections with the heretical Cathars and the Lollards. Its chief treasure was presented by the Black Prince after his victory at Poitiers – a great gold and silver table studded with jewels, 'furnished full of precious relics, and in the middle of it a holy cross of the wood of the True Cross'.

The Dom at Cologne was also a magnet for the reverent. It possessed the embroidered skulls of the three Magi, who had brought their bountiful caskets of riches, frankincense and myrrh to the cradle of the infant Christ at Bethlehem. The Empress Helena had found these relics, too, in the Holy Land, and they had been transported by way of Constantinople and Milan to their final resting place; the donor and thief of the relics was said to be the alchemist Albertus Magnus, rumoured to possess a talking head, in the manner of the Celtic god Bran, which acted as an oracle. However that might be, the remains of the Eastern Wise Men were held in a shrine created by Nicholas of Verdun, which had sculptures of their gifts to Jesus, of His baptism in Jordan and of His Second Coming. The Magi also have their own chapel with stained-glass windows from the fourteenth century; they are celebrated again in the choir. In the Dom, too, is a Chapel of the Holy Cross, which contains a romanesque crucifix from the tenth century, while the cathedral Treasury displays a Byzantine reliquary containing a piece of the True Cross.

For pilgrims to Italy, the Santa Casa on the hillside at Loretto was the house in Nazareth where Christ was born, miraculously wafted there from Palestine by flights of angels. This spot was believed to be the fact of the mystery of the Incarnation, particularly when the crusaders were driven from the Holy Land. Its presence outshone the venerable relics in other Italian cities – except Turin, which held the Holy Shroud, pressed from the naked body of Christ taken from the Cross.

Rome itself had always been ambiguous towards the symbols of the Grail, tasting in them flavours of heresy. Outside Saint Peter's and the Vatican, there are two churches particularly significant in this quest. The medieval chapel of Saint John at the Latin Gate was replaced by an octagonal Renaissance church. Its paintings show the saint drinking from a Gnostic chalice containing the serpent; also escaping from a cauldron of boiling oil to write his *Book of Revelation*. And at Saint Lawrence Without the Walls, frescoes picture the holy man giving the Grail to the Spanish legionary who would carry it on its journey to end in Valencia.

Within the Vatican, Fra Angelico depicted Pope Sixtus II bestowing the Grail on Saint Lawrence. And there is a statue of Saint Longinus in Saint Peter's, while a yellow jasper chalice in Saint John in Lateran – possibly the cup of the Last Supper – is held to have been brought by Saint Jerome from Jerusalem. Yet the most holy relics are kept hidden in the four huge pentagonal hollow piers, designed by Michelangelo himself, which bear the weight of the soaring dome of Saint Peter's. Always chary of putting too much faith in relics that work miracles, let alone actual objects from the Passion, the papacy has varied its policy of concealing and showing its blessed treasures over the centuries.

As well as the remains of its name saint, Saint Peter's holds the Holy Veil of Saint Veronica, probably acquired after the Fourth Crusade. It also claims the iron tip of the Holy Lance, although this relic is like the hydra with many heads. And to the skull of Saint Andrew, also reported to be in Scotland, Pope Urban VIII added a large piece of the True Cross, which was transferred from the Church of Santa Croce in Gerusalemme. These sacred remnants are still housed within the labyrinthine piers, if they were not dispersed in 1527 at the sack of Rome.

From time to time, the relics of Saint Peter's – particularly the Veil of Saint Veronica, at Epiphany and Easter – had been disclosed. It was a form of Grail, granting absolution to those who saw it and adored 'the very mystery of this likeness', in the words of Pope Innocent III. Dante even recognised the urge of the Christian faithful to view this revelation in the 'Paradiso' of his *Divine Comedy*. He compared the sight of the Veil to Saint Bernard's wish for grace from the Virgin Mary, the Queen of Heaven:

> *As he who perhaps comes from Croatia*
> *To look upon our Veronica*
> *And still desires it despite her fame,*
> *But says in thought, as long as He is shown:*
> *'My Lord Jesus Christ, the true God -*
> *Was this way your appearance made?'*

For however creditable was the provenance of a holy relic, it could only be a symbol. It was a sign pointing towards a personal vision of God. Without that perception of grace, nobody could reach the divine, whatever the arrow to the Virgin Mary or to the Almighty. Moreover, the Middle Ages were renowned for mass belief – the Children's Crusade was the worst example of common credulity. Crowds and congregations wished to see miracles performed, and acts of healing often happened at shrines and reliquaries through faith, hallucination or hypnotism. The example lay, after all, in the New Testament. Saint Lazarus, raised from the dead, was a popular icon in the south of France. Curing the sick, making the deaf hear, the blind see, the dumb speak and the lame walk, casting out demons and evil spirits, these were expected in medieval as well as Biblical times.

More popular even than the Grail romances were the Lives of the Saints. These were stories of a quest, of spiritual rather than knightly adventures, of jousts against demons and battles against the Devil as engaging as those of Arthur and Charlemagne. And beatific vision was the insight of the holy men, whose long fasts persuaded them that they were being fed by manna as if from a Grail. Saints Cuthbert and Columba were often visited by angels in their dreams, as well as nourished by their faith. Furthermore, experiences of the soul leaving the body were widespread among the elect. These might occur in the form of a rising dove, a flight of cherubim or even an ascending globe of fire, as Saint Benedict reported on the death of Germanus. The Grail was so portrayed, and in such ways did the Knights of the Round Table also envision its form in its many guises.

In the ecstasy of prayer, some saints were seen to levitate or appear in two places simultaneously. Saint Columba had gifts of second sight and prophecy, a Christian Merlin from the Arthurian legends. Describing his gift, he said, 'There are some, though few of them, who have been granted divine grace, so that they can see clearly and distinctly at one moment as under a sunray the whole circuit of the world surrounded by the ocean and the sky. The inner part of their mind is miraculously enlarged.' This was the same as the blinding vision of the Grail, the moment of communion with the One Maker of the cosmos. As Pope Gregory also said of Saint Benedict: 'He saw the whole world because, by the supernatural light of the Creator, the soul is enlarged, and being suffused with the light of God, it is inwardly exalted above itself. Looking down, it sees what it could not understand as a small matter.'

For the Church, beatific vision and a personal contact with heaven through ecstatic prayer was illumination for a saint, but heresy for an Arthurian knight or a rebel against the authority of Rome. Experiences of the godhead must remain within the pale of orthodoxy. Although revelation was admitted through dreams as well as through fasting and prayer, these apparitions might be demoniac as well as divine. The dreams of the otherworld which occurred to the saints often presented themselves in Jewish, Greek or Celtic forms, as in the stories about the Grail Castle. Their culmination was in *The Divine Comedy* of Dante, partly devised from his inspiration about the nature of the inferno, purgatory and paradise, partly from his invocation of the current European myths of the otherworld outside the Bible.

Some of the dreams recorded about the saints might have been sources of Grail romances. Roger of Wendover declared that in 1206 Saint Julian ordered Turchill of Tunsted to prepare for a journey. When he was asleep, the saint took his spirit from his body and served as a guide through hell and heaven, as Virgil served Dante. Evading demons and tortures, Turchill saw Celtic and alchemic cauldrons in four courts, some burning with fire, others filled with snow and ice, and still more holding boiling sulphur or black salt water. Souls were purged in these vessels of regeneration before passing on to the golden temple on the Mount of Joy, where they ate copious and delicious food from the nearby Earthly Paradise.

Opposing pictures of purgatory and paradise were the perceptions preached by the medieval Church. These images possessed the Christian mind, entering into reveries and dreams. They also provided the real power of the Church of Rome on earth. Excommunication did not only consign the soul to hell; it also denied the sinner his feudal and property rights until he was absolved. Suspects might be accused of witchcraft as well as heresy. Unorthodoxy could be proof of interior demons. Emperors and apostate kings had crusades preached against them as if they were infidels. As well as the miracles of healing at the shrines of the saints and the Holy Blood, the spectacles of aristocratic repentance at the great cathedrals were the dramatic masterpieces of the age. Dressed in a shift, flogged for misdeeds, those of the high-born who offended Rome – like Raymond VII, Count of Toulouse – might have to journey to Canossa or to Notre-Dame in Paris to submit to the Church, abjure heresy and show that the decree of Rome was more powerful than the sword.

Relics, miracles and public penitence might impress the masses, but the abuse of these presentations and redemptions would lead to the great split within the Christian Church and the destruction of its general images. Miracles were too easily made, indulgences were widely sold, forgiveness for sins came with bequests rather than sorriness. There was a schism in the papacy, with rival claimants in Avignon as well as in Rome. The popes began to recruit their own troops to defend their possessions in Italy. Military funds were needed not to send another crusade to the Near East, but to defend Tuscany and Umbria, ruled by the Vatican. The coins paid for tokens or parchments of absolution debased the treasures of the faith.

In the early Middle Ages, no matter if the Holy Blood or the bones of the saints were genuine. Popular belief supplied the origins, and to the theologians, such signs and wonders were only symbols on the way to God through the goodwill of the Church. Yet with the waning of the Middle Ages, rebel and purifying creeds would act as the Knights of the Grail had done in the romances. By trial and self-discipline, they would attack corruption and licence, seeking their own salvation in the refinement of their vision of heaven.

The Two Grail Trails of France

The crossroads of the Grail trails of France is at Vézelay. The crypt of the cathedral church there holds the bones of Saint Mary Magadalene. According to local historians, the relics wee removed by the 'holy theft' of the monk Badilon from her hermit cave at Sainte Baume near Marseilles, although the clerics of the nearby basilica of Saint Maximin also claimed the sacred remains of the beloved companion of Jesus, where they are still kept in a Gallo-Roman sarcophagus that serves as an altar. In Marseilles itself, the church of Saint Victor used to flaunt its possession of the spiced jar of unguent with which the Magdalene anointed the feet and the wounds of Christ. These two French repositories denied the claims of the Abbey of Halberstadt and of Saint John the Lateran at Rome that each housed the blessed relics. Both asserted that they were the final resting places of the Saint, who had died as a penitent in the Cave of the Seven Sleepers outside Ephesos, before being taken to Byzantium to be buried beside her brother Lazarus in a monastery on the Bosphoros, only to be spirited away by Conrad, the Bishop of Halberstadt, after the sack of the imperial city during the Fourth Crusade.

Two early lives of the Magdalene, written in the ninth century by Saxer and Raban Maar, the Archbishop of Mayence, moved her cult overland from the Mediterranean to the Atlantic, where she was meant to have landed with the Grail and many pilgrims. The myth spread north through Bruges, Vézelay, Semur-en-Auxois, Troyes, Châteaudun, Chartres, Verneuil-sur-Avre, Bayeux, Bellevault, Besançon, Le Mans, Châlons-sur-Marne and Reims to Fécamp in Normandy on the Channel, the first stronghold and port of the invading Vikings under Rollo, and then across the sea to Glastonbury and Cambridge, where a college was founded in her name. William of Waynflete, the founder of Magdalen College at Oxford where five statues of her can still be seen, read the Maar manuscript and revered the saint as much for her knowledge as her repentance. She had been regarded in the Gnostic *Gospel of Philip* as 'the symbol of divine wisdom', while Maar stressed that her jar of ointment symbolised the secrets of the heart as the sanctuary of faith and charity, the very container of spiritual life.

Yet in Vézelay, Saint Bernard had preached the Second Crusade, after founding the Cistercian Order of white monks and having the Knights Templar of the octagonal red cross blessed at the synod of 1128 at Troyes, the original city of the Grail romances. Their function was the protection of pilgrims to the holy places, not only to Palestine, but also to Santiago de Compostela in Spain, where so many prospective crusaders found themselves fighting the Moors before they managed the voyage on towards Jerusalem. Although the Benedictines from Cluny had already established the Knights of Saint John as the protectors of the sacred way, the Templars were also needed in the holy war in Spain. The

bones of the repentant woman saint brought pilgrims to
Vézelay; the arms of the Hospitallers and the Templars took
them through the town from the coronation place of the kings
of France at Reims to the Cathedral of Saint James at
Compostela. As far as the French border, a way lay through
Neuvy Saint-Sepulchre, Charroux, Civray, Aulnay, Saintes
and Dax to the pass at Roncesvalles where Roland had died.
At each of these places, there remained symbols of the Grail.

Odo of Cluny particularly connected the ancient myth of
the Grail as the womb and the sin of Eve with Christ first
appearing to the Magdalene after the crucifixion in His healing garden as the Doctor of her soul. His hymn for his fellow
monks celebrated her story:

> After the scandal of her frail flesh
> From a cauldron she made a cup afresh
> Into a vase of glory, she altered
> The vessel whose worth she had bartered
> To her Doctor she ran, spent and sick,
> Bearing her vase so aromatic.
> All the illnesses she had endured
> By the word of the Doctor so were cured.

In the south of France, the legend was that Mary
Magdalene had landed at Les-Saintes-Maries-de-la-Mer near
Marseilles, the Sarras of Arthurian myth where Joseph of
Arimathea also brought the Grail on his way to Britain. The
cult of the Magdalene was so widespread that the number of
her shrines or churches increased in the five centuries after
the eighth from thirty to one hundred and fifty; they were
often associated with the veneration of the Black Virgin. The
Gnostics adored the Magdalene as the favourite disciple of
Jesus. Her history was told in *The Golden Legend*, the most
popular medieval version of the Lives of the Saints. She and
her brother Lazarus and her sister Martha owned castles and
lands near and in Jerusalem. One home was a tower at
Magdala on the Sea of Galilee; another at Bethany. She was

engaged to John, the other beloved disciple; but when Jesus changed the water into wine at Cana, John left with Him, and Mary became promiscuous before being redeemed by Jesus, who also brought back her brother Lazarus from the dead.

Her role at the Crucifixion identified her as the Grail-bearer. The Gospels made her out to be the leader of the three women who came with spices to anoint the body of Christ in His Tomb, only to find it gone. The Magdalene was also with another Mary, the mother of James, at the Crucifixion, 'beholding from afar', although not with the Virgin Mary. She would have seen Joseph of Arimathea catching the Holy Blood in a vessel from the Cross, although she did not herself prepare Christ for burial, as the Tomb was empty when she arrived there. Yet He did appear to her alone later, and one legend allowed Him then to give her the Grail. Other legends made her accompany Joseph to Sarras with his Grail containing the Holy Blood.

Many medieval windows and tapestries, however, depicted the Magdalene and Mary, the mother of James,, holding golden vessels rather like the three Magi; these contained the spices for His Body, and they gave out one of the properties of the Grail, the sweetness of delectable aromas. On the sea voyage to France, the Magdalene, as well as her companion Joseph, was frequently shown as carrying a cup or precious vessel. Although the Grail Princess with the chalice in the processions at the Castle of Corbenic or of the Fisher King was not identified as the Magdalene, her legend was surely in the imagination of the romancers.

With the Magdalene came many early Christians, including her brother Lazarus, the first Bishop of Marseilles; her sister Martha, who quelled the dragon of the Rhône at Tarascon; and the first Bishop of Aix, Saint Maximin. She retired to a cave on a cliff at Sainte Baume, the holy balsam for the Body of Christ. There she contemplated for thirty years until angels took her on the point of death to the hermitage of Maximin. He had her body embalmed and put in a mausoleum. It was later transferred to a sarcophagus in the church that bore his name, where the incorruptible flesh gave off sweetness and her cheek was still rosy where Jesus had touched it during the Resurrection. The flask of the Holy Blood which the Magdalene had brought with her was seen to liquefy every Good Friday. Although Vézelay also claimed her body, one arm was left at the fortified church of Les-Saintes-Maries, where it was put in a precious reliquary and is said still to perform miracles of healing, while blessing the waters of the Mediterranean that brought her safe to Provence.

In the cathedral at Bourges, there is an actual picture on stained glass of the only Grail recognised by Rome. Within the chapel of the doubtful martyr Saint Philomena, Pope Sixtus II is shown handing over the golden chalice to Saint Lawrence for transport to Spain. Precious buckets for washing the blood off the new-born Christ are also shown, as is a golden-topped altar between two pillars, on which are placed a chalice and a crucifix below the sacred hanging lamp of the Temple. More political, however, is the window of 1517 by Jean Lécuyer, which shows the martyrdom of Saint Denis, the cult figure of the Capetian kings. In sixteen panels, his life, torture and resurrection can be read. Given the Grail and absolution by visiting Saints while in prison, he was roasted and decapitated before he rose again, holding his severed head, as John the Baptist did. Walking with it from the scaffold at Montmartre north to the abbey which bears his name, he then expired and left it his remains.

The collection of the supreme Suger, the abbot of Saint Denis from 1122 until 1151, prophesied and inspired Grail literature. Suger was determined to see that his abbey was the rival in beauty and relics to the Sancta Sophia in Constantinople. He made Saint Denis the patron saint and protector of the health of the Capetian royal family. The abbey was the home of all the coronation regalia as well as of the healing bones, the Oriflamme and the crowns of Charlemagne and Saint Louis. When the French kings died, as they must, they were also buried at Saint Denis, and many of their marble tombs still remain in the abbey church in spite of the pillage at the time of Robespierre. What was dispersed then was the treasure created by the inspired and powerful abbot.

A Renaissance picture, now in the National Gallery in London, shows Suger raising the Host at Mass to give to the kneeling king. The altarpiece and cross above it are beaten gold and ablaze with jewels. Angels are carved above the saints, touching a hanging lamp and bowl which resemble the holders of the Holy Shroud and Veil at Constantinople. Two vessels from the first century still survive in Paris, an Egyptian onyx cup carved for the Ptolemys and a green serpentine bowl, now surrounded by a circle of precious stones inlaid in gold, made for King Charles the Bald. Another Persian bowl of aventurine, from the sixth century, commemorates Saint Eloi. Yet the four vases of rock crystal, agate and sardonyx, including the Merovingian Vase d'Aliénor at the Louvre, were the preview of the Grail. Suger himself declared of a Byzantine chalice of the second century, now in Washington: 'Because we must offer libations to God, with gems and gold, I, Suger, offer this vase to Our Lord.'

Suger also anticipated the Grail as a stone fallen from heaven with his conversion of a porphyry amphora from imperial Rome into the body of a golden eagle, to be used in his liturgies. He wrote a Latin verse in pride at his change of the classical vase into a Christian vessel:

> *This gem merits its inclusion*
> *In gold and precious stones.*
> *It was of marble, but now is*
> *More precious than marble ever was.*

In a sense, Suger was another Saint John the Baptist, announcing the coming of the Grail. A modern pilgrim will not see those treasures any more at Saint Denis. They were melted down or dispersed, ending up in the museums of

Paris, London and Washington, when the abbey was pillaged during the French Revolution. The ransacking of the royal tombs led to stories of *sans-culottes* playing skittles with the bones of the Valois and Bourbon royal houses. Certainly a painting by Hubert Robert illustrates coffins being lifted from the regal mausoleums, which were then shattered or dismantled. The abbey church fell into ruins; Napoleon began its restoration, which was carried through by Viollet le Duc. The many royal tombs there at the present time have been restored or brought from other places in France. The most haunting is the ornamental marble urn by Pierre Bontemps; it was safeguarded in the Abbey of Hautes-Bruyères and holds the heart of King Francis I, as Melrose Abbey still holds the Heart of Bruce.

Set against one wall is a tombstone of Michel de Troye, the grand prior of Saint Denis in 1517, holding a chalice in his hands as on the Grail stones of Scotland. Near him hangs a copy of the Oriflamme, the banner with a cross and five ragged tassels which was flown to lead the French army into battle. There is also a fragment of the Holy Lance, transferred from the Sainte Chapelle. Among the windows which Suger had painted is a nineteenth-century Apocalypse scene in which the doves of the Holy Spirit, carrying hanging golden lamps and backed by a green stone, descend on Saint John lifting up the Word of God. Outside the main entrance, Christ in majesty rules at the Last Judgement, while eight maidens holding their vessels up or turning them down are carved on the supports. These are the Wise and Foolish Virgins, although they have been identified as the cupbearers of the Grail procession. On the metal doors between are scenes of the Passion. All three blessed Marys are portrayed, with the Mother of Jesus even present at the Last Supper and superseding the significance of the Magdalene. And over another side door as well on a wooden statue within, Saint Denis is shown carrying his head as a holy object in his hands, a life after death.

At the meeting of the pilgrim and crusading way with the

Magdalene cult route at Vézelay, the bones of that saint are still preserved in the crypt inside a reliquary supported by two angels. Memories and symbols of her abound, one of them linking Saint Bernard himself to the quest for the Grail, brought by her compassion to France. An animal shield in the chapter demonstrates a Grail surrounded by fleur-de-lys and drops of blood or tears, bearing the words of the monk Nicholas, the secretary to Bernard: *Optimam partem elegit* ('She has chosen the best part). This reference to the Magdalene is commemorated by hosts of memorial plaques and dropped chains, which are testimonies to her powers of healing and liberation.

Charlemagne himself gave the castle of Semur-le-Auxois to the monks of Saint Maurice, who kept it until the French Revolution. The most ancient chapel in the basilica of Notre-Dame there is dedicated to Saint Mary Magdalene, and was restored along with Notre-Dame de Paris and Carcassonne by the great architect Viollet le Duc in the nineteenth century. Two windows with seven diamond panels made six centuries previously recount her life and legends. She and her sister Martha can be seen praying with Joseph of Arimathea in front of a golden Grail on a red cushion on an altar; then taking a ship to Sarras, where the saint dies and is entombed in her sarcophagus. On the marble Renaissance altar, Christ is shown after His Resurrection appearing to the Magdalene. Yet perhaps the most enduring version of the cult may be in the chapel of her brother Lazarus, above a sculpture of her helping to lay Christ inside his tomb. Stained-glass windows of 1927 by Louzier commemorate American doughboys, wounded or killed in the First World War. An angel of God swoops down on three veiled women, as at the foot of the Cross. By them are two vessels of mercy, a golden censer and platter, a modern healing grace.

From Semur, past the great Cistercian abbey of Fontenoy, the cult of the Magdalene spread to Troyes, the city of Chrétien, who first gave the Grail its medieval identity. The oldest church in the city is the Saint Magdalene, part of which dates from the end of the twelfth century, the time of the writing of *Perceval*. My visit there was a revelation. The word *graal* is a Provençal word. Southern troubadours were popular at the Court of Champagne. Most likely, they knew of the story of Joseph of Arimathea and the Magdalene from the Mediterranean south at La Baume. The oldest church in Troyes was built to commemorate that legend, and Chrétien would have known why. In a Renaissance extension of the building, the stocking-makers of Troyes presented in 1506 scenes in stained glass from the life of the woman saint, surmounted by a pair of small windows showing twin cherubs holding ornate Grails. In one panel, the two blessed Marys bear precious jars of spices for the wounds of Christ. In another, Jesus reappears to Saint Longinus and Joseph, before His apparition to the Magdalene, a Grail lying at her feet. She and Joseph and her family are then banished from the Holy Land, only to have Christ bless them again as they are converting the King of Sarras at a royal feast. Finally, the woman saint is laid in her sepulchre, with Bishop Maximin praying for her soul.

Although these windows postdated the author of *Perceval*, they reflected faithfully the early story of the Magdalene on cathedral windows of previous centuries. There is every chance that Chrétien knew of this *Story of the Grail*, the subtitle of his book, because of her church in Troyes. An early stained-glass window showing Longinus piercing the side of Christ with the Holy Lance and Joseph of Arimathea catching His Blood in a Grail is in the cathedral of Saint Peter in Poitiers; it dates from 1165, before the writing of *Perceval*. Other churches and basilicas in Troyes still confirm the prevalence of the legends. In the Church of Saint John, where Henry V of England married Catherine of France, there are windows of the Last Supper, of John the Baptist's head on a platter, of the three Magi bearing gifts, of the Circumcision of Jesus and, more rare, of manna falling from heaven, collected in bowls by the believers. Saint John himself dying in a vat of boiling oil, a cauldron of destruction and rebirth, can be viewed on a thirteenth-century window in the city cathedral.

In the basilica of Saint Urbain, there is a Grail stone as in Templar Scotland. A Renaissance bishop holds the chalice in his hands, while four Sanskrit reverse swastikas adorn his robes. More interesting, there is a reliquary altar in the chapel of Saint Joseph. On the wooden carving which houses the sacred remains, two doves drink from a chalice, as we will see at Charroux, at the Byzantine tombs of the archbishops of Ravenna and on the black font of Winchester Cathedral. In the chapel to the husband of the Virgin Mary, there is also a relief in stone of the crucified Christ, from whom Mary Magdalene and Joseph of Arimathea are collecting the Holy Blood. To emphasise the other road to God, there is also a statue of Saint Bernard, holding his foundation abbey at Clairvaux in his hands.

Most strange, however, are the links between Chrétien, the romancer of the Grail, and the Treasury of the cathedral of Saint Peter and Saint Paul at Troyes. There, a contemporary window shows two of the Apostles showered with blessings from an angel, bearing above them a Grail full of small stones and a golden lamp on chains. A later reliquary of the Magdalene carried between two angels testifies to her holy memory of the city. But an extraordinary alms purse connects the Arthurian legend with the pursuit of the divine. On it, we see two women seated before an altar, which bears a naked heart. Above, a flying oblong Ark sends down a fork of lightning or grace. What the portrait of Saint Bernard there would make of this confusion between human love and religion, only Chrétien de Troyes might resolve.

To the north, halfway to Reims, at Châlons-sur-Marne, the evidence of the cult of the Grail continues in the early windows of Notre-Dame-en-Vaux. A magnificent Last Supper, centred on the platter of the Paschal Lamb before the figure of Christ, bears comparison with the contemporary work of Leonardo da Vinci. Another window celebrates Saint James in a pilgrim's habit leading the Spanish crusaders to victory against the Moors at the Battle of las Navas de Tolosa. At another window dedicated to the Compassion of the Virgin Mary, Joseph of Arimathea catches the Holy Blood of the crucified Christ, while a large-scale Mary Magdalene holds a golden chalice as other women receive Him after His deposition. Her story is also repeated, collecting His Blood at the foot of the Cross, sailing to Sarras with Joseph and her sister Martha at the prow, their two golden Grails with His Blood blessed by an angel on arrival and used to heal the sick. Most curious is an apparition of Jesus to the Magdalene, in which He plunges the Holy Lance of Longinus into a transparent bucket, as if washing it off.

At Châlons, too, are the double windows of the Brotherhood of the Blessed Sacrament at Saint Alpin, who saved the city from Attila, King of the Huns. These are rare testaments to the Cathar and Huguenot heresies, which led to the bloody religious wars of France. As in the Grail romances, the crux of the conflict was the granting of grace directly from God. Was the Host a mystery of the Roman Catholic priesthood? Or were communion and the chalice open to all believers? The Protestants controlled Châlons in the early sixteenth century, and the Brotherhood of the Blessed Sacrament was formed. The windows show manna falling from heaven and the institution of the Last Supper. The Brothers, dressed as Apostles, take communion directly from the Son of God, as the *perfecti* and the Cathar faithful did at their divine feasts. Christ is shown putting His hand to His mouth, signifying that He is the Word of God speaking individually to each believer through the Bible. And in another Renaissance window, two colourful panels of the miracle of the loaves and the fishes along with the turning of water into wine at Cana emphasise the bounty of God to all who attend the celebrations of Him.

The royal and crusading way began at Reims. There was the baptism of Clovis, founder of the kingly line of France. There was the cult of Melchizedek, the priest and king, who combined divine and temporal power. There was the legend of the Holy Spirit in the form of a dove which brought the sacred balm from heaven, as in *Parzival*, to anoint the heir to the throne at his coronation. There were the sacred relics from the Treasury of Charlemagne, with the Virgin Mary crowned in heaven; the black ball of the world was at her feet, the Ark of the Covenant appeared in her window, and Mary Magdalene waited in attendance upon her. This was the start of the holy road to war and repentance in Spain.

In his *History of the Franks*, Gregory of Tours described the baptism of the pagan ruler Clovis at the end of the fifth century. A dove flew down bearing in its beak an ampoule of divine unction, which was used thereafter to anoint twenty-five of the kings of France, especially when their other sacred place at Saint-Denis fell into English hands. In the Treasury kept at the Palais du Tau, there is a relic taken by Napoleon from Charlemagne's Aachen, the Emperor's own talisman of sapphire, emerald, ruby, pearl and gold, containing a sliver of the True Cross. As well as the reliquary of the blessed ampoule, the sacred jewelled golden chalice of the coronation is displayed, a survivor of the French Revolution. This masterpiece of the late twelfth century is a Grail of its country. Yet the most significant representation in the cathedral of Notre-Dame is the coming of Melchizedek, giving a wafer of bread and a cup of wine to the Patriarch Abraham, who has returned from victory over the enemies of the King of Sodom. As the Book of Genesis told the story:

> And Melchizedek king of Salem brought forth bread and wine: and he was priest of God Most High.
>
> And he blessed him, and said, Blessed be Abraham of God Most High, possessor of heaven and earth:
>
> And blessed be God Most High, which hath delivered thine enemies into thy hand.

In the sculptures, the bearded Melchizedek in his long robes offers a wafer with his right hand, while holding a large chalice in his left. Behind him, a cloth covers a table altar.

Standing before him is Abraham in a chain-mail armour and helmet, surcoat, swordbelt and spear, with his hands joined in prayer. Another knight faces us, holding up his right arm which is broken off at the wrist: he may represent the King of Sodom. His armour is as scaly as a dragon, his round ridged shield resembles the sun, its rays spiking from the boss. This ensemble is remarkable for the thirteenth century, because the knight directly receives communion from priest and king without the benefit of the Church, which does not yet exist. Such an ancient assertion by the kings of France to have divine sanction was brought forward to the age of chivalry, crusade and expanding royal power. For Melchizedek was again praised in a Psalm of David for his prowess in holy war.

> *The Lord hath sworn, and will not repent. Thou art a priest for ever, after the order of Melchizedek.*
> *The Lord at thy right hand shall strike through kings in the day of His wrath.*
> *He shall judge among the nations. He shall fill the places with dead bodies; He shall strike through the head in many countries.*

Nearby, in the small rose window of the Litanies of the Virgin Mary, the Ark of the Covenant is displayed as one of her attributes – the same conjunction of Melchizedek and the Ark can be seen at Chartres, proving the prevalence of these early medieval cults. The Ark is shown as a brown pouch with a red diamond in its middle, hanging from two carrying poles. On its golden tabletop sit two brown and yellow birds, owls, phoenixes or eagles, representing wisdom. A blue sun encompasses it. Two other symbols of the Grail are worked into the window: the Virgin Mary as a spiritual pitcher, pouring out holy water; and as a vessel of devotion.

Equally significant is the sculpture of the coronation of the Virgin on the gable of the central doorway of the west façade of Reims Cathedral. God the Father, holding the Holy Book in his left hand, crowns her with his right hand beneath a sunburst from a central boss, as on the shield of the scaly knight with Melchizedek. Beneath her feet is a large black basalt ball, representing the cosmos, reminiscent of the sacred meteorite in the Ka'aba in Mecca. Above her is a large statue of the Magdalene beside Saint Peter, while below, as at Chartres, are statues of King Solomon and the Queen of Sheba. The same themes linked the sacred places on the pilgrim paths of the Middle Ages.

At the rival great cathedral of Chartres, King Melchizedek is carved holding a cup with a stone inside, a correspondence with the Grail of Wolfram von Eschenbach. On a capital in the north tower, two mythological birds are shown drinking from another chalice. Curiously, two reliefs of the Ark of the Covenant, which had stood before the navel of the world, the foundation stone of the Temple of Solomon, are also carved at Chartres, with a Latin inscription suggesting that 'You are to work through the Ark' (*Archa cederis*). For the Jews, that holy receptacle was the keeper of all the mysteries of life and death. The cathedral also keeps the tunic worn by the Virgin Mary on the day of the birth of Christ, as well as the skull of Saint Anne, her mother. Its beautiful window of stained glass dedicated to the Magdalene was donated by the water-carriers of the city.

On the way to the Channel lies an early church of the Magdalene in Verneuil-sur-Avre. It is crowned by an unearthly censer or pepperpot spire, as if it were a descending Grail that scatters light. The stained-glass windows of the choir show Joseph of Arimathea with the Holy Vessel blessing Saint Mary and other pilgrims before their voyage from the Holy Land. An inscription on another window identifies Marseilles as their landing place, where shepherds already kneel on the rocks in worship and wonder. Although the building, like that at Troyes, dates from the twelfth century, the windows are part of the revival of the cult of the saint inspired by Viollet le Duc, as at Semur and Châteaudun.

At the latter place, the abbey church of the Magdalene is stripped as bare as her reputation has been. Yet the exquisite round romanesque arches beside those with slight points in the shape of perfect breasts make this white stone edifice the most beautiful of the shrines still left to the saint. There is no altar at Châteaudun, as if religious faith had been removed from the Magdalene. In a battered frieze, her sole statue has had the Holy Vessel broken from her hand. Yet above her gouged head is the scallop shell of the pilgrims on their way to Santiago de Compostela; for her church was traditionally built over a crypt of the fifth century dedicated to Saint James and hollowed out of the rock. And strangely, on the hexagonal medieval font of baptism, there is carved a mixed pagan and Christian relief of the back of a naked figure emerging from a cornucopia. Man or woman, it holds up the lid, which supports two round stones, of a flowering Grail.

Viollet le Duc acquired his adoration of the restoration of supreme medieval shrines as a young traveller in Italy, where he found the vandalism due to neglect even greater than the barbarism of the French Revolution. 'The period of the Renaissance was a brilliant flash of lightning,' he wrote to his father. 'Destruction before, destruction afterwards.' Appointed as Inspector-General of Diocesan Buildings in France, he was inspired by the writer Prosper Mérimée to begin his mission of restoration at Vézelay, which, as Mérimée told him, was in danger of demolition. 'We can only fear that, at the first tap of a hammer, all will not fall.' Together, they saved many of the pilgrim churches of the thirteenth century, including the other Magdalenes at Châteaudun and Semur. The great cathedrals of Notre-Dame in Paris, Lausanne, Reims, Amiens, Carcassonne and Clermont-Ferrand and the basilicas of Saint-Denis and Saint-Just at Narbonne were the responsibility of Viollet le Duc alone, as were many other religious buildings. He thought that modern French painters should study medieval art as a language, 'not only its words but its grammar and its spirit'. He looked for the given moment in re-creating the past. He himself was in love with old stones, although as Mérimée wrote, that love was always rational and reasonable. 'I go around them with ever more precautions, ever more cares, I look for their sickness, their sufferings, we understand each other better in the end.' He even joined the revived medieval *compagnonnages*, the Masonic guilds, which had originally built Chartres and the illustrious Gothic cathedrals that he was set on re-creating in their former glory.

Another seaborne Grail of running Holy Blood reached Fécamp on the Norman coast. The scabs scraped off the body of Jesus by the knives of Nicodemus, which appeared in some of the romances in the Grail Castle procession, were held to be sealed in lead, hidden in a hollow fig-tree and launched from Phoenicia to keep them safe from Roman invasion. The tree took root at Fécamp without disclosing its secret, in the manner of the flowering thorn at Glastonbury. When Rollo, the first Duke of Normandy, began the construction of the huge abbey church there in the tenth century, on the site of a nunnery sacked by the Vikings, a miracle was necessary to bless the place. An old man appeared in a vision and left one of the knives of Nicodemus on the altar, incised in Latin with the inscription, 'In the name of the Holy and Indivisible Trinity'. Later, at a Mass in a nearby village church at Saint-Maclou-la-Brière, the wine in the chalice was turned into blood, signifying the presence of Christ. When the abbey was rebuilt in the twelfth century, the knife of Nicodemus and the two lead cylinders of the Holy Blood were found in a hollow pillar eighteen years before the discovery of the tomb of King Arthur at Glastonbury. Some of the precious relic was sent to Norwich Cathedral, but it disappeared during the Reformation. The lead tubes remain in the abbey church of the Holy Trinity at Fécamp. They are housed in a tabernacle behind the high altar, on which three angels are carved holding vessels to catch the sacred fluid from His wounds. Below are testimonies to miraculous cures: *MARIE PROTEGEZ NOUS. HOMMAGE AU PRECIEUX SANG.*

While I was there, in the Chapel of the Virgin opposite the shrine, an aged priest was raising a silver-gilt communion cup and celebrating Mass. On the wooden altar in the Calvary chapel are carved the golden symbols of the Passion, the Crown of Thorns, the Holy Nails and the urn which caught the Blood of Christ. And even more remarkable is a marble relief over the Chapel of Saint John the Baptist. His severed head is carried on a platter by two angels. Fécamp houses many of the venerable sights from the Grail procession, although the bone of Saint Mary Magdalene which was claimed to be there in the Middle Ages has disappeared. The abbey church of the Trinity also holds a chapel to the Magdalene, while in the modern village church at Saint-Maclou, where the wine turned to blood a thousand years before, windows like those at Verneuil still show a Grail arriving from the sea at Marseilles, confirming the French link between south and north in the cult of the Holy Blood.

Our Lady of the Holy Blood also arrived up the coastline at Boulogne in the seventh century. She was a centre of worship until her destruction in the French Revolution. This Black Madonna and Child, one metre tall, came by small boat with a copy of the Gospels in Syriac Greek script. The beaching seemed to confirm the legend of the coming of the Magdalene by sea. The image of Mary on her ship with the Child Jesus was used on pilgrims' badges on the way to Compostela or Rome, and also as the heraldic arms of the Port of Edinburgh at Leith. They underlaid the facts of the early Celtic missionaries to Europe with the Word of God as well as the myths of the passage of the Grail to Britain.

Yet in legend, romance and belief, Joseph of Arimathea and the cult of the Magdalene were carried across the Channel to Glastonbury. Outside the abbey there, where King Arthur's bones were held to be buried along with the holiest relics in all Britain, a Hospital of Saint Mary Magdalene was built in the thirteenth century to house ten poor men or pilgrims. The simple chapel is still there, as spare as a hermit's cell, pointing the way to the Grail. The medieval chronicler John of Glastonbury associated the neighbouring church at Beckery, dedicated first to the

Magdalene and then to Saint Brigit, with King Arthur. Basing himself on the *Perlesvaus*, declared to be written by a monk of Glastonbury, John declared that Arthur's vision of the Grail happened in the chapel of the Magdalene. There he saw in a vision the miracle of the sacrament, the Virgin Mary offering up the Child Jesus to the priest for sacrifice. She then gave to the King a crystal cross, which was preserved among the holy relics of Glastonbury. He changed his coat of arms into a green shield with a silver cross, placing Mary and her infant upon it – an image of Christ which the Celtic monk Gildas had declared that Arthur bore at the Battle of Badon. Gildas himself was revered at Glastonbury for writing *The Loss and Conquest of Britain* there, while the abbots adopted Arthur's supposed shield as their own after discovering his remains in the abbey.

As for Joseph of Arimathea, he is still commemorated in Glastonbury as the saint who brought the Holy Vessels from Sarras to Britain. John identified their shapes in an odd alchemic and Gnostic passage which he ascribed to a prophecy of Melkin the Bard, the teacher of Merlin. At Avalon, there was a pagan cemetery, supervised by thirteen celestial spheres, which was enclosed within the wattle chapel originally founded by Saint Patrick. 'There Joseph de Marmore, named "of Arimathea", took everlasting sleep . . . with him in the tomb [are] two white and silver vessels filled with the blood and sweat of the prophet Jesus.' These two cruets, as they are now called, can be seen in the windows of the Church of Saint John the Baptist at Glastonbury and in All Saints' Church at Langport. In the Church of Saint John, a recent window showed the bringing of the two cruets by Joseph to Britain as explicitly as the many windows in France portrayed Joseph and the Magdalene bringing them to Sarras. Joseph can be seen at the Crucifixion, then collecting the Holy Blood from Christ's Body after He was rescued from the Tomb, then sailing to Glastonbury with the two precious containers, and planting his staff on Wearyall Hill that sprouted with the flowering thorn, symbolising His Crown and

Wounds. Actually, the medieval abbey also claimed to possess a part of the Crown of Thorns, encased in a splendid reliquary, still preserved in Stanbrook Abbey. A bronze bowl now in the Taunton Museum in Somerset lays claim to be a local Grail, as does a sapphire-blue glass dish with eight-petalled star flowers; also the Nanteos olive-wood cup, which, like the Ka'aba stone at Mecca, is worn away by the kisses of the faithful, looking for healing and divine guidance.

Another centre of pilgrimage on the Channel was the mystic Mont Saint-Michel. The expanding French monarchy needed a warrior saint to hallow its exploits, as the dragon-slaying Saint George blessed the endeavours of the English. French troops began to process behind the white cross of Saint Michael as well as the Oriflamme of Saint Denis. By the end of the twelfth century, the holy race of the Franks had, according to Robert the Monk, been chosen by God 'as His people and His heritage'. The cult of the warrior Saint Catherine with her sword and crown was replaced by the reality of Saint Joan of Arc, the blessed virgin and victor, as the Archangel Michael had been as the leader of the armies of God at the fall of Lucifer and against the Anti-Christ. His feast day had been instituted by Charlemagne, and in the eighth century he appeared in visions to the blessed Bishop of Avranches, demanding a monastery in his honour at the top of the ocean pinnacle in Brittany. Under the Norman kings, the Mont rivalled Fécamp, Reims and Vézelay as a sanctuary for the faithful.

Under the enlightened abbot and Norman historian, Robert of Thorigny, a contemporary of Chrétien de Troyes, the Mont became a centre of learning. Its vast scriptorium still testifies to that medieval illumination. It was rivalled only by the scriptorium which the aged Alcuin had established at Tours in the abbey of Saint Martin, a legionary turned priest from Roman Gaul, whose cult declined as that of the Archangel Michael rose. Unfortunately, the Huguenots destroyed that abbey, although the Mont, with its superb fortifications, never fell to its religious enemies. At

Tours, only the Charlemagne tower still stands, in memory of the Emperor's teacher Alcuin and his profound scholarship. In a side chapel of the abbey church of Saint Michael in the Mont, reserved for prayer, an altarpiece demonstrates the three most usual forms of the Grail. The five scenes of this medieval ivory and painted Passion depict Christ's torments before He is crucified. The centrepiece shows two of the venerated relics: Longinus the blind centurion plunges a spear point into the side of the Son of God, then rubs his eyes with the Holy Blood and can see again; an angel with a golden cup collects the issue of His nailed feet. The three Marys – the Virgin Mary, the Magdalene and the mother of James – are at the Cross. The next scene shows Christ taken down from His torture in front of the three Marys, but this time the Magdalene wipes the wound on His hand with her long golden hair, which will be squeezed into a covered chalice – the Grail which she and Joseph of Arimathea would transport to Sarras, for he, with a pilgrim's pouch, and Nicodemus are also shown on the base carving. In the fifth scene, Christ is seen stepping from the Tomb over sleeping soldiers, one with a battle-axe, while two angels swing golden lamps on chains or censers of bounty above Him, the blessings of heaven. The Holy Lance, the angelic Grail and the Joseph and Magdalene Grail are joined in this altarpiece by the showers of grace.

Orléans was on the pilgrim's way from Paris to Compostela. Yet as at Tours, little is left to show that. There is still a Magdalene Road and Gate, through which Talbot and the English garrison retreated after the wounded Saint Joan of Arc had forced her way into the city. The old Cathedral of the Holy Cross was ransacked by the Huguenots, who also destroyed the ancient basilica of Saint Aignan. The heart of King Francis II was thrown to the dogs. The cathedral is now the shrine of Saint Joan; vulgar windows to her glory make gaudy her brave simplicity. Yet in her way, the warrior maid deserved to replace the repentant rich sinner at the foot of the Cross.

The trail in search of the Magdalene may well end in the Museum of Religious Art in Liège. There the earliest and most charming painting of her dates from the eleventh century. While the kneeling woman donor of the picture plays at cat's cradle with a rosary and the infant Jesus, held in His Mother's hands, the Magdalene in her red dress holds a golden vessel, her head surrounded by a halo of rays. In the background is one of the first representations of a Garden of Paradise, in front of ramparts and a quay with river boats beyond. Again this pervasive cult of the repentant saint, the bearer of the Holy Blood to France, prefigured the romances of the Grail.

The Way of the Crusaders

Pilgrims on the crusading trail from Vézelay to the north of Spain passed through Autun, where they can still be seen on the tympanum of the cathedral with their shoulder bags sporting crosses and scallop shells. On one capital of the Flight into Egypt, the child of Christ is shown on his mother's lap as she rides on a donkey led by Saint Joseph. Uniquely, the Blessed Virgin holds a globe in the palm of her hand, while Jesus puts his fingers on this stone cosmos. But such an indication of the quest for the divine is only a signpost on the path to Neuvy Saint-Sepulchre, where the Blood of Christ is still kept, and on to Charroux and Civray, where two of the earlier depictions of the Grail in France remain to this day.

At Neuvy, the Abbé will demonstrate the two drops out of the three of the Holy Blood which survived the French Revolution. These were presented to the basilica by Cardinal Odon of Châteauroux after he had acquired them in the thirteenth century in Palestine. They are kept within a phial inside a modern reliquary: a kneeling golden angel carries the precious burden. Yet another form of the Grail is always on show in Saint Joseph's chapel off the ten pillars which support the high dome of the round structure, modelled on the Church of the Holy Sepulchre in Jerusalem. There is an immense stone urn with a copper cover surmounted by the Cross – a true font of blessing and rebirth.

Further along the way to Compostela, the pilgrims arrived at the wonder of the abbey of Charroux. Its supreme surviving tower on its soaring octagonal arches derived from Charlemagne's chapel at Aachen, more exact a replica of the Church of the Holy Sepulchre than at Neuvy. Most remarkably, one stone carving has been left out of the museum within the abbey ruins where the other statues may be found, including one of the Foolish Virgins squandering the riches of nature by turning her pitcher upside down. Secluded there, three jewelled reliquaries may also be seen, one of which housed the Saint Vertu presented by Charlemagne. To the west of the crypt of the round tower, however, an eleventh-century incised relief has been placed so that the rays of the morning sun illuminate it. Among fronds of lilies, two doves are drinking from a chalice. If there is one supreme time and place of Grail pilgrimage in France, it is sunrise at the tower of Charroux.

Among the seventy-five relics which made the abbey of Charroux such a magnet in the Middle Ages were a piece of the True Cross, a version of the Holy Face of Lucca, and the Saint Vertu, now kept in the cathedral at Poitiers. The name of this last remnant of the body of Christ was a euphemism. The Pope called it the Holy Prepuce, actually the foreskin of Christ taken from Him at His circumcision. The original benefactor of the abbey, Charlemagne, might well have wished to own a part of the virility of God as a symbol of his own blessed power and virtue, and as the sire of a race of sanctified rulers in the manner of King David of Israel.

Before Charlemagne took the little piece of sacred skin from the Church of Saint Mary in Aachen to present it to Charroux, it had a strange provenance. It was reputedly given to him by an angelic boy in a vision during the saying of Mass in the Church of the Holy Sepulchre in Jerusalem. There he saw the right hand of God descend, as can be seen on the portico of the cathedral of Saint Peter at Saintes, also on the route to Compostela. The Almighty placed a small thing on the communion chalice, the Saint Vertu, capable of curing and restoring to life. In point of fact, Charlemagne never visited the Holy City in his life.

The popes also claimed that they came into the possession of the sacred foreskin after the sack of Constantinople. Yet they lost it from Saint John Lateran with the sack of Rome by the troops of Charles V. Hidden in a cave near Calcata in Latium by an imperial soldier, it was said to have made many miraculous cures after its transfer to the local church, and it was revered in a procession round the town on New Year's Day, the Feast of the Circumcision. Its reliquary of gold, enamel and gemstones was supported by a pair of angels; that precious object is still in the Vatican Museum without its contents. The Saint Vertu of Italy has now disappeared from its wonder-working, although not from folk memory, unlike its fellow at Charroux.

Seven miles to the west of Charroux, carved Templar knights continue to guard pilgrims above the entrance doors to the painted church of Saint Nicholas at Civray. Standing on the rim of a half-moon, their nailed feet tread down the devils and pagans that threaten the faithful, while protecting Christ ruling in heaven below them. Inside, there is a rare twelfth-century fresco of a holy man reaching out towards an altar bearing two candles and a chalice. An angel holding the scroll of the Word of the Lord flies down, bringing grace. This is the only mural of the period on the route to Compostela showing the Grail.

Aulnay to the south-west is the best preserved of all the stopping-places along that pilgrim road. On its west portico, crusading knights recline guarding the Paschal Lamb on its round platter. On another tympanum, Saint Peter is shown as crucified upside down. He is seen as a descending figure of the divine, his two torturers hammering the nails into his feet and standing above him on the arms of the cross – a theme that could be interpreted as a revolt from the authority of

Rome, even though it was traditional. Further to the south towards Bordeaux, at Saintes, there is an architrave of slaughter above the entrance to the cathedral of Saint Peter. Primitive men butcher each other above two Templar symbols, the Lamb of God carrying the Cross, and the Hand of God pointing down with two fingers curled back from a sunburst, the supposed vision of Charlemagne in Jerusalem. In the Middle Ages, Saintes was as famous as Hailes as being a sanctuary of the Holy Blood; but as in England, the remembrance of the faith lost has long gone.

In my discovery of the two French Grail trails that crossed at Vézelay, I was looking at the roof of the ancient Abbaye des Dames. Two doves alighted on the cross on its pinnacle. One of them had a morsel in its beak. It was an actual sight of what Wolfram von Eschenbach had described in his *Parzival* as the Grail. Although I had viewed so many versions of the Sacred Vessel in paint or stone or stained glass on my way to Saintes, I felt that I shared somewhat in the literal faith of the Middle Ages. There was the Holy Spirit descending as a dove from heaven. In its beak, a blessed stone or a sacred wafer. The mind only had to believe the vision.

At the ancient Roman spa town of Dax, towards the Pyrenees, I found perhaps the earliest Grails that were carved in France. They were placed on the outer wall of the apse over delicate romanesque columns at the church of Saint-Paul-les-Dax. The intense simplicity of this eleventh-century work showed a primitive and total faith in teaching by pictures. On the first, three women, including the Magdalene, carrying three jars of ointment, approached the Tomb; its lid was being raised by two angels. Above them, two heavenly hands swung two censers on long chains, while a third hand held an octagonal cross in front of a divine torch. On the next frieze, the twelve disciples and Jesus were sitting at the Last Supper. Thirteen pairs of feet were showing under the tablecloth, while dishes and mugs were being set on the table along with three bowls, each filled with a fish, the symbol of Christ.

The third and last frieze was the most remarkable. Split into two scenes, Christ was shown surrounded by seven soldiers with hammers and swords. Then He was put on to a large octagonal Cross looking rather like a windmill. On one side of Him, Saint John was standing; on the other, holding a book, a Mary, either the Virgin or the Magdalene. Between them at the foot of the Cross was Saint Longinus, piercing His side with a spear, while Joseph of Arimathea in a pointed cap was catching the sweat and blood from under His armpit on a taper, to transfer it into a pot held in his left hand. These were the symbols of the Grail, which would meet pilgrims on one of their last halts in France before proceeding to Compostela. And all these sculptures showed signs of the Holy Vessel a century before Chrétien de Troyes wrote his *Perceval*. By foot and not by footnote, I was finding evidence of the cult of the Grail before it was written down. The concept did not reach Chrétien only from the words of Celtic historians, myth-makers and minstrels. This was a far-flung legend that was concentrated in Champagne. By fresco and window and image in stone, the message reached the primary messenger of words, as the Angel Gabriel came to the Virgin Mary at the Annunciation before the birth of Christ.

A Forgotten Way and Cult

The pilgrims on their path through France towards Spain had other goals. Although the rusty sword stuck in the rock at Rocamadur was not the Durandal of Roland any more than it was the sword of King Arthur in the stone, yet the Black Virgin there was as celebrated as the one in Montserrat in Catalonia. The Calvary to her shrine up the steep steps on bleeding knees was for the guilty almost as purging as the journey to Compostela or Vézelay, where also the penitents threw off their chains in front of the bones of the Magdalene. Throughout the south of France and northern Spain, the cults of the Black Virgin and the Magdalene were often confused in the desperate need of the sinner to be shriven.

First, the pilgrims had to cross over many rivers on the way by some of the few bridges over their torrents. At Cahors, the Valentré Bridge with its three towers, said to be the Faustian gift of the Devil, resisted the English during the Hundred Years War and Henry of Navarre in the religious wars. The Templars in their decline, when they were hardly defending the pilgrims any more and had become bankers, had made Cahors into the money market of all Europe, before it gave way to the Temple in Paris. At the bridge over the Tarn at Moissac, further south, the abbey church of Saint Peter has a masterpiece of the Vision of the Apocalypse according to Saint John over its doorway. Also there, as at Auch, is a fine life-size carving of the late sixteenth century, the putting of Christ's Body into the Tomb. Ignoring the Gospels, the Virgin Mary has joined the scene with the other women. The Magdalene holds up her sacred vessel, overshadowed at the feet of Jesus as she was to be by the Mother of Christ.

Even further down the way to Compostela, there are two cathedrals of Saint Mary, at Auch and at Oleron. Although the first did not begin building until 1489 and was dedicated to the Virgin Mary, it still represented the cult of the Magdalene, who is shown bearing her vase on one of the hundred and thirteen oak choir stalls, which are an epiphany on the history of the Grail. The carvings demonstrate the Renaissance love of the classical past as well as religion. Between the Old Testament prophets and the apostles stand the Sibyls and the Virtues. So the Sibyl of Cumae, also revered by Virgil, holds up the cornucopia and horn of bounty, while Eucharistic Faith holds up a chalice and a vision seen by the pure Knights of the Round Table, a crucified Christ emerging from the cup, contained in a tiny circle as large as a wafer. Many prophetesses appear with open coffers and bowls of plenty. The Tiber Sibyl holds up a severed and speaking head, while Judith holds the mute head of Holofernes. As at Chartres and Reims, King Melchizedek is shown on the stalls; he offers a large ewer with a lid and carries a pilgrim's pouch. Saint Longinus is there with the Holy Lance, while Saint Peter uplifts a large Christian fish. Most curious of all is the carving of Saint John, bearing a chalice with the small dragon serpent of wisdom climbing out of it.

The Magdalene is also predominant in the eighteen Renaissance stained-glass windows by Arnaud de Moles: one of them shows Saint James dressed as a pilgrim. In the central bay of the main apse, with the standing Virgin Mary and Saint John, the Magdalene appears kneeling at the foot of the Cross and touching the wound on His nailed feet. In the Resurrection window, Christ touches her brow in His visitation to her alone, while she holds a small golden bowl with a carved lid in the fingers of her left hand.

At Oleron, however, the cathedral of Saint Mary in the hills above the castle at Pau is a silent witness to the slow obliteration of the cult of the Magdalene. On its tympanum of the twelfth century, carved large, is a primitive scene of the Deposition from the Cross similar to the one on the apse of Saint-Paul-les-Dax. Joseph of Arimathea supports the body of Christ, while Nicodemus takes out His nails with pincers. Saint John holds a curved hammer, ready for use if needed, while the Virgin Mary stands to the side. As on the ivory altarpiece at Mont-Saint-Michel, the Magdalene wipes the wound on Christ's hand, but with her palms, not her hair.

Yet the modern commentary in the church only refers to the Magdalene as 'a woman saint'. The cathedral itself may be named after her, for she was the most venerated Saint Mary in the early Middle Ages at the time of its building. It was founded by Viscount Gaston IV of Béarn, a hero of the First Crusade and the *reconquista* of Spain, because his catapults and towers on wheels enabled Jerusalem and Saragossa to be taken. His statue, or that of the Emperor Constantine crushing a pagan from horseback, springs out of the side of the tympanum: the smashing of the face makes the rider anonymous, although below him, two chained Saracens forever grimace.

At Orthez, modern pilgrims may still cross over the famous fortified bridge with its central tower spanning the road and eat at the Auberge Saint Loup on the other side, as travellers have done for five centuries. The road to Compostela leads on through Sauveterre, where the Church of Saint Andrew has the most charming small romanesque façade within the fortified town. At the foot of the Pyrenees, there is the long winding climb to Roncesvalles beginning at Saint Jean-Pied-de-Port, where medieval pilgrims used to arrive by riverboat. But at the scene of Roland's defeat by the pagan Basques, not the Moorish infidels, only a small fifteenth-century church of Santiago shows itself, together with a wayside cross. In place of the old monastery, which was so hospitable to pilgrims, there are modern blocks for teaching prayer; also hostels. Within them is encased the Gothic chapterhouse of the founder King of Navarre: he still lies with his Queen there. Roland, incidentally, is said to be buried at the pilgrim Atlantic port of Blaye, in the estuary of the Gironde opposite Bordeaux. His body may lie beside the two surviving towers of the triangular Château des Rudel; its famous son, the minstrel Jaufré, died in the arms of his love, Melissende of Tripoli, after falling sick in the Mediterranean crossing to her crusading County in Syria.

The two Grail trails of France which cross at Vézelay – the ways of the crusaders and the Magdalene – also meet at the approaches to Spain. For she was an inspiration to the holy warriors against the Moors, who must have found the Christian faith of the little enemy mountain towns overwhelming. Every cluster of houses, tenaciously clinging to rock or slope, boasts a church or an abbey or even a cathedral. The Muslims may have built a spate of mosques in the south of Spain, but they were confronted by so many spires in the Pyrenees that their attack would have seemed to be blocked by a stockade of stones, even if these were not as terrifying as the thickets of impaled victims which met their eyes when they invaded the Transylvania of King Vlad the Impaler. To the modern traveller, the evidence of that long-gone holy war still bristles against the sky. And the cults which crossed at Vézelay – the sword borne by the knights against the infidel, along with the Grail of grace carried by the Magdalene – can still be found together on the borderland of the struggle between the Cross and the Crescent.

The cult of the Magdalene also spread west along the Mediterranean coast from Saint Maximin-La-Baume and Marseilles, where she traditionally landed with the Grail. At Béziers, there is a large church dedicated to her with an octagonal tower constructed by the apse. Viscount Trescard was murdered in the holy building, and at the massacre of the population of the city in 1209 during the Albigensian Crusade, the worst slaughter took place in this sanctuary, where the Cathars had fled, seeking a vain mercy. The grim words of Arnald-Almaric, the Abbot of Cîteau, to the vengeful crusaders against the heretics still resound: 'Kill them all: God will look after His own.' During the French Revolution, the church was turned into a workshop for making bayonets, but now the only sign of war on its outer wall is a crusading knight within a large medallion, while a gigantic scallop shell design reminds the pilgrim today of the holy way to Spain.

In Narbonne, the old Bishop's Palace has a Magdalene tower and chapel, now converted into an archaeological museum. A faded fresco of the Deposition from the Cross has almost expunged the saint, while two clearer angels swing their censers on chains above her. At Albi, there are a pair of Magdalenes carrying her vase, almost lost among the exuberant Renaissance portals. But at Carcassonne and Perpignan, there are no traces of her. Below the Langue d'Oc, the land of the Catalans honoured the Black Virgin in another tongue.

Just so do modern times endeavour to wipe clean the ancient cult of the Magdalene, the Saint Mary of the Middle Ages with her one hundred and fifty shrines. Why was this done? The medieval Church was at its most successful in making Christians feel guilty. Its control over barbaric passions lay in the necessity of expiation only granted by the priest. And much repentance was demanded in that cruel and plundering age. For the warlords and the knights, whose greed made them into considerable sinners according to the Bible, the Magdalene was their perfect forgiveness – a stained woman, blessed by Christ Himself. In a strange way, she became associated with Queen Guinevere in the Arthurian cult: both erring ladies needed pardon.

Yet in later ages of materialism and psychiatry, guilt would be at a discount and pardon would become merely a confession from a couch. The Vatican would think that purity was a better message, particularly for women; Hail Marys should be repeated for transgressions, rather than walking with bleeding feet along rocky paths. Jung himself, one of the fathers of analysis, would study alchemy and the Grail in order to find out the wellsprings of those legends in the human psyche. In the course of this progress, the cults of the Magdalene and the Grail were to be lost or mistaken.

With the waning of the Grail at the end of the Middle Ages, the Magdalene was gradually taken over by the Virgin Mary or Our Lady, although the Gospel of Saint John never put her at the Tomb. The three Marys there were a later invention. Yet churches were renamed; the Gospels and the golden legends were forgotten. The Mother of Jesus was shown superseding the Magdalene at the foot of the Cross; also washing His wounds there and taking care of His Body at the opening of the Tomb. By the nineteenth century, she was dominating the Magdalene at most of the second Mary's sites in France, such as Meaux, where the windows of the Lady Chapel even show the Virgin at the feast at Cana and with the disciples at Pentecost. The attraction of the repentant sinner who brought the Grail to Sarras was replaced by the vision of the purity of Our Lady. So the sinful woman, already forgiven by Christ, was remade without spot or stain.

Chapter Nine

The Waning of the Grail

> In the Middle Ages the choice lay, in principle, only
> between God and the world, between contempt or eager
> acceptance, at the peril of one's soul, of all that makes up
> the beauty and the charm of earthly life. All terrestrial
> beauty bore the stain of sin.

> J. Huizinga, *The Waning of the Middle Ages*

In the classic work by Huizinga, *The Waning of the Middle Ages*, the nobility was clearly shown as acting out a vision and a dream. The feudal courts saw themselves as Knights of the Round Table and so were elevated towards the sublime. Yet there were rules in that passionate and violent age, 'always vacillating between tearful piety and frigid cruelty, between respect and insolence, between despondency and wantonness'. One of these formalities was a curious reduction of the Grail procession. At the ceremony of the Mass, where the congregation could not take communion, a disc of silver, ivory or wood called the Pax was passed around for everyone to kiss after the Agnus Dei. This communal observance was the nearest material symbol on offer to the laity of the approach to the divine.

The spirit of the Middle Ages wanted to lay out each conception in mosaic. A holy thought should become an image; reaching for God be seen as a sign along the way. There was a danger in confusing the spiritual with the temporal, the bones of the Saints with the examples of their lives. Even secular tournaments with jousting knights were called 'a great indulgence conferred by arms', as if pardon came with victory. As in any crusade, an absolution for sins was the incentive for holy war. Although the Church of Rome knew that images were merely for the illiterate, these were not condemned. They were the spelling lessons towards the Word of God. And religious extravagance was tolerated, as long as it did not lead to radical change. Beatific visions of Christ were admitted, if they remained within the teachings of the Church.

Extreme and material visions of the Saviour were included. 'A man feels quite deluged in the blood of Christ and faints. All the red and warm blood of the Five Wounds flowed through the mouth of Saint Henry Suso into his heart. Catherine of Siena drunk from the wound in His side.' Such ecstatic enlightenments were still considered Christian revelations. Jean Berthelemy, indeed, was literal and cannibal in describing the Eucharist in *Le Livre de Crainte Amoureuse*:

> *You will eat Him roasted at the fire, well baked, not at all overdone or burnt. For just as the Easter lamb was properly baked and roasted between two fires of wood or of charcoal, so was gentle Jesus on Good Friday placed on the spit of the worthy cross, and tied between the two fires of His very fearful death and passion, and of the very ardent charity and love which He felt for our souls and our salvation. He was, at it were, roasted and slowly baked to save us.*

A certain voluptuousness and paganism had always been a part of the *chansons* of the troubadours. Religious music was used for love poetry. And the most popular of all the lays, the *Roman de la Rose*, mixed carnal love with the Passion of Christ quite shamelessly. In the opulence of the courts before the Renaissance, even the ascetic quest for the Grail would become a luxurious voyage. In tapestry and royal theatre, chivalry would appear as a drama of gilt and circumstance.

There were nine cult heroes in the romances and images of

the late Middle Ages. Three were leaders from the Bible: Joshua, King David and Judas Maccabeus; three were from classical times: Hector, Alexander the Great and Julius Caesar; and three were historical Christian warriors: King Arthur, Charlemagne and Godfrey de Bouillon. These were particularly celebrated on the tapestries from Arras and Tournai commissioned by the nobles of Burgundy. In a curious fantasy of history, all wore contemporary costumes dripping with silks and brocades, spiked with lances and long-toed pointed boots. Weapons, ships, musical instruments and tools were also of the time, as were legends and alchemy. In one Flemish tapestry of the fifteenth century presently in the Palazzo Doria in Rome, the young Alexander was flown up to heaven through the spheres of air and fire on a winged chariot, blessed by God the Father. This was a sacred adventure before the Greek conqueror would acquire dominion over nature and the earth. In the tapestries about Christ, display trampled over purity. Particularly sumptuous was *The Adoration of the Magi*, woven in Brussels of gold and silver silk thread, and presently in the cathedral at Sens. A naked baby Jesus sits on his mother's damask robe. There is no manger, but a carved throne. The Magi wear regal oriental costumes and bear wrought and jewelled caskets, gifts of infinite bounty. One donkey and one cow munching hay are background figures, with two loutish faces peering through a window at this palatial scene of the presentation of the riches of the East.

Even the agonies of the Passion are described as part of *The Glorious Life of Christ*, an Arras work for the cathedral of San Salvador in Saragossa. His entry into Jerusalem is a triumph. His crucifixion is a stylised tableau with the traditional symbols of the Grail, the Holy Lance of Saint Longinus and the sponge of vinegar taken from the cup and held up to Him. In addition, a curious scene of the three Holy Marys shows them placing two golden Grails of spices on the broken tomb, while an angel announces to them that Christ is already risen. One gilded cup has the stone fallen from heaven dropping into it, pointed out by the Virgin Mary, whose growing cult was a strange paradox in the laxity of that age.

The crusades were depicted in dramas and pageants. At the French court of Charles V, the fall of Jerusalem in the First Crusade was redone in 1378 for the Holy Roman Emperor. Fifteen tapestries on Godfrey de Bouillon decorated Pleshey Castle, while Henry III of England commissioned wall-paintings on the same theme. And William Caxton not only printed the Bible and Malory's *Morte D'Arthur*, but also an English translation of the romance of *Godfrey de Bouillon or the Siege and Conquest of Jerusalem*. However decadent the contemporary action, crusading retained its popular appeal.

Although the Church condemned tournaments, the nobility revelled in them as the expression of ideal chivalry. As concepts of the Grail and the crusades became more lavish, so extravagant military orders rose to replace the Hospitallers, the Templars and the Teutonic Knights. In instituting and financing the Order of the Golden Fleece, the dukes of Burgundy gilded the rough virtues of the ascetic knights of the Holy Land. Instead of protecting pilgrims to the sites of the Passion, this body of elect aristocrats attended rituals and had love affairs. Holy wars were hardly their concern. Status and entertainment were replacing swords and engagement. Betterment was becoming the enemy of the good.

Penance and savagery had always underlaid the quest for the Grail and for Jerusalem. This purpose was now encrusted by ornament and boast rather than rigour and vow. War, as in the other classic work by Huizinga, *Homo Ludens*, was being reduced to play. The Grail romances had changed the holy combat and the joust unto death into fables, and the Burgundian court altered the chivalric quest into an orgiastic entertainment. The process would culminate in Tudor times at the extravagant Field of the Cloth of Gold. Cannon had already come to end the era of the armoured knight. England and France had fought a Hundred Years War, when women saints were burned alive and chivalry was the mask of brutality. This fantastic tournament was a necessary charade for Henry VIII of England to persuade himself that the old noble values still survived into a mechanical age, when the gun was already mightier than the blade. Yet it was already the travesty as well as the tapestry of peace. The Order of the Garter was worth no more than the Golden Fleece. Ceremonial was the memorial of a fierce faith lost.

The Dying of the Crusades

The luxury which tainted the purity of the quest for the Grail slowly suffocated the impulse for the crusades. At Lille in Burgundy in 1454, the year after the fall of Constantinople to the Turks, Duke Philip the Good gave a banquet for the Feast of the Pheasant. On the neck of the drugged bird, Philip swore to join a crusade to the east with one other ruler. Two hundred nobles vowed to accompany him. Yet they did not reach the Holy Land. The victory against the advancing Turks under Sultan Mehmed I was achieved by thousands of Hungarian believers, not by their rulers, who seemed to have lost stomach for the fight against the infidel in filling their own.

The intention to leave on crusade remained among the kings of Europe, but the conquest of lands nearer their borders usually intervened. After his capture of Paris, the dying Henry V of England interrupted the priest reciting the penitential psalms to declare that if his life was spared, he would leave to rebuild the walls of Jerusalem. His pledge was too late and too antique. The real problem was no longer taking the Holy City, but repulsing Muslim assault on Central Europe. As the later Pope Pius II put it in a letter to Nicholas V: 'Now Muhammad reigns among us. Now the Turk hangs over our very heads. The Black Sea is closed to us, the Don has become inaccessible. Now the Vlachs must obey the Turk. Next his sword will reach the Hungarians, and then the Germans.'

The last great crusade towards the Levant had ended in the total disaster at Nicopolis in 1396, when the previous Duke of Burgundy, Philip the Bold, had subsidised thousands of French and other European knights to join King Sigismund of Hungary's efforts to drive the Turks back to the Black Sea. The land war had turned into a defensive operation. The advance of Islam would have to be stopped finally by the walls of Vienna. In the north of Europe, the crusades against the pagan Slavs by the Teutonic knights were being defeated by the rising power of Poland. Only in Spain did the *reconquista* gradually move from the northern mountains to the southern beaches, and then on to a naval war against the Ottoman admirals and the fleets of Barbary.

The dimming of the light of the crusades lay in turning them into papal wars that were financed by the corrupt sale of indulgences. After the Albigensian suppression, the papacy stressed the policy that the enemy had to be defeated at home before he could be attacked abroad. When Gregory IX wrote to King Louis of Hungary, he assured him that the tyrant Visconti had to be deposed in Italy to prepare for a holy war against the Turks. Pius II repeated the same message, stating that battles against Ferrante of Naples and Sigismondo of Rimini were the same as attacking the Turks. The vows of crusaders who had elected to sail to the Near East were commuted to service in Lombardy. And the coffers of Saint Peter's assigned tenths while donations collected for the recapture of Jerusalem paid for besieging cities in Tuscany or Sicily.

The failure of many of the crusades against fellow Christians who were declared to be heretics appeared to point the finger of God at the motive behind their calling. Heaven seemed to be signalling its disapproval. This was particularly true of the five crusades against the Hussites in Bohemia, which heralded the rise of Protestantism in Europe. Jan Hus himself said that these fiascos were witnesses of the internal corruption of the Church, a theme taken up by the reformers of the Renaissance.

The conquest of the infidel in the Near East had already been translated to the subjugation of the pagan Slavs and

Lithuanians on the Prussian borders. The Teutonic Knights had taken over the mission of the Templars, leaving the seaborne Hospitallers to hold Rhodes and, with its fall, Malta against Islam. From their headquarters in Marienburg, the Teutonic Knights had become more representative of German national expansion than of a Christian crusade. From the fourteenth century onwards, they excluded foreigners. 'The Order is a German Order,' the Grand Master wrote, 'in which nobody who is not German, but only Germans, healthy and trained people, who are in all respects born to the shield, are included by custom.' The imperial knights, the *ritter* and the *Reisen* of *Parzival* were becoming provincial rather than international, and yet their order took them back to the immortal days of King Arthur and the Grail. Their Table of Honour was described in 1375 by Jean de Chastlemorand:

> *The Grand Master, seeing that this Reise had been hon-
> ourably completed, on the day of Candlemas feasted the
> knighthood that were with him and highly; and for the
> honour of the day, after Mass in his castle at
> Marienburg he had spread the Table of Honour, as it
> was his will that there should be seated at it twelve
> knights of the several kingdoms . . . and they were
> served, for the high dignity of the day, as was their due.
> And thanks be to God to those twelve they explained this
> order of the Table and how it came to be established.
> And then one of the knights of that religion gave to each
> of them a shoulder badge on which it was written in let-
> ters of gold 'Honneur vainc tout!'. And the next day the
> knights took their leave of the Grand Master, and
> returned each to his own country.*

Yet this order which retained the traditions of Camelot was doomed by the nationalism it encouraged. The Poles were becoming powerful. Heretical Hussite ideas, which opposed the Catholic hierarchy and demanded direct access to God, were spreading from Bohemia. Marienburg was defended in the early fifteenth century, but it was lost in 1457, surrendered by paid mercenaries. Poland, rather than the Holy Roman Empire or the Church of Rome, became the sovereign of the order. The crusade to the East in the north of Europe was over.

The Breaking of the Grail

In literature as in art, the Grail was only a series of descriptions or images. They were milestones on the way of the pilgrim towards the vision of God. But the official signs and blessings of the Church, the relics of the Passion and of the Saints, the sale of indulgences and the pardon for sins, were becoming incredible and discredited. In the amazing and popular *Travels* of Sir John Mandeville, completed in 1356, pilgrimage was taken to the limits of fable. The author displayed both the belief and the scepticism of his age in visiting the sacred remains scattered among the abbeys and the cathedrals.

At the Church of the Holy Sepulchre in Jerusalem, Mandeville wrote that 'in this temple was Charlemagne when the angel brought him the prepuce of Our Lord Jesus Christ of His circumcision. And after King Charles let bring it to Paris to his chapel, and after that he let bring it to Poitiers and after that to Chartres.' As for the head of Saint John the Baptist, the back of the skull was in Constantinople, the jaws in Genoa and the chin at Rome. 'And some men say that the head of Saint John is at Amiens in Picardy, and other men say that it is the head of Saint John the Bishop. I wot never, but God knoweth. But in what wise that men worship it the blessed Saint John holdeth him apaid.'

That was the point of faith. However true the provenance of the relic, the belief of the pilgrim in the Messiah or Saint from whom it was meant to come transformed the object into the search for revelation. The trials of the voyage were the quest for a Grail of sorts, even if the history of the sight seen was dubious. In so far as the worshipper of the fragment of the head of the Baptist believed in his holiness, the saint would repay him for his sincerity. As it was, Mandeville praised the simple Christianity in the land of the African Prester John, the son of Feirefiz in the *Parzival* of Wolfram von Eschenbach. There the people were said to sing the mass as the Apostles had, 'as Our Lord taught them [in] a good faith natural'.

This hankering for the simplicity of a reformed religion was transformed by Mandeville into a travesty of the Eucharist, which he set in the Isle of Rybothe or Tibet. He seemed to mock its pope and its carnivorous ritual. At the death of the father, the son cut off his head and fed his body to the birds – angels of God in the Tibetan liturgy. The brains were served to friends of the family, the skull used as a memorial vessel. 'And that cup the son shall keep to drink of all his lifetime in remembrance of his father.' This echo of the words of Christ, 'Do this in remembrance of me', was heretical in the extreme, a curious questioning of the doctrine of transubstantiation by bringing up the rites of the Zoroastrians, whose descendants still expose the bodies of the dead to be eaten by vultures in open burial towers.

Chaucer certainly had read his Mandeville before he composed *The Canterbury Tales*. The first comic epic in the English language was written two hundred years after the murder of Saint Thomas à Becket. Pilgrimages to his tomb were even more popular than to Our Lady of Walsingham. To the Church, of course, such piety was bliss, for it hallowed the triumph of religion over the secular state. In the *Tales*, the first pilgrim, the Knight, was praised as a crusader, 'late y-come from his viage'. His son the Squire had only been on a false crusade, the recent pillage of Flanders. The Wife of Bath had been three times to Jerusalem and to other shrines, without doing her character much good, although she found a homily on her travels:

And eek I pray Jhesu shorte their lives
That will not be governed by their wives.

175

But the profiteers from the Christian faith and the pilgrimage were mocked and run down, the Summoner and the Pardoner, the Monk and the Friar, although the Prioress and the Second Nun were allowed their virtue and their anti-Semitism, as the crusaders were. Corruption in religion, particularly the sale of the faith, was endemic, as the Pardoner confessed:

> *I wol nat do no labour with myne handes . . .*
> *Nay, I wol drynke licour of the vyne*
> *And have a joly wenche in every toun.*

Such effrontery led to the inescapable reaction. When the great Dutch humanist Erasmus visited Canterbury in the company of his learned friends Dean Colet and Sir Thomas More, he thought of Christ comparing the scribes and the Pharisees to whited sepulchres that were outwardly beautiful, but inwardly full of dead men's bones and of all uncleanness. He demanded:

> *What would Jesus say could he see the Virgin's milk exhibited for money, with as much honour paid to it as to the consecrated body of Christ; the miraculous oil; the portions of the True Cross, enough if they were collected to freight a large ship? Here we have the hood of Saint Francis, there Our Lady's petticoat or Saint Anne's comb, or Saint Thomas of Canterbury's shoes; not presented as innocent aids to religion, but as the substance of religion itself – and all through the avarice of priests and the hypocrisy of monks playing on the credulity of the people. Even bishops play their parts in these fantastic shows, and approve and dwell on them in their rescripts.*

Walsingham in Norfolk was called the English Loretto, because it held in its wooden chapel a reproduction of the Sancta Casa. This primitive shrine was blessed when the crusaders brought there the milk from the breasts of the Virgin Mary. Erasmus also visited the sacred place, and he was impressed by the contrast between its simplicity and the riches deposited there. The sea winds blew through the bare boards. Worshippers were admitted into the unfinished church by a narrow door on each side. The chapel had little light, and only from wax candles that had an agreeable odour. Yet 'if you looked inwards, you would say it was the mansion of the gods, it glitters so with jewels, gold and silver'.

That was the contrast of pilgrimage. The more holy the place, the more it was overloaded with precious memorials. The truth lay between the essence and the encrustation. Outside Walsingham there were two holy wells of miraculous healing rather like the ancient wishing wells in Ireland. The pilgrims knelt on the forestones, dipped their hands in the sacred flow of water and requested their heart's desire. This act did not mean that they would achieve their demands. When Ogygius questioned the custodian of the sanctuary at Walsingham, he found the building of the roof, the thatch and the crossbeams rather too new. He was then shown a decayed bearskin and the reliquary of the Mother of Jesus. 'So being persuaded, and excusing our stupidity, we turned to the heavenly milk of the Blessed Virgin.'

Such inquiry would turn into heresy. The German reformer Martin Luther, for instance, went in 1510 on a pilgrimage to Rome. His purpose was to expose the sale of indulgences. Paradoxically, he sought to put justification by faith before the good works performed by pilgrims visiting sites of uncertain reputation. John Calvin of Geneva would go much further. To him, pilgrimage was a useless action. The direct approach to God through one's own faith was the best way to the Creator. There were no symbols or images needed on the path to Him. These representations should be destroyed as Moses had destroyed the idols and the Calf of Gold. Personal vision was the road to the divine.

When Henry VIII broke with the Church of Rome over the divorce and execution of his various wives, he loosed iconoclasm on his holy places, as the Byzantine emperors had done before. Statues of the Virgin were burned in London; a movable image of Christ at Boxley Road in Kent was broken into pieces. At Walsingham, two of the clerics were hanged, drawn and quartered, and the shrine itself was desecrated. Before he died in the Tower of London, Philip Howard, Earl of Arundel, wrote in an epitaph:

> *Owles do shrieke wher the sweetest hymnes*
> > *Lately were sunge;*
> *Toades and serpentes holde their dennes*
> > *Wher the palmers did thronge.*
>
> *Weepe, weepe, O Walsingham,*
> > *Whose dayes are nightes,*
> *Blessings turned to blasphemies,*
> > *Holy deedes to despites.*
>
> *Sinne is wher our Ladie sate,*
> > *Heaven turned is to hell,*
> *Sathan sittes wher Our Lord did swaye,*
> > *Walsingham, oh farewell.*

A Divided Legacy

Even at the ending of the mass veneration of bodily and blessed objects, tradition and fanaticism kept them alive. As Huizinga pointed out, the deep faith of the Middle Ages was never afraid of disillusionment or profanation through handling holy things coarsely:

> *The spirit of the fifteenth century did not differ much from that of the Umbrian peasants, who, about the year 1000, wished to kill Saint Romuald, the hermit, in order to make sure of his precious bones; or of the monks of Fossanuova, who, after Saint Thomas Aquinas had died in their monastery, in their fear of losing the relic, did*

not shrink from decapitating, boiling and preserving the body. During the lying in state of Saint Elisabeth of Hungary, in 1231, a crowd of worshippers came and cut or tore strips of the linen enveloping her face; they cut off the hair, the nails, even the nipples. In 1392, King Charles VI of France, on the occasion of a solemn feast, was seen to distribute ribs of his ancestor, Saint Louis; to Pierre d'Ailly and to his uncles Berry and Burgundy he gave entire ribs; to the prelate one bone to divide between them, which they proceeded to do after the meal.

With the Reformation, Europe would be split between the Protestant north and the Catholic south. As with any radical change, extremes tipped the balance, and art lost to puritanism. The Swiss reformer Zwingli declared that the Eucharist was an idol. Material or carnal things such as icons or relics could not hold within them the transcendence of God. In Scotland, France and the Netherlands, images were smashed and churches were desecrated. The adoration of relics and elaborate ceremonies was seen as worship of the Devil.

The religious revolutionaries were the heirs to the medieval heresies and the personal quest for the Grail of divine revelation. The Brethren of the Free Spirit were the catalysts between the dissident Cathars of Provence, the Taborites of Bohemia and the German Anabaptists of the Renaissance. They believed that every created thing was divine. A person who truly searched for the Creator should look into himself, where He already was. On death, that speck or spark of God was reabsorbed into the essence of the everlasting. Throughout eternity, man was God and in God. There was no need of a priest or Church on earth to mediate in the salvation of a soul. Each had to seek out and find God, who already occupied the body of all beings.

To the doctrine of the divine within every living thing was added the myth of Eden. Humankind would return to the state of Adam and Eve in the Garden of Paradise – where there was no property or poverty or oppression – after the destruction of Orthodoxy, the victory of the Anti-Christ and the reign of Jesus for a thousand years. The adepts of the Free Spirit would enjoy that state of paradise now and should rule the elect, chosen from other believers. They could recall the Golden Age, which Jean de Meun had hymned in his popular *Roman de la Rose*, or the Grail Castle of the romances. Such visions and egalitarian dreams had been behind the Peasants' Revolt in England, where the preacher John Ball had asked his famous question:

> *When Adam delved and Eve span,*
> *Who was then a gentleman?*

God's law meant that all authority should be overthrown and all goods held in common. Such doctrines inspired the extremists among the Hussites, after their victory in Bohemia. These Taborites believed in an Apocalypse in which only their towns would be spared, while the rest of the world was condemned. And from them broke off a more fanatical sect, the Adamites, who supported a holy war against the rest of humanity. They saw themselves as the angel with the fiery sword at the gates of Eden. They burned and massacred the inhabitants of all the neighbouring villages until the Taborite commander was forced to exterminate his own zealots, for fear that their message would subvert the whole of human society.

The Reformation opposed pilgrimages to holy places and the veneration of relics such as the True Cross. These stimuli to the crusading movement, however, did not prevent the Protestants from using religious zeal to mount their own crusades. Luther, indeed, supported the extermination of the Anabaptists in their fanatical paradise in Münster, and the rebellious peasants. To him, the Pope was the Anti-Christ, and Catholics and Muslims were both heretics in alliance with Satan who should be pursued by war. As for the Jews, he anticipated their mass conversion, then turned on them in fury in his Wittenberg pamphlet, *On the Jews and their Lies*, the first popular work of anti-Semitism. He wanted all synagogues burned, prayer forbidden, Jewish homes razed, and forced labour inflicted on the people of that faith. He was instrumental in driving the Jews from Saxony and many German cities. Faced by Protestant persecution, the Jews looked for protection to the Catholic bishops and the Holy Roman Emperor, whose pogroms were intermittent. And grouping themselves in ghettos became the Jewish way of survival in the European city, beginning in Venice and spreading north and east, a forced segregation which would make their bunched communities even more vulnerable.

The Reformation split Scandinavia, north Germany, Holland and Britain from southern Catholic Europe, and initiated centuries of strife by land and sea, in which national interest could hardly be distinguished from religious differences. For the Counter-Reformation proved as sanguinary and savage as the excesses of the Reformers against priests and nuns. The stake was now the fate not of Saint Joan of Arc, but of the Protestant martyrs described by Foxe, and the captured sailors of the Elizabethan navy. The Inquisition was not used only against the Muslims and the Jews, but also against the breakaway Christian religions – now identified with the conspiracies of the Devil.

As the Reformation incited the Counter-Reformation, so the fanaticism of the Protestants had its revenge. In 1544 the Council of Trent allied the removal of religious discord with the crusade against the infidel. And for the next hundred years, until the end of the Thirty Years War in Middle Europe and the English Civil War, elements of the crusading ideology would surface in the propaganda of the conflict of the faiths. Notably, the year after the great Christian sea victory at Lepanto, the French religious wars began with the Massacre of Saint Bartholomew's Day, when the Catholics turned on their fellow Huguenot citizens with the ferocity shown by the crusaders when they first took Jerusalem, or by

Perceval against the Moorish knights in the *Perlesvaus*. The mercilessness, maiming and torture used by the French spiritual rivals towards those of another faith was as dreadful and inexcusable as in the crusade against the Cathars – a national self-mutilation in the name of nothing very much, but believed too much.

The crusading imagery was more credible in terms of imperial ambition. When the Spanish Armada left in 1588 to conquer England, red crosses billowed on its vaunting sails and the mission was blessed as if against the Turks at Lepanto. Its disaster was seen by the King of Spain as a divine judgement on him. And in effect, it was a perversion of the crusading faith, for the way to London was hardly towards another Jerusalem. Indeed, a survivor of Lepanto would write the first modern novel of genius, *Don Quixote*, which would mock the ideals of chivalry and crusading, translating them into the visions of an aged knight, tilting at windmills. What Godfrey de Bouillon had inspired, Cervantes would prick, although the crusades in Spain had created the nation.

The Emperor Charlemagne, from a 14th century French illumination.

One of the three Magi holds up a Grail at the birth of Jesus. From a fresco in the museum of San Vitale in Ravenna.

Above left: A ritual sacrifice beneath the Crucifixion, with Saint Longinus and the Holy Lance, also the sponge on the reed being offered to Christ. From the Floreffe Bible, *c.* 1170. Courtesy of the British Library, London, MS Add. 17738, f. 187.

The king and priest Melchisédek at his table of sacrifice, flanked by Abel and Abraham. A mosaic of the seventh century, Ravenna.

Above: The Fisher King is maimed by the bleeding lance. From a 14th century French manuscript, *Le Roman du Saint-Graal.* Courtesy of the British Library, London, MS Add. 10292, f. 74.

Right: The golden cup at the feast of King Arthur at Camelot, before it was snatched by the Red Knight in *Perceval.* From a 14th century French manuscript. Courtesy of the British Library, London, MS Royal 14, F 111, f. 89.

The Virgin Mary and Child with the donor and Saint Mary Magdalene holding her Grail. From an 11th century oil painting on wood at the Museum of Religious and Mosan Art at Liège.

Saint Mary Magdalene (*right of picture*) holds the Grail as a chalice and a stone from heaven towards the Infant Jesus, with Christ crucified in front on the Krell'scher high altar, Nuremberg.

Above: King Arthur bids farewell to his knights as they leave on the Quest of the Grail. From a 13th century French illustration.

Right: The dying Roland with his horn and holy relics in the hilt of his sword Durendal is taken to Heaven from Roncesvalles by the hand of God, bearing a Grail. From a 13th century Spanish illustration.

The Abbot Suger at the High Altar with the kneeling King of France by the Master of Saint Giles. Courtesy of the National Gallery, London (No. 4681).

The Grail Table at Herrenchiemsee.

The mechanism for lowering the Grail Table to fulfil the orders of King Ludwig the Second of Bavaria.

The cupola of Venus at Linderhof.

Postcards of the First World War.

Memorial to the
German War Dead,
1914–1918

Hitler as Galahad and a
Teutonic Knight.
From a propaganda
illustration of the
1930s.

A human god, dressed in a fish skin and holding a bucket and a cone. From Sir Austen Henry Layard's drawing of a monumental stone relief from the Assyrian city of Nimrud, about the 9th century BC.

Joseph of Arimathea holding up two sacred vessels. From a 15th century stained glass window in All Saints' Church at Langport, Somerset.

Aeneas is healed by the sacred cup and bowl of the mother goddess. From engravings designed by Francis Cleyn and executed by Wenceslaus Hollar and Pierre Lambert for John Dryden's translation of Virgil's *Aeneid* (London, 1692).

Above left: The Church rides on its four-headed Horse of the Apocalypse, catching in a Grail the Blood of Christ released by Saint Longinus with his spear. From the crucifixion of the 12th century in *Hortus deliciarum* by Herrard of Landsberg.

Left: Greek picture of the religious mysteries. From the pottery collection of Sir William Hamilton.

A woodcut by Dürer of Saint John the Divine's apocalyptic vision of the Son of Man with the Grail symbols of the sunburst and the seven stars, the sword and the seven golden candles in their holders.

Right: Woodcut of the Book of the Grail presented to the King. From the 1516 edition of Malory's *Morte d'Arthur.*

The Romano-British Great Bowl of Mildenhall. Copyright British Museum.

Below: The alchemical wedding in a Grail of love with a blessing from sacred vases and the Holy Ghost.

The Gunderstrup Cauldron, dating from the 1st Century AD. Courtesy of the National Museum, Copenhagen.

An alchemical furnace. From *De alchimia* of 1529 by Geber.

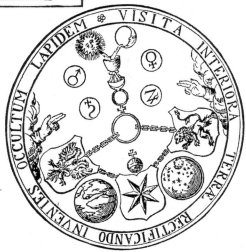

The Emerald Table of Hermes Trismegistus. From *Geheime Figuren der Rosenkreuzer* (Altona, 1785). At the top of the medallion of the Order of the Rosy Cross, the sun and the moon pour fire and the elixir of life into the cosmic cup.

GRAIL CASTLES

Right: Neuschwanstein in Bavaria.

Inset right: The Castel del Monte, built by the Emperor Frederick the Second.

Below: Mont Saint-Michel.

The Castle and monastery of Javier on the way to Santiago de Compostela.

Above: America offering her riches to Europe, a severed head at her feet. An anonymous illustration from Flanders, about 1600.

The book cover of a Scout Guide of 1919.

A religious procession, Italy, 1930.

The Nibelungs hold up their table of treasures.
From Fritz Lang's film, *Siegfried.*

Chapter Ten

The Grail in Spain

'Hell do you call it?' Don Quixote said. 'Do not call it
that, for it does not deserve the name, as you shall see.'

Miguel de Cervantes, *Don Quixote* (The Cave of
Montesinos)

The Road to Santiago

The small northern kingdoms of the Asturias, Navarre,
Aragon and León with Castile were the front line of the crusades against the Islamic incursion into southern Europe.
Their fierce belief was their morale and left little room for
heresy and the individual search for God. They thought they
held in various places the true Grail presented by the Pope to
Saint Lawrence. Their adventures as knights were real
against the Moors, not performed in a legendary quest for
grace. They achieved their benediction on the field of battle
with the aid of Saint James and the military orders, who
helped the knights of Santiago defend the pilgrim way to
Compostela. Their religion was a defence of the faith and an
aggressive assertion of its power through war.

In the third century, Saint Lawrence had been the devoted
pupil of Pope Sixtus II in Rome and had assisted his master
during the Mass. Sixtus was martyred by the Emperor
Valerian during a persecution of the Christians. Lawrence
asked the Pope why he was going to his death without his
teacher, who had raised the Host with him before the congregation. Sixtus answered that Lawrence would also die

within three days, but after doing great deeds for the Church.

The Roman Emperor then pressed Lawrence to surrender the holy relics of the faith. One of them, the legend declared, was the cup which Christ had used at the Last Supper. Lawrence would not give it up to the Romans. As he stood before the judge of the court, he pointed to the crowd of the poor, declaring that they were the true goods of the Church. He was then put on the hot gridiron and burned slowly to death, speaking like Dionysius or Jean Barthelemy on the Eucharist. 'See the one side is roasted enough,' he was alleged to have said. 'Turn me on the other side and eat.' He delivered the sacred cup to two Spanish legionaries to take to his parents at Lloret above Barcelona, from where it was transferred to the converted Visigothic rulers of Huesca in Aragon, the first of many resting places near the Pyrenees.

The oldest of the romanesque cathedrals in Spain was at Jaca, the first capital of Lower Aragon and the key to the Somfort Pass. Its carvings reflected the influence of the south of France and swayed the minds of the masons working on other cathedrals all the way west. The remnants of its carvings are playful and do not bring up the Grail, although the Saint Lawrence vessel was held there for some time. At the cathedral of Huesca, however, the Gothic tympanum stresses the legend of that Holy Chalice, as it was kept there as well as in Jaca. On one side of the crowned Virgin Mary holding the infant Christ, the three Magi bear gifts to Him, yet on the other side, the risen Christ appears by a Tree of Life to the kneeling Magdalene, the bringer of the Grail to Sarras. Above, two angels sprinkle grace from their usual hanging lamps or censers.

At the eleventh-century monastery of San Pedro el Viejo in Huesca, another Adoration of the Magi is carved over the doorway to the cloisters. The emphasis is on the gifts they carry for the newborn Son of God. There are also scenes on the capitals of Christ receiving the bitter cup from an angel in

Gethsemane; of the breaking of bread at Emmaus; and of the Last Supper. Buried there, and not in the pantheon of the kings of Aragon in the mountain monastery of San Juan de la Peña, is King Alfonso I of Aragon, named the Battler. He was given the name of Anfortius or Anfortas, the Grail King, in his crusade to begin the *reconquista*. He became a Templar in 1130 and bequeathed a third of the whole kingdom of Aragon to that military order. The archives of the Crown of Aragon confirmed the legend of the gift of the Grail by the Pope to Saint Lawrence; it was held in Huesca until the loss of the city to the Arabs after the defeat in 711 of Jerez de la Frontera. Hidden in a series of caves in the Pyrenees, it eventually reached San Juan de la Peña for its safe keeping.

From necessity, the cathedrals and monasteries of northern Spain were built as fortresses as well as houses of God. The approaches to San Juan de la Peña are through gorges and forests. Its thick walls, constructed from the siege knowledge of the Templars, back onto a cliff and a cavern with a trickling pool, which would become the inspiration for the descent of Don Quixote into the Cave of Montesinos. Within this massive structure is a delicate cloister with capitals showing some of the mysteries of the New Testament, particularly a graphic pouring of water from a pitcher into bowls to be turned into wine at the feast of Cana; also the fish on the dish at the Last Supper.

On the way to Santiago, other castellated monasteries defend the route: Javier and Leyre, where the Magdalene can again be seen on the tympanum, kneeling at the foot of the Cross with the Virgin Mary and two other women behind her. And at Sangüesa, the church of Santa Maria la Real defends the pilgrim bridge with three women saints by the entrance door overlooking the passing of the faithful. Among this dour and defensive architecture, nothing is more surprising than the delicate Santa Maria de Eunate, on the pilgrim road towards Puente la Reina, where a perfect pediment bridge still takes voyagers across the river. Near a Templar commandery, the small Eunate church was built in the sacred octagonal shape of the military order; the eight sides of the arches of the cloister enclose the eight walls of the church with its little curved apse. Standing isolated, yet surrounded by sheep grazing on brown grass, this holy place is the most contemplative on the blessed road.

The Sanchos, the kings of Nájera, expanded their realms to Pamplona, and eventually to León and Castile, creating a northern Spanish kingdom stretching from the Atlantic to Catalonia. Led by his falcon chasing a partridge into a cave, the young King Sancho III discovered at the end of the cavern a painted statue of the Virgin Mary with a lamp burning before her and the two birds at peace. Kneeling down, the King asked her protection, then rode out to win a victory against Islam at Calahorra. With part of his spoils, he began the building of the Monastery of Santa Maria la Real, which remains a marvel on the road to Compostela. Its Cloister of the Knights, containing a Garden of Paradise, a carved and painted choir, the royal pantheon of tombs, and the sacred cave where the image of the Virgin was found, are still testaments to the faith along this way to salvation.

Along the track at León, there is a Grail in the museum to rival the Saint Lawrence example, which ended in the cathedral at Valencia. Similar to those that the Abbot Suger collected for Saint-Denis near Paris, the Chalice of Urraca, who was the daughter of King Ferdinand I, is a Roman sardonyx cup and dish united by gold mounts adorned with pearls and gems, which form a Christian liturgical chalice. In the city, the south transept portal of the basilica of San Isodoro shows the Deposition of Christ from the Cross, with Nicodemus using the pincers to take out His nails, Joseph of Arimathea receiving His Body, and Mary Magdalene kissing the wound on His hand. At the side, the Magdalene appears again with the Virgin Mary and Mary the mother of James to watch astonished as an angel opens the empty Tomb. Furthermore, two angels lift the dead Jesus heavily towards heaven in a muscular Ascension.

On the pilgrim path lies the Atlantic port of Oviedo; its kings of the Asturias fought the *reconquista*. They claimed to possess the Spanish Ark of the Covenant, the Arca Santa, which included the Holy Blood, a part of the Holy Shroud, the milk of the Virgin Mary and hairs from the scalp of the Magdalene. The wooden chest was said to have originated in Jerusalem, finding its way somehow to Toledo and then to Oviedo, where its arrival by sea was guarded by a wolf. Once shown to El Cid, the Roland of his nation, it was later covered with a silver lid, which depicted Saint Longinus piercing the side of Christ to receive His Blood. A portion of this, miraculously recreated in a silver chalice and paten, was donated by the sovereigns of all Spain, Ferdinand and Isabella, to the mountain villagers of O Cebreiro, who still believe that their home was the legendary Sarras, where Galahad arrived on his Ship of Solomon with the Holy Grail. Arthurian romances still flourish towards Santiago.

Although the cathedral of Saint James is entered through the Doorway of Glory, the extraordinary Goldsmith's Doorway of the eleventh century terminates the quest for the grace of God in the north of Spain. One scene upon it demonstrates Adam and Eve driven from the Garden of Eden by the angel with the fiery sword – surely a forecast of righteous war putting human frailty to flight. A second scene depicts Christ pardoning the Woman taken in Adultery. She may well represent the Magdalene. With their ferocious judgements, the crusades of the north of Spain never forgave human weakness, as Christ did Himself. Yet in the search for grace, the Knights of the Round Table did not win the vision of God by their combats or their swords, but by their repentance.

At the Mediterranean end of the Pyrenees, Catalonia also played its part in repelling the Moors, as Charlemagne had done. Its religious shrine was the massif of Montserrat, where strange jagged pinnacles pierce the sky in an unearthly austerity. Richard Wagner was so impressed by its appearance and its name – another version of the Mount of

Salvation – that he set his Grail Castle in his opera *Parsifal* on the site of the monastery there. Its Black Virgin, La Moreneta, is revered as the patron saint of the Catalans; although the French army destroyed the original priory, the polychrome wood statue was saved. The caves of the original hermits are gouged into the white cliffs, including the one where shepherds were said miraculously to have found the Black Virgin, as Sancho III found his in Nájera in another cavern. There is no record of how the two Virgins reached their rock niches. In matters of faith, a fierce belief is enough to establish a truth or win a holy war as well as a seat in heaven.

The Grail of Conquest

The *reconquista* of Spain from Islam by the Christian north began before the crusading movement, but was mightily helped by it. The idea of a continual holy war promoted by the papacy, the Frankish knights and the Cluniac monks provided spirit and recruits for the cause. Many crusaders passed through the Iberian peninsula on their way to Palestine and never reached their goal, fighting their Muslim adversaries on the way and remaining to occupy the hard-won lands. Both the Templars and the Hospitallers were originally welcomed as ascetic warriors against the Moors, but these military orders were largely replaced by home-grown varieties. For the emphasis of the primary orders was still on the Holy Land. Spain was a place to stop off, not to defend. The Knights of Calatrava took over that abandoned frontier fortress from the Templars. They were originally Cistercian monks, who put on the sword. By the thirteenth century, they had become the effective standing army of the kingdom of Castile. They wore black armour and a white surcoat with a red cross fleury, its leaves bent back until they formed the M of the Virgin Mary.

The other leading Spanish order was the Knights of Santiago, formed to protect the pilgrims on their way to pray at the shrine of Saint James at Compostela. Their duty, according to the Archbishop of Toledo, was the sword of defence. 'The sword reddens with the blood of Arabs, and faith burns bright with the love of their mind.' Their rule was adopted from the Templars, but they were not a monastic order. Uniquely, they were allowed to marry and have families and personal possessions, although these were surrendered to the order on the death of each knight. They transcended the borders of Spain, reaching France, Italy, Hungary, Palestine, and especially Portugal, which would form its own knights of service, the orders of Évora and Aviz, and later the extraordinary Knights of Christ, created from the ranks of the fleeing Templars.

The frontier war with Islam in Spain led to a continuous crusade. A class of popular knights emerged, any Christian who had enough money to buy weapons and a horse. They were known as *cabelleros villanos*, and these medieval cowboys often reached a noble status by their deeds, as the rustic Perceval did in the first Grail romance. A successful mounted warrior could aspire to high estate. The Spanish frontier was an early version of the American frontier, with the Moors playing the role of the Indians. It produced the virtues of an independent raiding society, which built communities and cities behind its forays and its new castles. Particularly important in the Christian north was the port city of Valencia in Aragon, where the only material Grail blessed by the papacy was to come to rest.

The conquest of the interior of Spain in the thirteenth century, which effectively excluded the Muslims to the kingdom of Granada in the south, was a crusade, a looting expedition and a migration helped by ethnic clearance. 'Waves of friars, contemplatives, military monks, canons, parish priests, and nuns, transported like a numerous garrison into this borderland, gave tangible shape to the Christian self-image, making it a living thing.' The Word of Christ was imprinted upon the land through its new settlers, although tolerance was ordered by a royal edict. 'We decree that

Moors shall live among the Christians in the same way that . . . Jews shall do, by observing their own law and not insulting ours.'

The crusading impulse in Spain and Portugal led to the spread of Arthurian literature there. As early as 1170, King Alfonso VIII of Castile married Eleanor of England, whose father and mother, Henry II and Eleanor of Poitou, were strong supporters of the troubadours and the Grail stories. Soon Arturus was used as a Christian name in Salamanca, while the fabulous history of Britain and the Battle of Camlann began to appear in state records. As the lance was the devastating weapon of the Spanish knights in their charges against the cavalry of Islam, it was soon given a holy point of vengeance as well as healing. In the *Demanda di San Graal, la lanza vengadora* was worshipped as it projected from a golden vessel or hovered above that Grail. Many traditions of the Arthurian romances and ballads were copied: those concerning Lancelot would influence Cervantes. But the great Spanish epic of chivalry was *Amadís*, which imitated the legend of Lancelot without acknowledgement. And in the Catalan tale of *Tirant lo Blanc*, the characters praised the Round Table and described the murals of the palace at Constantinople, covered with scenes from the Quest for the Grail, as were the walls of the castles of Aragon and Castile in tapestries by the fifteenth century.

If the Pope was the preacher of holy war against the infidel, the Arthurian romance was the theatre. Its scenes of fantasy and devotion inspired crusaders into acts of extra-ordinary heroism. This everlasting crusade against the Moors went further in Portugal. By the middle of the thirteenth century, King Sancho II had conquered Islam as far as the Algarve. His shock troops were the military orders, Franks and Germans as well as his own knights. As Robert the Bruce did in Scotland, the Portuguese Crown incorporated the refugee Templars on their downfall into the Knights of Christ. For that small country was the first since the Normans to imagine a Mediterranean empire, an extraordinary ambition that would grow into a global reality.

At Castro Marim and Tomar, the Knights of Christ took over the Grail architecture of the Templars. The sacred octagon of the central choir at Tomar was surrounded by a polygon with sixteen sides. The design was based on the Mosque of Omar and the Dome of the Rock, mistaken for the Temple of Solomon, the Church of the Holy Sepulchre and the Aachen chapel of Charlemagne. Frescoes including Templar crosses covered the vault. The eight-sided shape was repeated in Spain, particularly at the Church of Vera Cruz near Segovia, where a similar structure housed a piece of the True Cross, brought back by the Templars from Jerusalem. And the Grail was already in its final home. When Valencia was taken from the Moors in 1399, the Lawrence Grail cup from Rome was carried there for the coronation ceremonies of the conquering Don Martin. It has remained in the cathedral, a simple agate carving the size of a sliced orange. It is set on a seashell base on a silver pedestal with four legs. Its handles and goldwork contain two emeralds and twenty-six pearls. An Arabic inscription on its base praises Allah, 'the Merciful One', perhaps a reference to the cup found by the Prophet in the seventh heaven. As the church windows in Rome still show, this chalice was the only Grail recognised by the Catholic Church, usually so opposed to the doctrine of the individual approach to God.

Another legend took the Grail to Toledo, where its literary origin was discovered by Wolfram von Eschenbach in *Parzival* and Cervantes in the visions of Don Quixote. The story went that the Roman Emperor Titus, on his sack of Jerusalem, removed the objects of the Passion to Rome, and these fell into the hands of Alaric the Visigoth when he in his turn, in 410, sacked the city of Rome. The cup and platter of the Last Supper were transferred to another cavern beneath Toledo by its last Visigothic rulers. They foresaw the future victory of the Arabs in the Iberian peninsula. The myth of Toledo still asserts that the mysteries of the Temple of

Solomon and of the Passion, the Ark of the Covenant, the emerald Table of Solomon and the cup from the Crucifixion, were buried somewhere at the frontier fortress against Islam during the crusades. Certainly at the Tavera Palace there, a visitor is told to view the Virgin Mary's footprint on a holy stone, perhaps fallen from heaven.

A special contribution from Spain to the quest for the Grail were the intense religious experiences, when the mystic saints took the Grail from Jesus Himself. In the words of Saint Gertrude of Helfetha:

> *On one occasion, when I assisted at a Mass at which I was to communicate, I perceived that You were present, by an admirable condescension, and that You did use this likeness to instruct me, by appearing as if parched with thirst, and desiring that I should give You to drink. And while I was troubled and could not even force a tear from my eyes, I beheld You presenting me with a golden cup with Your own Hand. When I took it, my heart immediately melted into a torrent of fervent tears.*

Saint Theresa of Avila continued these beatific visions of a holy chalice and a jewelled Grail Castle into the sixteenth century, before Cervantes in *Don Quixote* struck them down.

The struggle against Islam was continuing outside Spain. Even before the final conquest of the outpost kingdom of Granada, ports were being seized in North Africa. But they were unprofitable. For exploration was becoming far more interesting than assault on the infidel. The fleets of Europe would reduce the Mediterranean from being the cauldron of world trade into a begging-bowl held out to the Atlantic and Pacific Oceans. The colonisation of the Americas by the Spanish and the Portuguese was followed by ships and settlers from France, England and Holland. The process would be repeated across Africa, India and the islands of Asia. The bullion of Mexico and Peru and the spice trade of Zanzibar and Java now flowed across the great oceans, with some of the wealth siphoned into the Mediterranean, which had previously served as the exchange and mart of the overland gold, silver, herb and spice routes.

Like a slower Puck, the European sea powers cast their girdle round the earth in eighty years or so, and strangled their founding sea within the noose of the far-flung rigging of their voyages. According to the eminent historian Braudel:

> *The opening up of the Atlantic destroyed the age-old privilege of the Levant, which for a time had been the sole repository of the riches of the Indies. From that point on, every day saw a widening of the gap between the standard of living of the West, which was going through a revolution in technical and economic progress, and the eastern world of low-cost living.*

As the caravel and the carrack took the place of the caravan, and as the ocean superseded the desert, so the commercial centres of the Near East became less attractive for the new imperialist nations of western Europe. There was more profit to be had in the slave trade of Africa than of Circassia, and even more opportunity to convert the multitudinous infidels in the Gold Coast and Dahomey than in Beirut or Tripoli. The Levant was no longer the *souk* where Asia bargained with Europe. Its commercial and industrial importance was in decline. The New World of the Americas and the spice islands of Asia attracted the greed and the desire of the fading knights of the Old World. Although they still had to find a truce line with Islam in the Mediterranean and Central Europe, their Grail lay beyond the Atlantic and Pacific Oceans.

Don Quixote

Miguel de Cervantes Saavedra fought at the Battle of Lepanto, the great Christian victory of a Holy League against Islam. The son of a wandering chemist and surgeon, he lost the use of his left hand in that victory, and was wounded twice in the chest. His scars of battle were enhanced by five years of slavery beneath the Moors, before he was ransomed from Barbary pirates. Altogether, he knew well the triumphs and illusions of the finale of the crusades, the reach between the promise and the hard cold cell.

Certain episodes in *Don Quixote* recalled the medieval preoccupations with another world. The Don and his squire Sancho encountered Death riding on a cart with a human face, an angel with painted wings, an emperor and a Cupid and an armoured knight with a feathered hat. They represented the strolling play of *The Parliament of Death*. 'Being a demon,' the leader of the troupe said, 'I am capable of anything.' Although an imp with bladders frightened Quixote's horse Rocinante so that he was thrown to the ground, Sancho persuaded his master not to fight Death and fallen angels and emperors, even in show. There was not a real knight among them.

In another adventure, Quixote fought a joust with a Knight of the Mirrors, wearing an alchemical costume of green, white and yellow feathers. For once, he won the passage of arms only to have his victory taken away by sorcery. 'Learn what magic can do,' he declared to Sancho, 'and how great is the power of wizards and enchanters.' For he saw in his fallen foe the face of his old bachelor friend from his home town. And so Cervantes poked fun not only at the *danse macabre* of medieval melancholy, but also at the legends of Merlin, alchemy and magic which still persisted in his age.

These questionings came to their apogee when Don Quixote was lowered into the Cave of Montesinos, where marvels were said to happen. He was guided there by a student of works of chivalry, whose job was to compose books for the printers, all of them of great use and most entertaining. He had done *The Book of Liveries* and a book of inventions, based on Vigilius Polydorus. Quixote was hoisted into the underworld and returned after three days and nights in a coma of beatific visions. On awakening, he declared that he had seen the Elysian Fields and a Grail Castle with walls of crystal. From it emerged the robed wizard Montesinos, who swore that he was held under a spell by the French enchanter Merlin.

Quixote then told of the speaking corpse of Charlemagne's nephew who died at Roncesvalles and was laid out on a slab. His salted heart, like that of the Bruce or the Douglas, was carried in a Grail procession by black-robed women with white turbans. Other guests in the castle included Queen Guinevere and her maid, who poured the wine for Lancelot 'when from Britain he came'. Sancho laughed at the Don's testimony, but here Cervantes mixed credibility with fantasy as Wolfram von Eschenbach had in *Parzival*. He claimed that the original history of Quixote was actually written by a certain Spanish Arabic Jew, Cid Hamete Benengali, as Flegetanis of Toledo was claimed as the original author of the German master-work. And Cervantes made Hamete evaluate in notes on his text the worth of the vision in the Cave of Montesinos, declaring that he could not believe in everything which had happened there to the valiant Don Quixote. Until now, all the adventures were possible. But the one in the cavern was beyond reason. Yet Quixote could not lie. Therefore, the wise reader must decide for himself. However, it was reported that Quixote retracted his vision on his deathbed, confessing that he had invented the Arthurian pieces because of what he had read in other romances.

Here Cervantes appeared to invent the modern novel of deconstruction. He would not declare that he did not believe in the legends of chivalry. He would only write that a fictitious scribe doubted them and that the invented Don Quixote had denied at his dying a particular adventure. The reader had to decide on the text himself.

In two final references in *Don Quixote*, Cervantes had his knight and squire Sancho reach the River Ebro, which looked like liquid crystal. The don was reminded of the Cave of Montesinos, although Sancho considered the visions there to be lies. Even so, an enchanted bark floated downstream, like a Ship of Solomon. Knight and squire boarded it to meet a company of millers. Quixote declared the water mills to be a fortress where knights or princesses were held captive, and he brandished his sword, but fortunately the boat capsized in the mill race and the Don and Sancho were rescued by the millers' poles.

Later, Quixote encountered the bronze speaking head from the Grail legends. It was set on a jasper table and said to be cast by an enchanter, Escotillo. When the Don asked the head whether the happenings in the Cave of Montesinos were a dream, it replied, 'There is much to be said on both sides.' The head was revealed to be mechanical and broken up by orders of the Inquisition, 'the sentinels of our faith'.

When previously attacked by a canon of the Church for believing in the chivalric romances such as *Amadís*, Quixote said that his questioner, not he, was bewitched. To try and persuade anybody that Amadís and the other knights had never lived was the same as saying that the sun did not shine, ice was not cold and the earth did not bear fruit. If all the romances were lies, 'there was no Hector nor Achilles nor Trojan War nor Twelve Peers of France nor King Arthur of England who still goes about in the shape of a raven and is expected to reappear in his kingdom at any time'.

Here Quixote did speak of the truth of the Quest for the Holy Grail, which he called *Grial*, and the love of Guinevere and Lancelot. He then described another vision of a Grail Castle, in which he was the Knight of the Lake. Plunging into a seething cauldron of water, he found himself again in Elysian Fields of paradise in front of a jewelled castle made of diamonds, rubies, pearls, gold and emeralds. There beautiful maidens bathed and fed him and told him they were held under a magic spell, until a knight would release them. This perception, Quixote said, made him a better man, brave, polite, generous, courteous and bold. If the Arthurian legends were the stuff of dreams, they became actual in the change of character of their believers. This was another way of saying that the romantic search for the divine was still a valid way to God, a moral journey in its own right. Even if the knight on his quest in Spain in the seventeenth century was out of date and a figure of fun, his trials were real enough, as were his sufferings, and these purified his spirit. When illusions became deeds, they made a better man.

These arguments could not survive the final verdict of Cervantes, when he killed off his glorious character. The deluded knight was received back into the Christian faith. Chivalry and the crusades were finished, although not the inward quest for the divine.

Death came at last for Don Quixote, after he had received all the sacraments and once more, with many forceful arguments, had expressed his abomination of books of chivalry. The notary who was present remarked that in none of those books had he read of any knight dying in his own bed so peacefully and in so Christian a manner. And so, among the tears and laments of all who were there, he gave up the ghost. That is to say, he died.

The enduring popularity of the work made Don Quixote live for ever. Cervantes' mockery of actual pilgrimages on earth concentrated the quest for revelation on the interior journey towards the soul. The Cave of Montesinos would become the examination of self-despair and dream. The voyage would lie through the individual brain and bowels towards redemption.

Chapter Eleven

The Grail in Italy

> The present heroism is bound to become grotesque, the
> strongest faith is bound to become madness, when the
> ways leading to the transcendental home have become
> impassable.
>
> Georg Lukács

The earliest carving of the Grail in Italy is on the tomb of
Archbishop Theodorus at Sant'Appollinare in Classe, near
Ravenna, but no longer on the sea. This mysterious relief of
the sixth century combined Greek and oriental Christianity
and cosmogony. On either flank, a dove sits on a plant with
two flowers of four petals each, representing the Gospels. In
the middle, a stone supporting the crescent moon drops into
a wrought bowl. Within the cup of the moon is the base of the
eight-pointed cross, while the dove of the Holy Spirit
plunges down with the point of its beak into the top of the
crucifix. This trinity of symbols of the Holy Spirit blesses
bowl, stone, moon and cross, the main signs of the religious
faiths of the Near East.

The Byzantines translated the horn of plenty and the pagan
gifts of the gods into Christian symbols of the Grail, the gift
of the Holy Spirit. Ravenna abounds in the earliest signs of
the Holy Vessel. Dating from the fifth century, their style and
content would influence all Europe. The key two mosaics are
those of a gold chalice with handles put on a white tablecloth
in front of Melchizedek, the ancient king and priest, while
Abel offers to him and God the first fruits, a sacrificial white
lamb. On the cloth are a pair of round loaves in the shape of

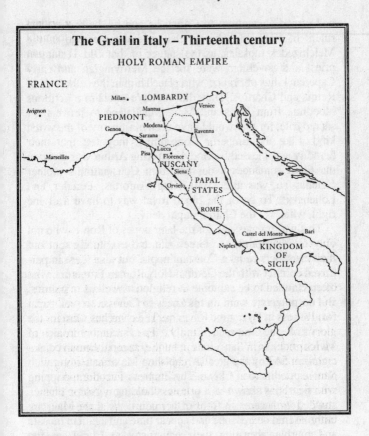

The Grail in Italy – Thirteenth century

HOLY ROMAN EMPIRE

sun-discs and a pattern, two misaligned squares making up an octagon within a circle, the sacred building shape of the Baptisteries at Ravenna, which both have exquisite and naturalistic mosaics of Jesus being baptised in Jordan with the Holy Spirit as a dove descending on Him. Opposite the mosaic at Sant'Appollinare in Classe stands the bearded Emperor Constantine IV granting privileges to his bishop's minion, while holding a bowl. The first Emperor Constantine had turned Byzantium to Christ: he and his heirs were the rulers of state and church: that was the message of the Melchizedek mosaics, as the statues of that Old Testament priest and sovereign were for the Merovingian and early Capetian kings of France, who placed him in the cathedrals of Reims and Chartres. They did not have to claim a fictitious bloodline from Jesus and Mary Magdalene to prove their sacred role, for that would have been blasphemy of the worst kind. Like the Emperor Constantine, they felt that their heredity was blessed by God. Even King Arthur was given in the Grail romances a descent from Constantine's mother Helena; so was the Grail King Anfortas, Peredur and Lohengrin. To be of the blood royal was to have a divine right, whatever the Church might deny.

This was no message for the later popes of Rome, who not only fought against the Greek rite and eventually sent out their crusaders to take Constantinople, but also were in perpetual conflict with the German Holy Roman Emperors, who often claimed to be supreme in religion as well as in politics. But no potentate went on his knees to Canossa to seek papal forgiveness in Byzantine Ravenna. The churches were for the glory of the imperial family. The second mosaic of Melchizedek is in San Vitale, a huge octagonal church consecrated in 547 by the great Archbishop Maximian along with Sant'Appollinare in Classe. The Empress Theodora, dripping with pearls, is shown as a priestess holding a golden chalice studded with gems in front of her court: the three Magi are embroidered on her robe and appear time and again in mosaic and marble, thrusting their generosity at Christ, as the Byzantines did. Theodora faces her husband, the Emperor Justinian, who holds a large gold paten, instead of Archbishop Maximian, whose ivory throne and last resting place remain an encyclopedia of early signs of the Holy Vessel. There are two doves drinking from a flowing Grail on his sarcophagus, and on his ivory throne we see the feast at Cana, with much water flowing from huge pots into wine: the miracle of the loaves and the fishes occurs with many scones and one fish-head: four Evangelists surround the Virgin Mary, and two of them bear a dish, one with little loaves and one with the Lamb.

The evangelisation of the Grail from its pagan classical roles is further made clear in San Vitale, where a piece of Roman mosaic depicts two peacocks and six game birds surrounding a curved chalice with two handles; they do not however drink from the vessel, as two of the eight doves do below the arguing Apostles in the brick mausoleum of the Empress Galla Placidia, built in the shape of a cross. Two winged cherubs on a Roman tombstone in the cloisters only reach up to an urn full of fruits, while in the moving frescoes of the fourteenth century at Santa Chiara, three Christian angels use cups to catch the Blood from Christ's wounds, as on the reliquary at Fécamp in Normandy. Other mosaics in Ravenna show female saints in a procession, confirming the theory that the women in the Grail procession in the Castle of the Fisher King may derive from a Greek ritual. Saint Lawrence also appears at Galla Placidia advancing towards the burning gridiron, bearing the Holy Writ and a golden cross, although not the Holy Vessel given to him by the Pope and sent on to Spain. The emphasis at Ravenna on the Gospel of Saint John puts only the Magdalene with Mary the mother of James at the Tomb of Christ in Sant'Appollinare Nuovo; the later intrusion of the Virgin Mary into the scene is a Renaissance phenomenon. Other Byzantine symbols of the Grail may be found in the city of the Italian sea-power responsible for the sacking of Constantinople on the Fourth Crusade: in the courtyards of the great Piazza of San Marco in Venice. These cosmic carvings were brought back from the eastern Mediterranean by a decree of the Doges, which required Venetian ships to use ancient stone works as ballast on their voyage home.

The legend of Saint Lawrence had sanctified the carrying of the Grail to Spain, and the later opposition of the papacy to its message, which was the independent search for God, could not diminish the popularity of the Arthurian romances.

In the 'Inferno' of Dante's *Divine Comedy*, indeed, the Matter of Britain led to the downfall of Paolo de Rimini with his sister-in-law Francesca:

> One day we read in pastime how in thrall
>> Lord Lancelot was to love, who loved the Queen.
>> We were alone – we thought no harm at all.
>
> As we read on, our eyes met now and then,
>> Our cheeks were changing both from red to pale,
>> But just one moment overcame us, when
>
> We read of the smile, wanted by lips that could not have me,
>> Such smile, by such a lover kissed away.
>> He who may never more try now to leave me.
>
> Trembling all over, kissed my mouth. I say,
>> The book the writer, he did pander me
>> Like Galeotto. We read no more that day.

Yet even if forbidden love consigned sinners to hell, the warrior saints making up the shape of a shining celestial cross were praised in the 'Paradiso' as they were on the tapestries of Flanders: Joshua and Judas Maccabeus, Charlemagne and Roland, or Orlando, Willehalm, or Guiglelmo, and Godfrey de Bouillon. Holy war was still the path to salvation, however much the Church of Rome was misusing the finance and the direction of its crusades.

The Sack of Rome

By the beginning of the sixteenth century, Erasmus noted that people had completely turned against buying forgiveness for their sins through indulgences. They said that this was nothing but commerce. 'The justification changed all the time. At one moment it was war against the Turks, then the military needs of the Pope, then the Jubilee.' There was no limit or end to the haggling. Princes took a part of the proceeds, as did officials, commissioners, deans and preachers. 'Some were given money to talk, others to keep silence.'

The money that reached Rome was being used for the wrong causes. It was being raised under false pretences. Erasmus, in his *Consultatio*, was clear about these errors:

Every time that this farce has been acted out by the popes, the result has been ridiculous. Either nothing came of it, or the cause actually deteriorated. The money, people say, stays stuck to the hands of the popes, cardinals, monks, dukes, and princes. Instead of the wages, the ordinary soldier is given licence to pillage. So many times we have heard the announcement of a crusade, of the recovery of the Holy Land; so many times we have seen the red cross surmounted on the papal tiara, and the red chest; so many times we have attended solemn gatherings and heard of lavish promises, splendid deeds, the most sweeping expectations. And yet the only winner has been money.

A contemporary tale spoke of Cesare Borgia losing a hundred thousand ducats at cards, the sum raised from granting absolution for offerings given towards a crusade. 'There go the sins of the Germans,' he said.

Although the cardinals advising Pope Leo X in 1517 still believed that many would 'gladly purchase eternal life for a small price' if they saw others fighting for God in earnest, the French replied that nothing would now come of any attempt to sell absolution. People had been deceived so often that calling for a crusade was now seen as a clever trick to extract their money. Even the faith in wonder-working relics was diminishing, these lesser Grails of the Holy Blood or bones of the Saints being replaced in the knightly romances by talismans and magic stones.

Yet while the Reformation grew in power and questioning, Rome remained the spiritual centre of the Christian faith and the focus of European pilgrimage. Although holy relics were widespread across Europe, the papal city held the choicest of them. This was recognised by a Netherlands romance of the fourteenth century, in which the hero, Seghelijn of Jerusalem, became Emperor and Pope and transferred all the sacred objects of the East, including the True Cross, from the city of the death of Jesus to the Curia and the Tiber. The most precious of these relics were to be housed in the gigantic hollow piers of Saint Peter's.

Yet while these pillars were still incomplete, Pope Clement VII reaped the dragon's teeth sown by the sale of pardons. The Holy Roman Emperor Charles V attacked Rome in 1527 with an army of levies, many of them Lutherans determined to destroy all Catholic symbols of the search for divine grace. While the Pope and the Curia defended the Castel Sant'Angelo, the Swiss Guard was decimated trying to defend His Holiness. The patients in the papal hospice were thrown into the Tiber, while nuns were sold to brothels. As for the holy relics, a letter to the Duchess of Urbino claimed that they were all scattered. 'The Veronica was stolen. It was passed from hand to hand in all the taverns of Rome without a word of protest. A German stuck on to a pike the lance point that pierced Jesus' side, and ran mockingly through the Borgo.'

A second letter, from Cardinal Salviati to the papal envoy in Madrid, confirmed the profanation, so similar to the sack of Constantinople on the Fourth Crusade and by the Turkish Sultan. The great chapel of Saint Peter and Pope Sixtus was burned, as was the Holy Face of Saint Veronica. The heads of the Apostles were stolen, the Sacrament thrown in the mud, the reliquaries ground underfoot. 'I shudder to contemplate this, for Christians are doing what even the Turks never did.' A contemporary Lutheran soldier confirmed the looting of chalices, monstrances and precious religious ornaments; but he denied the finding of the Veronica. His testimony was corroborated by the Roman Marcello Alberini in his *I Ricordi*. The Veronica, the heads of Saint Andrew, Saint

Peter and Saint Paul, and 'the miraculous effigy of the Saviour in the Sancta Sanctorum' were not desecrated in the sack of the Holy City.

Certainly, these relics were on public display soon afterwards, especially the Holy Lance and the Veronica, which Robert de Boron declared had cured the Emperor Vespasian of leprosy, before he went to Jerusalem to rescue Joseph of Arimathea from prison. Even the sceptic French essayist Montaigne referred to the fervour and grief of the crowds which saw the Veil and the Lance in procession. Whether they survived the Emperor's pillage of Rome hardly mattered. They were held to have done so. They retained their credibility and inspired mass worship. They were still as fundamental in the display of Catholic piety as the symbols of the Passion were in the Grail processions of the medieval romances.

This was true in the rival city states of Italy. The *Procession in Piazza San Marco* by Gentile Bellini, now hanging in the Academia in Venice, showed the sacred relics of Christ seized from Constantinople carried under a canopy in a precious Grail casket attended by scores of monks and dignitaries. The Holy Face of Lucca, said to have been created by Nicodemus, was displayed secure in an octagonal chapel of green, white and gold from the early twelfth century; the dukes of Normandy and Saint Catherine of Siena were pilgrims there. In his 'Purgatorio', Dante was told by the Demons above the lake of boiling pitch that not even the *Santo Volto* could save the Luccan sinners from their fate. The actual bones of Nicodemus were given to the Pisans for their help in the First Crusade and remain in his marble tomb in the duomo of the Italian city. In spite of the sack of Rome, traces of the Passion and the jewelled reliquaries built to house them were still venerated across the land.

Not every bowl is a Grail, but if it has a sacred meaning or use, it recalls that holy vessel. In Christianity, there are many representations of the Grail other than the cup used in the Mass. For instance, on both of the marble pulpits of the

Duomo and the Baptistery in Pisa, we still see the Grail in the shape of a great chalice. Yet the infant Christ is being washed in it by kneeling maidens, while His exhausted mother, the Virgin Mary, lies back under a crinkled stone coverlet. The same scene from the childhood of Jesus on a stained-glass window at Bourges Cathedral has a golden pail as the Grail. And in a faded fresco by Benozzo di Lese, again at the museum in Pisa, we watch the newborn Jacob and Esau after their cleansing in a large dish with sides.

This was the Christian version of the cauldron of birth and regeneration, as the font was the symbol of receiving the grace of the Holy Spirit. In the spectacular carved marble vase of the font at San Frediano in Lucca, or the huge urn of Neuvy Saint-Sepulchre, where the Holy Blood is also housed, we understand the full significance of baptism. This is confirmed by the numerous reliefs in the cathedrals of Europe which showed Christ's blessing in a rock pool in the River Jordan by Saint John the Baptist, whose severed head on a platter became another picture of the Grail.

The shapes of the three gifts borne by the Magi were transformations of the sacred vision. In the marble reliefs at Pisa, the trio of wise men from the East ride camels as well as horses. One of them carries an oblong box in the shape of the one meant to house the Ark of the Covenant depicted on the pillar outside the cathedral at Chartres. Yet in the Italian version, the Magi appear to be offering the divine baby some round stones fallen from heaven instead of the usual caskets or censers representing the treasures of this world.

In Dante's 'Inferno' and in the many hells depicted within the churches of Europe, the damned are boiled alive in vast vats and pots, tormented by devils. As with the cauldron of Annwn, they demonstrate the judgement of life. Human beings pass into oblivion and reduction through eternal pain, or into resurrection. For as at Chartres and Bourges, female saints can be discerned in barrels, being baptised into the faith, or being boiled alive. Either a blessing or a torture, the vat of water was a means of change.

The only time that the sinful King Arthur carved on the architrave of the duomo in Modena was permitted to view the Grail in the romance of *Perlesvaus*, he saw it in five different forms. These were not described. They could only be understood by those who knew the mysteries of the sacrament. The Christian equivalents of the Grail are the only sources of inspiration known to many of us: the reliquary for remains of the Passion, or the Communion dish for His Body, or the chalice for His Blood. The Renaissance chapel of the Sancto Sacramento in the duomo at Lucca has the effigy of a rotunda above an altarpiece of the Lamb of God holding the cross in front of a sunburst. The rotunda contains a silver-gilt Grail medallion with a flared top. Two phials of the Holy Blood, said to have been found behind the Holy Face when it landed on a magic airborne craft in the mouth of the River Magra, are housed behind that metal plaque. The dome of the little rotunda is supported on four green marble pillars. At their base are two more chalices with a stone dropping into their rims; also two censers or relic-holders, and two pairs of twin jars. These are the usual symbols of divine giving, which we understand, and which represent the grace of the Holy Blood.

At Bocca di Magra, the Carmelite Fathers still claim that their replica of the Holy Face is the true one, for it contains below the nape of the effigy's neck two niches for phials. Yet as far back as Dante, Lucca was believed to have the original *Santo Volto* and the two bottles of His Passion. The claim of the basilica of Santa Maria up the Magra river to possess the Precious Blood appears to be a recent assertion, given the quality of the mannerist painting above the ugly marble reliquary holding the sacred drops: two angels bear a glass container with three cherubs sporting beneath them. The basilica is worth a visit, however, for the Renaissance relief beside the tabernacle of the supposed Blood of Christ. On its pale marble are carved many of the Grail symbols, such as the spear of Saint Longinus; these include two of the rarer ones: the Hand of God offering the Bitter Cup to the kneeling Jesus in the Garden of Gethsemane, and the Presentation in the Temple, where the child Jesus is received by an elder over the Ark, which is lit by a sacred lamp surmounted by the dove of the Holy Spirit in a burst of six rays. Two pairs of twin pillars show the scene on the relief to be the cube of the Temple of Solomon, Jachin and Boaz helping to support the ancient shrine of Israel.

Further to the south, a miraculous appearance of the Blessed Blood led to the building of perhaps the most magnificent duomo in all Italy. In 1263, a Bohemian priest called Peter of Prague was a Doubting Thomas, who had reservations about the bread and wine of the sacrament changing into the Body and Blood of Christ. After a pilgrimage to Rome to pray at the tomb of Saint Peter, he stayed at Bolsena on its mountain lake in order to celebrate Mass in the grotto tomb of Saint Christina. As he held the host over the chalice towards the congregation, it turned into the Holy Body and Blood, as it had in the visions of some of the Knights of the Round Table. Traces of the actual blood which fell on the stones below the altar are preserved above the altar of the Miraculous Eucharist in the basilica of Saint Christina at Bolsena; beside them is carved an eight-pointed cross. The footprints of the saint are kept on a floating rock, which also came to ground in Bolsena. At her feast day, at the vespers of Saint James on the pilgrimage route to Compostela, dancing women still break four crystal vessels full of perfume, similar to those used by Mary Magdalene to wash the feet of Christ.

The chalice cloth imbued with those blessed bloodstains is housed in the special Chapel of the Corporal in the duomo at Orvieto. A doorway was built in the cathedral to carry in the precious linen; a sculpture over it commemorated the occasion. Pope Urban IV decreed the celebration of Corpus Christi in honour of the miracle, as well as commanding the building of the duomo. Saint Thomas Aquinas was with him at Orvieto during these blessed times and wrote hymns for the new feast day. The sacred cloth is housed in the most superb reliquary in the region. Its twelve panels of silver gilt and blue enamel display episodes from the Life of Christ and Peter of Prague's transformation of the spiritual into the actual at Bolsena – perhaps too direct an approach to the divine substance for the Church not to include it in its ceremonies. In the Capella Nuovo, indeed, the stunned anguish on the faces of the Risen in the fresco by Signorelli still shows the great difficulties of a religious faith which insists on the link between the flesh and the soul, even in resurrection.

There are many signals of the Grail on the portals of the duomo at Orvieto, and another carving of the Ark of the Covenant. This time the Ark appears as an oblong studded chest beneath a holy lamp at the scene of the Presentation in the Temple – an earlier version of the one at Sarzana. A wise priest reads a text, while the other priest returns the holy child to his mother, the Virgin Mary. As on the pulpits in Pisa, Mary is also seen in her bed after bearing her son, while Jesus lies in his manger and two kneeling maidens attend a Grail of birthing for Him. Again, a relief of Christ demonstrates His baptism in the natural vat of the Jordan river, the dove descending upon His head.

In Orvieto also, a polyptych by Simone Martini shows the Magdalene holding her pot of ointment and presenting the Dominican bishop of Savona to the Virgin and Child. Another fresco by Luca Signorelli there depicts the Magdalene kneeling below the Body of Christ and kissing His right hand. His head is resting in the lap of His mother. The same pose for the Magdalene was used by Botticelli in his *Lamentation* now hanging in the Alte Pinakothek in Munich. Yet the most graphic presentation of her was in Grünewald's Isenheim altarpiece, where she reaches up sobbing towards the base of the Cross with her clenched fingers, her aromatic vase at her feet.

Yet the duomo in Orvieto is less a place of the Grail than is the Church of San Lorenzo de Arari. This simple romanesque building holds two remarkable frescoes of the fourteenth century. One recounts the life of Saint Lawrence, read in four episodes right to left, as in Hebrew. The first panel shows him healing the sick, although Christ as a boy bears the Grail, no larger than a round purse or stone, for the holy man. The second panel depicts his condemnation, the third his burning on the gridiron, the fourth his rescue from purgatory of the sinners who believed in his message of redemption. An even more remarkable fresco of the Virgin and Child recalls the Grail as a giver of divine life. Mary is feeding the infant Christ openly with her right breast, while her aurora is made of the leaves of the Tree of Life, and two angels hover above with a heavenly crown.

In three of the Arthurian romances, the *Queste*, the *Perlesvaus* and the *Morte D'Arthur*, the Mass of Our Lady, the Mother of God, was heard at the ceremonies of the Grail. Through her womb, an inverted bowl, the Virgin Mary gave birth in blood to Jesus; through her breast, as in the fresco in Orvieto, she gave milk to the Son of God. In the medieval text the *Litany of Loretto*, she was described as three vessels, spiritual and honourable and singular in devotion. In the little rose window at Reims, she had further attributes: the Ark of the Covenant, the Morning Star and the mystic rose, the palm and the olive tree, the sun and the moon, the exalted cedar and the stainless lily, the refuge of sinners and the doorway to heaven, the golden house and the ivory tower of David, the royal crown and the throne of wisdom, the Holy City and the faithful dove. Also in the cathedral windows at Troyes, she was shown as the mirror lamp of justice and the sacred fountain.

As well as containing within her flesh the Body and Blood of the infant Christ, the Virgin Mary gave out delight and nourishment to all: she was sanctity and security, wisdom and justice, refuge and prophecy. Her symbol was the rose with five petals, sacred particularly to the Knights Templar, who were also virgins dedicated to the protection of the Cross. And in the medieval *Minneliedern*, the songs often compared the Virgin Mary to the Grail. At San Lorenzo de

Arari, signs of the Holy Vessel may be seen as a gift from God, as a scale of judgement, and as female food for the spirit. With the eternal inventiveness of Italy, the patterns of the Grail there confirmed its infinite varieties, as if the importance of its message – the individual quest for God – were being disguised from the Catholic Church.

The actual Grail of Italy – the *Sacro Catino*, or Holy Cup – is in Genoa. William of Tyre, who was a historian of the early crusades, wrote that the Genoese, the ferrymen to the Holy Land, were given the cup in 1102 in Jerusalem to honour their services after the capture of Caesarea. Yet as the city cathedral was dedicated to Saint Lawrence, who can still be seen roasting on his gridiron above the main door of the duomo, other traditions made the *Sacro Catino* come from Spain, where it was sent by the martyr, remaining by repute in Valencia. The Genoese claimed that the sacred trophy was part of the booty of Almeria which they helped to take from the Moors in the twelfth century; alternatively, a tribute from the fall of Tortosa. Whatever its origin, the *Sacro Catino* was so venerated in the Middle Ages that it was guarded by twelve knights, modelled on the disciples and the dozen Peers of the Round Table of Charlemagne.

The Holy Cup was thought to be carved from a huge emerald, as was the tablet of the alchemist Hermes Trismegistus. When Napoleon conquered Genoa, he had it taken back to Paris for analysis. Broken there, it was discovered to be made from Roman glass of the time of Jesus Christ. One piece of the sacred vessel was kept in France, the others returned to be repaired. Presently on display in the city museum with the relics of Saint Lawrence and the ashes and head of Saint John the Baptist, the six-sided goblet with a gold rim is placed on a wrought-iron tripod. Its bowl is shallow, opaque and dark green. It is a memorial of how the Near East sent to Europe the mystic concept of the personal search for God, even at the time of the assault from the West.

The Patrons of the Grail

The literature of the Grail had depended upon the courts and principalities which paid the troubadours to sing it and the monks to write it down. This remained true, as the Middle Ages were moulded into the Renaissance, in providing the new words and symbols of the personal search for the divine. We may still read and see what was commissioned then. Riven by the wars between its city states as well as the ambitions of the French and the Habsburgs of Spain and Germany, Italy became the cornucopia of grants to artists for the glory of rulers and governments, as well as God.

The supreme patron of Florence, Cosimo de'Medici, was a banker. Through international finance, he endowed and influenced the arts on a scale that surpassed even Mæcenas. He was the first magnate in business to sponsor the arts, and though his collections were mainly of classical antiquities, he commissioned works from the leading artists of his time. He bought paintings by Masaccio, Fra Angelico, Uccello, Donatello and Giotto. He gave generously to the family church of the Medici, Brunelleschi's San Lorenzo, the saint who had transmitted the Grail to Spain. He supported libraries, monasteries, convents and foundling hospitals. In acquiring power in his native city from the *Signoria*, he always showed a modesty and a respect for art. He rode a mule in an effort to hide his wealth. Only his successors, such as Lorenzo the Magnificent, displayed the luxury of the Burgundians. In 1533, indeed, when the daughter of the Emperor Charles V married a Medici, the garden courtyard of the palace in Florence was transformed into an Earthly Paradise, a symbolic Garden of Eden.

As well as building for his patron the circular roof of heaven on the duomo in Florence, Brunelleschi manufactured a mechanised paradise in the monastery of San Felice in Piazza. Writing his *Lives of the Artists*, Vasari could not contain his admiration:

The Grail in Italy

Imagine a heaven full of moving figures and an infinity
of lights that go on and off like lightning! Brunelleschi
suspended a huge half-globe from the beams of the roof.
This was like a barber's bowl, edge down, made of thin
planking. Within the outer edge of the rim were fixed
brackets exactly the size of children's feet. Two feet
above each there was an iron fastening to secure a
twelve-year-old child so that he could not fall even
though he wanted to. About the rim were spaced twelve
children clothed as angels with gilded wings and wear-
ing wigs of gold thread. They took hands and waved
their arms, and so appeared to be dancing while the
basin was turning about. Little lamps seemed like stars,
and the brackets were covered with cotton wool to look
like clouds. Within the globe was a bar ingeniously sus-
pended, which had eight arms, each holding a nine-
year-old child, well secured but yet free to turn. In the
centre of this bouquet of angels was a copper mandorla,
which came down, moving softly, to the stage. A boy of
fifteen dressed as an angel then stepped from the man-
dorla and approached the Virgin and made his
announcement. Then the entire pageant was drawn up
in order. There was, besides all this, a figure of God the
Father in a choir of angels fixed near the convex side of
the basin. It did truly represent paradise.

This spectacle of the bounty of heaven, with half-globes
and mandorlas appearing as dramatic Grails, was similar to
the Burgundian practice of translating mystic quest to lavish
entertainment. Lorenzo de' Medici turned the lethal jousts of
the Arthurian knights into an egoistical civic show, held in
the square of Santa Croce of the Holy Cross. At the tournaments, each armoured warrior on his charger was preceded
by a squire with a symbolic banner: the painter Verocchio
painted one of Cosimo himself. The Duke wore a red and
white surcoat; also a plume of gold filigree set with diamonds
and rubies in his black velvet cap before it was substituted for

a helmet with three blue feathers. In the centre of his shield with the three gold lilies of France, the protector of Florence, shone the huge family diamond. Cosimo won the tournament while the other knights fell off their horses, rather as the Emperor Nero had won the Olympic Games for both his lyre-playing and his chariot-racing. 'I was not a very vigorous warrior,' Cosimo did admit with aristocratic modesty, 'nor did I hit hard.'

What he did confirm was that life in an Italian city-state was insecure for the wealthy without control of the government. It was equally insecure for the artists whom he chose to patronise. Two years after Cosimo's death, the raging Dominican monk Savanarola tried to destroy the religious as well as the secular art developed by the Medicis: he even persuaded Lorenzo di Credi to slash his own pictures in his studio. In a Bonfire of the Vanities, relics, books, ornaments and works of art were consumed. A furnace of puritanism scorched Florence until the mob turned against the new rigour and its preacher. In 1498, Savanarola was hanged from a gibbet and roasted on flames below. 'Prophet!' the crowd shouted. 'Now is the time for a miracle.' There was none.

Such a violent reaction from the long tradition of religious art had its history. The Byzantine emperor Leo the Isaurian had been an iconoclast who had burned artists and the library of Constantinople, in which he shut scribes and attendants. The reforming monks of the Middle Ages were equally no friends of images. Saint Francis of Assisi wanted no painting in the churches of his order – 'no wall in honour of Saint Poverty and Saint Humility'. Pope Nicholas V looted the Colosseum for lime; two thousand cartloads of statues and marble from the Roman monument were rendered down in the ovens. The Counter-Reformation would imitate the puritanism of Luther and ban the nude from religious frescoes. Michelangelo's figures in the *Last Judgement* in the Sistine Chapel would have their private parts covered with draperies. In Venice, Veronese would be hauled before the

Inquisition, accused of heresy and forced to paint out some figures in a religious picture. Art now had to be correct in faith.

North of the Alps, the reaction against the symbols of Christianity was even more extreme. The Protestant mobs turned against religious art and all images as if they were Vandals or Vikings. 'Nothing has survived,' Erasmus wrote, 'neither in the cloisters nor on the portals, nor in the convents. The pictures were covered with whitewash; what could burn was thrown on the bonfire, the rest was smashed. Neither monetary nor artistic value was any protection.' Erasmus himself moved to Freiburg under the personal protection of the Catholic Archduke of Austria. Protestantism threatened to turn Switzerland and Germany into a wasteland of culture. The Renaissance humanism represented by Erasmus was usurped by the Reformation of Luther, who despised the classical values of his contemporary.

Although in the north of Europe, the patronage of art became the province of wealthy merchants, guilds and bankers, the Catholic princes still kept their power. Artists saw no wrong in working for contradictory camps or feuding financiers. Lucas Cranach could be the court painter for the electors of Saxony and the designer of great guns for Duke Henry the Pious and still be the godfather of Luther's first son as well as the illustrator of his Reformation pamphlets. The commercial Fugger family in Augsburg were the Medici of the north, making Holbein's birthplace a Renaissance city on the far side of the Alps. Yet all the while, religious subjects were becoming less popular. The medieval craftsman linked with the patron in the common service of God was developing into the Renaissance artist who found that competition for his skills bred inspiration and income. Mutual labour in praise of the divine was being fragmented into various works at a price.

Benvenuto Cellini, perhaps the finest sculptor in precious metals of his age, served the Pope as a gunner at the Castel Sant'Angelo during the Sack of Rome. He melted down many of the sacred reliquaries in the papal treasure, so that these could be spirited away as ingots. He kept the leavings for himself, to create statues for the enemy of Rome, the King of France. He had no sense of piety or dedication to heaven. His extraordinary autobiography was hardly a spiritual journey towards a personal glimpse of the divine, merely the search of the Renaissance artist for the highest bidder.

The Changing of the Grail

In the art of the Italian Renaissance, the symbols of the Grail became more rare, perhaps because they were heretical. The most striking were to be found in *The Baptism of Christ* attributed to Leonardo da Vinci and Verrocchio, which remains in the Uffizi Gallery at Florence. Beside the Jordan river, Saint John pours blessed water from a bowl on to the head of Christ, already crowned with a sun-disc of a halo. Above, two hands release the dove of the Holy Spirit, radiant with shafts of light. Representations of the severed head of Saint John the Baptist on a platter were few, although it does appear in *Madonna and Child with Saints* by Lorenzetti in the Church of Sant'Agostino in Siena. In Tintoretto's *The Annunciation* in the Scuola di San Rocco in Venice, another dove within a sun-disc of holy rays can be seen flying down on the Virgin and leading angels to tell of the birth of the Saviour. And in *The Adoration of the Magi*, painted by Vivarini and now in the Frick Collection in New York, and by Gentile da Fabriano, again in the Uffizi, the caskets and cruets of the oriental givers of riches to the Son of God are emphasised in their opulence. And the Magdalene appeared in her red dress in Piero della Francesca's fresco of Saint Mary in the cathedral of Arezzo. Her crimson robe was repeated by Botticelli in his *Mary at the Foot of the Cross*, while her long red hair, wiping the wound on the nailed feet of Jesus, was shown by Giotto in his *Crucifixion* in the Scrovegni Chapel at Padua.

There, three flying angels catch Christ's blood in small grails, while Longinus smears the fluid from his lancepoint onto his blind eyes. And in the *Lamentation* there, the Magdalene cradles the wounds on the feet of Christ, while His mother holds His head.

In the Assisi chapel dedicated to the saint, she shows her love of Christ the Gardener as He moves off with His spade. Further episodes of her legend are painted, including the scene after her death, in which angels transport her body to be buried by Saint Maximin; she is covered only with her long hair and kneels transfigured in an orange shell. She became a cult to the flagellants and the Penitent Orders, particular at Borgo San Sepolcro and Bergamo. And she inspired women mystics, such as Margery Kempe, who saw her in a vision at the Church of the Holy Sepulchre in Jerusalem, and Catherine of Siena, who followed the 'sweet and loving' Magdalene, who never left the Cross and 'became drunk and bathed in the blood of the Son of God', some of which passed into her Grail. In Renaissance italian painting, the theme of the Magdalene stressed her remorse for her early voluptuousness and her luxurious life. At Bolzano, a fresco displayed her with her skirt slit to the hip, reprimanded by her sister Martha and her brother Lazarus for being with her lover, and in the Titian painting of her in the Pitti palace in Florence, she was depicted fleshily with naked breasts.

Most significant of all, in art as well as literature, was the reversion in romantic subjects to classical and secular values. The outstanding Botticelli painting of *The Birth of Venus* showed the naked Goddess of Love coming from the sea on a giant cockleshell, the symbol of the pilgrimage to Compostela swollen into the splendour of human desire. Such a daring transformation had always been part of the Arthurian tradition as well as Italian taste. In the *Storie Nerbonesi* of Andrea da Barberino, the hero, William of Orange, was made to order tapestries for his piazza in Paris from the four religions of the world, Jewish, Christian,

Muslim and classical pagan. Further in the text, scenes from the New Testament were mixed with the legends of Charlemagne, Joseph of Arimathea, Lancelot and the Holy Grail. Such a confusion was a heritage from the courts of the Norman kings of Sicily and of the remarkable Emperor Frederick II of Hohenstaufen, who built the extraordinary octagonal Grail Castle with eight surrounding octagonal towers at Castel del Monte above Bari. Designed like the Temple at Jerusalem and the Ka'aba at Mecca to be an axis of the world, the Castel was once said to have had at its central point another octagonal bowl carved from a single stone and holding the Holy Blood.

Almost unique among Holy Roman Emperors, Frederick II never commissioned a church. If there was a monument to his esoteric wisdom, it was the Castel del Monte. Built with the vigour and lack of ornament of the Cistercians, the holy order was particularly favoured by Frederick, who died, according to Matthew Paris, wearing its white habit. While the sacred octagonal shape might derive from Byzantine Ravenna and Charlemagne's chapel at Aachen, its triangular alignment with Frederick's other castles and cities near Bari was a tribute to his interest in astronomy and mathematics, which could make the Castel into almost a temple of the sun, as at Montségur. On a crusade which had more to do with diplomacy than fighting, he had himself crowned King of Jerusalem, asserting his divine right as strongly as Melchizedek. The preamble to his Constitutions of Melfi stated that he had been elevated by God 'beyond hope of man to the pinnacle of the Roman Empire and to the sole distinction of the other kingdoms at the right hand of the divine power'. No wonder that the Pope declared crusades against him in Italy. He thought himself almost immortal, and the verse which praised his virtues and magnificence on his tomb ended by declaring, 'Then Frederick, who lies here, is not dead.'

Although Italy had produced no outstanding Arthurian romances, the conversion of their style for Renaissance taste by Boiardo and Ariosto was a triumph. A large library had been accumulated by the dukes of Ferrara of the House of Este, and there the two poets were loosed among the themes of the Matters of Britain and France; also the legends of Alexander. For Boiardo, tales of Arthur were more interesting than those of Charlemagne, because fighting for love was better than for a crusade. As he declared in his masterpiece, *L'Orlando Innamorato*:

> *Britain in its glory and its grandeur*
> > *Was known for love and fighting in the fray.*
> *And so King Arthur there was raised to honour*
> > *And still his name is spread abroad today . . .*
> *Later King Charles held his high court in France,*
> > *But this was not the same, and nevermore.*
> *It locked the gates on love and arms and chance.*
> > *Its message and its faith was holy war.*

Ariosto made his figure of Roland in *Orlando Furioso* a knight driven to madness by his love of the princess Angelica, the daughter of the Great Khan. He concentrated more on the defence of Europe by Charlemagne against Islam than on the adventures of the Knights of the Round Table. One critic declared that 'as Virgil was the poet of Rome, Ariosto is the poet of Europe'. Certainly, he was so in the waning of the crusades. He wanted to revive the ideals of medieval chivalry, condemning the new artillery that mowed down the armoured cavalry as 'the worst device, in all the years of the inventions of humanity, which was ever imagined by an evil mind'.

Before the Sack of Rome, Ariosto saw the Holy Roman Emperor Charles V as another Charlemagne, the last imperial ruler with the vision to unite Europe in the struggle against the heathen. God had waited for his coming to power so that he might inherit the sovereignty of the New World of the discoveries as well as of the Old:

> *For, in the wisdom of the Almighty's ways,*
> *He waits until the world shall be made one*
> *Beneath an Emperor more just and wise*
> *Than any who since Augustus shall arise . . .*
>
> *For valour, whence all other virtues stem,*
> *God wills not only that this Emperor*
> *Shall wear upon his brow the diadem*
> *Which Roman Emperors have worn before,*
> *But, glittering with many a new gem,*
> *His sceptre shall encompass many a shore*
> *Which knows no season but the winter's cold;*
> *And there shall be one shepherd and one fold.*

In the light of this universal need for unity, Ariosto berated other Christian monarchs for warring on each other, not the infidel:

> *No longer now defenders of the faith,*
> *With one another Christian knights contend,*
> *Destroying in their enmity and wrath*
> *Those few who still believe; make now an end,*
> *You Spaniards; Frenchmen, choose another path;*
> *Switzers and Germans, no more armies send.*
> *For here the territory you would gain*
> *Belongs to Christ; His kingdom you profane.*
>
> *If 'the most Christian' rulers you would be,*
> *And 'Catholic' desire to be reputed,*
> *Why do you slay Christ's men? Their property*
> *Why have you sacked, and their belongings looted?*
> *Why do you leave in dire captivity*
> *Jerusalem, by infidels polluted?*
> *Why do you let the unclean Turk command*
> *Constantinople and the Holy Land?*

Ariosto would be disappointed. The Habsburgs of Spain and Austria would become the main defenders of

Christianity in the Mediterranean, while warring on other Christian rulers in Europe. Suffering a breakdown because of his incessant wars against the Muslims and the Protestants, Charles V would abdicate, instructing his heir Philip how difficult it was to protect an empire stretching from Spain to the Netherlands, and now to the Americas. Foreign aggression and internal revolution would prevent any last crusade against Islam, while it was 'almost impossible to lay down invariable rules, given the instability and uncertainty of human affairs . . . Go to war only when it is forced on you. It exhausts the treasury and causes great misery.'

United Christendom died in the divisions between the nations and the city states. The quest for the Grail and the grace of God became a personal thing, although their representations in art and literature still fascinated the Renaissance spirit. But these longings were transmuted in *Orlando Furioso* to dreams of bygone chivalry and vain hopes of its revival. Merlin was only a prophet and a sorcerer, pointing the way to the magic garden of Alcina, the sister of the fairy Morgana and King Arthur. Scotland, however, remained the home of Lancelot and still sent its Celtic warriors on crusades against the Moors:

> *For there the cavaliers of Britain roam,*
> *Valiant in arms, with knights of other lands,*
> *Some from nearby, and others far from home:*
> *Norwegian, Frankish and Germanic bands.*
> *Valour is needed by all those who come,*
> *For here a knight his death, not glory, stands*
> *To find; here Tristan, Galahad, Gawain,*
> *Lancelot, Galasso, Arthur foes have slain.*
>
> *And many a brave knight of both the old*
> *And new Round Table here renown has won,*
> *As many a monument to many a bold,*
> *Brave deed, and many trophies have been made*
>   *known . . .*

Yet Ariosto's chief and melancholy demeaning of blessed legends was his changing of the quest for the Grail and Eden into an arrival at an enchanted garden with a classical cornucopia. This was the *reductio ad paradisum*:

> *Where everyone in dance or joyful game*
> *The festive hours employed from early morn;*
> *Where of sad thoughts no shadow ever came*
> *To spoil this rosebud life without a thorn.*
> *There no discomfort was, no cup was empty,*
> *But endless bounty from the horn of plenty.*

Chapter Twelve

Alchemy, Merlin and Malory

Medieval alchemy prepared the way for the greatest
intervention in the divine world order that man has ever
attempted: alchemy was the dawn of the scientific age,
when the daemon of the scientific spirit compelled the
forces of nature to serve man to an extent that had never
been known before.

C. G. Jung, *Alchemical Studies*

From Alchemy to Science

Cosimo de' Medici, the Duke of Florence, came into possession of the Corpus Hermeticum after the fall of
Constantinople. He ordered Marsilio Ficino to give up his
translation of Plato into Latin and concentrate on these lost
works of the legendary philosopher, astrologer and alchemist
Hermes Trismegistus, the Merlin of the Orient. Tradition had
the *Hermetica* originally inscribed in Greek on an emerald
tablet in Egypt. They contained elements of Mithraism, neo-
Platonism and Stoicism as well as the *gnosis*, the understanding of all as one. They declared that man was an image
of the sun, which was an image of the cosmos, itself an image
of God. As with the Grail quest, the duty of everyone was the
search for the divine.

*For it is the height of evil not to know God; but to be
capable of knowing God and to wish and hope to know
him, is a road which leads straight to the Good; and it
is an easy road to travel. Everywhere God will come to*

223

*meet you, everywhere he will appear to you, at places
and times at which you look not for it.*

The idea of the knowledge of God being in everything and
every person had been an inspiration in the Arthurian
romances, particularly in *Parzival*. In one sense, the trials of
the Knights of the Round Table on their way to the Castle of
the Fisher King were the outward description of the inner tur-
moils of self-discovery. Finally to see the Grail was a vision
of the unity of oneself with the universe. The object seen was
in the shape of what one's knowledge made one able to perceive. The goal was union with the ultimate Creator.

*God makes all things for himself; and all things are
parts of God. And in as much as all things are parts of
him, God is all things. Therefore, in making all things,
God makes himself. And it is impossible that he should
ever cease from making; for God himself can never
cease to be.*

This Hermetic philosophy deeply influenced such
Renaissance scholars as Pico della Mirandola, Ramon Lull
and Giordano Bruno. It was an incitement to the alchemists,
who saw their scientific experiments with distillation and
chemical reactions as an endeavour to combine the material
with the spiritual in the knowledge of the wholeness of the
world. The Philosopher's Stone, which might turn base metals into gold, was merely a symbol for the transformation of
the body into an understanding of the Holy Spirit. Like the
stone fallen from heaven in *Parzival*, or the innumerable
blessed relics and chalices in European churches, any earthly
sign or wonder was merely a parable of the way to wisdom
and the Word of God. Indeed, in the *First Continuation* by
Gautier de Doulens, Gawain observed an apparatus similar to
the alchemic still. The blood from the Holy Lance flowed
down into a holder, then into a silver vessel, from which a
golden pipe carried it into another silver vessel. In spite of

this process, the Grail King assured Gawain that the lance would bleed until Judgement Day.

Although the Renaissance led to scientific experimentation, it also revived the interest in astrology as well as astronomy, in prophesy along with rational inquiry, and in alchemy as the father of the revelation of the secrets of the cosmos. In his *Ordinal of Alchemy*, Thomas Norton of Bristol wrote that people without a proper training in physics and metaphysics should not try to manufacture gold from an elixir, as he had done; for they would fail. When granting two of the royal physicians his permission to experiment in alchemy, King Henry VI of England noted that if they found the mystical elixir, it would cure diseases and wounds, lengthen life, and serve as an antidote to poisons. It might be as effective as the magic ointment used by Linet to set together the head of the knight hewn into a hundred pieces by Sir Gareth in Malory's *Morte D'Arthur*. *On Consideration of the Fifth Essence* by John of Rupescissa was more about distilling alcohol and helpful chemicals than making gold. And even the astrological magic proposed by Ficino in his *On Life* was more of a medical treatise than a star guide to human behaviour, as was the work of Paracelsus. As John Donne slyly noted about alchemical experiments:

> *No chemic yet the elixir got,*
> *But glorifies his pregnant pot,*
> *If by the way to him befall*
> *Some odoriferous thing or med'cinal . . .*

Isaac Newton himself would be as interested in alchemy as in the law of gravity. Ancient and modern inquiries into the workings of the cosmos were most confused. The discovery that the earth and the planets rotated round the fire of the sun, indeed, had originally been a principle of Hermes Trismegistus on his emerald tablet, while the commentary of Ortolanus on that text inferred the principle of condensation: 'Whatever is below is similar to that which is above.'

Most of the alchemists thought of themselves as rigorous researchers, and not necessarily heretics. As early as the twelfth-century *Anticlaudianus* of Alan de Lille, alchemy had seemed an allegory for the Christian visionary. The three stages of the process – the blackening and whitening and yellowing – were three mirrors that reduced forms to their original essences and ideas. Later, Sir Walter Raleigh wrote that the art of magic was the art of worshipping God. The Elizabethan sorcerer and experimenter John Dee told the Emperor Rudolph II at Prague that he used his Philosopher's Stone and the aid of angels only to intercede with God for the revelation of His Creation. Many of the transformations sought by the alchemists had, after all, been done by Moses' rod or Solomon's ring. Miraculous changes had been associated with Christ Himself, the Saints and even with the Mass, when the priest changed bread into the Body of Jesus. A popular belief was that if a man saw the consecrated host elevated above the congregation, he would be safe from all harm for the rest of the day. And as late as the seventeenth century, a weaponsalve was made to cure wounds at a distance by anointing the bloody sword so that the vital spirits of the hurt body would reunite in a sympathetic cure.

The quest for the Philosopher's Stone – the Grail in *Parzival* – gave to certain gems some marvellous properties. King Charles V of France had a precious stone which helped women in childbirth, as did the Duke of Burgundy. The heliotrope was given the power of making its wearer invisible. *The Book of Stones* by Bishop Marbode of Rennes, written in the late eleventh century, ascribed to jewels more power to cure than herbs. The sapphire, for example, cooled the blood, and when it was ground down, it soothed headaches and ulcers. Gervase of Tilbury brought up Solomon's ring to prove the wonder-working quality of gems. So the Arthurian romances abounded in magic gems and precious talismans as well as in the concept of the stone of bounty fallen from heaven. According to the *Wartburgkrieg*, the Grail was a precious stone that fell out of

Lucifer's crown when he was thrust from heaven.

No alchemical ring had more properties than the one in the *Morte D'Arthur* given by Dame Lionesse to Sir Gareth at her tournament for the Knights of the Round Table, although it increased her beauty. He would change colours in the wearing of it as in the process of the crucible and the still. As she said,

> *The virtue of my ring is, that is green it will turn to red, and that is red it will turn to likeness of green, and that is blue it will turn to likeness of white, and that is white it will turn to likeness of blue, and so it will do all manner of colours. Also he who bears my ring shall lose no blood.*

After many successes on the field, Sir Gareth gave up the chameleon ring and reverted to his final true colour of yellow – the gold of the end of the distillation of alchemy. The forerunner of Malory, Chrétien de Troyes, was rare in his discretion in *Yvain*, when the all-protecting ring given to the hero by his wife was never used by him, because he kept on his journey like a later Ulysses and did not return to her.

The three vessels of the alchemical process resembled three forms of the visionary Grail. The crucible purified and refined metal through fire and calcination, just as the chalice purged sin through the Holy Blood. The retort allowed chemical reactions and the changing of shapes and colours, and corresponded to the magic stone of miracle and spiritual enlightenment. The alembic, or the still, was the process of distillation, in which the essence was separated from the substance. It represented the Grail platter of bounty and nourishment.

Alchemic theories permeated the Arthurian romances. Merlin was the Mercurius of the alchemists, the spirit of the Philosopher's Stone and of the Grail vessel. For in the adventures of the Knights of the Round Table, the material and the ethereal were mingled. A bloody combat was followed by a magic encounter, ending finally in a prophecy or an ecstasy. And yet the Christian Church was incompatible with both the alchemist and the Knight of the Grail, pursuing an individual vision of the divine and the idea of man's unmediated relation to God. As the psychiatrist Jung would write in his *Alchemical Studies*, in Christ, the Almighty became man by His own will, while the Philosopher's Stone evolved into another bringer of light through human intention and skill.

> *In the former case, the miracle of man's salvation is accomplished by God; in the latter, the salvation or transfiguration of the universe is brought about by the mind of man. In the one case man confesses 'I under God', in the other he asserts 'God under me'. Man takes the place of the Creator.*

Merlin and Malory

When the Welsh Tudors came to power in England, the belief of the people in relics and miracles was still strong. The wonder-working of the *Lives of the Saints* was so popular that a compilation by the Archbishop of Genoa called *The Golden Legend* was translated by Caxton and printed in seven editions before the Reformation, along with Malory's *Morte D'Arthur*. The shrines of the saints at Canterbury, Glastonbury, Lindisfarne, St Albans, Walsingham and Westminster were crowded places of pilgrimage, as was the sanctuary of the Holy Blood at Hailes Abbey in Gloucestershire, where Bishop Latimer declared that the faithful believed 'that the sight of it with their bodily eye doth certify them and putteth them out of doubt that they be in clean life, and in state of salvation without spot of sin'.

The mystery of the Son of God was still the province of the priesthood. The changing of the wafer and the wine into the Body and Blood of Christ was their sacred alchemy. The accusations of the Lollards in their Twelve Conclusions of 1395 had little effect yet: 'Exorcism and hallowings, made in the Church, of wine, bread and wax, salt and oil and incense, the stone of the altar, upon vestments, mitre cross, and pilgrims' staves, be the very practice of necromancy, rather than of the holy theology.' These early reformers made no headway with their denunciation of saints such as 'the witch of Walsingham'. Indeed, miraculous cures were reported from the grave of the Lollard martyr Richard Wyche, although he had denounced such superstition. And even fifty years after the Reformation had commenced in the reign of Henry VIII, a Puritan pamphlet had to admit that 'three parts at least of the people [were] wedded to their old superstition still'.

For the Puritans and some of the leading ecclesiastics, the Mass was 'nothing better to be esteemed than the verses of the sorcerer or enchanter', as Bishop Hooper asserted, 'holy words murmured and spoken in secret'. Many followed Martin Luther in condemning the Catholic sacramental system, as he did in *The Babylonian Captivity of the Church*, declaring that 'the papacy is indeed nothing but the kingdom of Babylon and of the true Anti-Christ'. The Reformation was about a simple approach to God. Ritual and Latin must give way to hymns and sermons in the vernacular. The Word of God must be accessible, the approach to God plain and personal. Curiously enough, the quest for the Grail had always emphasised the direct search by each knight for the divine; but the mysteries of that sacred vessel were too subtle for the new Protestants, who rejected transubstantiation. To them, bread and wine were only symbols of the Body and Blood of Christ – as were, indeed, the many markers of the Grail quest in the Catholic churches of Europe.

When the Puritans came to damn such mysticism as the romances of King Arthur, the propaganda of the state decided to revive them. For the Tudors were Welsh kings, and the Scottish Stuarts would unite the whole island under the name of Britain – the title given to Albion by Geoffrey of Monmouth, when he claimed that King Brutus of Troy had first colonised the giant-ridden white isle of the northern seas. The seventh book of his *History* consisted of a prophecy spoken to King Vortigern by Merlin in the royal fortress in Snowdonia. Although the references were gnomic and occult, some of them seemed to bear on the future. 'The lion's whelps shall be transformed into sea-fishes' was taken as a reference to the drowning of the royal heir of King Henry I on the White Ship, while the death of the King in Normandy and the invasion of Ireland by Henry II were also foretold. Wace added to the legend of Merlin, writing of Arthur's death:

> *Merlin said of Arthur, as I understand it,*
> *That there would be doubt concerning his end:*
> *The prophet spoke truly.*

Yet to these reconstructions of the early Welsh bard Myrddin, now named as Merlin, Robert de Boron added a whole history of the magician. His *Merlin* was a sequel to his *Joseph of Arimathea*, an explanation of how the Grail reached Britain from France. A devil and a virgin were the parents of the precocious Merlin, who was given the power of changing shape and knowing the future. He became the royal adviser to Vortigern's successor Pendragon, and then to his younger brother Uther, who also inherited the throne. He had the trilithons of Stonehenge transported from Ireland and established a Round Table at Carduel for fifty knights, based on that of Charlemagne. Later, he created the test of the sword in the stone for Uther's unrecognised son, Arthur, so that he might become the King of Britain.

Merlin's character was that of a wise trickster, a guide to the Otherworld, a Lucifer and an enchanter. This personality was developed by Sir Thomas Malory in his ever-popular *Morte D'Arthur*, printed many times by Caxton and others after 1485 and the victory at Bosworth of the Welsh king Henry VII. This last medieval Arthurian romance resembled the first, an exercise in propaganda for the new dynasty, recalling King Arthur's conquest of Paris like that of

Henry V after Agincourt. In Malory's version, the British king not only defeated with Excalibur a giant and the Roman and Saracen leader Lucius, but was actually crowned as Emperor by the Pope in the Holy City, which surrendered to him. Curiously, he had the enemy magnates embalmed and buried in chests of lead in the Templar and oriental manner.

The conception of Arthur by Igraine, the Duchess of Cornwall, in the castle of Tintagel began the *Morte D'Arthur*. Merlin disguised Uther Pendragon as her husband the duke, who was slain on the night of their love, allowing Uther to marry Igraine. Merlin's price was to be responsible for the rearing of Arthur, for Uther had sworn on the Four Evangelists to grant Merlin his desire if he had his way with Igraine. Her sister Morgan le Fay, however, was put into a nunnery, where she was taught necromancy; she was ever the implacable foe of Arthur and of Merlin, her rival and his adviser. Passing the test of the sword in the stone, Arthur was only accepted as king after a long civil war, in which Merlin was his armourer, strategist and communications wizard. He procured Excalibur from the Lady of the Lake for Arthur: the magic sword was 'so bright in his enemies' eyes, that it gave light like thirty torches'. He brought reinforcements and placed them in ambush so quickly that the royal knights marvelled 'that man on earth might speed so soon, and come and go'. And Malory claimed a provenance for his accounts of ancient jousts and combats, giving Merlin a master in Northumberland named Blaise, who wrote down 'all the battles that every worthy knight did of Arthur's court'.

In one of his many shapes, Merlin appeared to the British king as a beautiful youth. He predicted Arthur's death because he had slept unknowingly with his sister and begotten Mordred upon her, in spite of an attempt, like that of Herod, to destroy all male children born on May Day. 'For it is God's will your body will be punished for your foul deeds; but I may well be sorry,' said Merlin, 'for I shall die a shameful death to be put in the earth quick, and you shall die a worshipful death.' He made the father of Arthur's Queen

Guinevere institute the Round Table for one hundred and fifty knights, first in London and then in Camelot, which was identified as Winchester. Malory confirmed that the royal court was always on the move; he made Arthur lament, 'Alas, yet had I never rest one month since I was crowned king of this land.' And then Merlin fell in love with the water nymph Nimue who served the Lady of the Lake. She tricked out of the wizard many of his secrets until she immured him alive under an enchanted rock. So the stone finally imprisoned the man of many shapes.

King Arthur found survival difficult without the warnings of Merlin. Morgan le Fay stole from him Excalibur and its healing scabbard of gold and precious stones, so that he was nearly killed by his own wonder-working weapon. And he would have been roasted alive by an alchemic mantle made of precious stones and sent to him by his necromantic sister if he had not insisted that the messenger wore it first; she 'fell down dead and never more spake word after and burnt to coals'. The *Morte D'Arthur* shifted from tales of Merlin and his king to the multiple quest of the leading Knights of the Round Table. In one adventure, Lancelot at the Castle Perilous discovered a magic sword by a corpse beneath a hill of silk and used it to cure a sick knight as a woundsalve, or as Perceval's bleeding lance healed the Fisher King. So many foreign knights were defeated and sent back to beg for mercy at Camelot that King Arthur could hold an alchemical feast at Pentecost with fifty warriors under a Green Knight, sixty under a Red Knight, a hundred under a Blue Knight, and six hundred under the metal Sir Ironside. The Black Knight was slain, or he would have been there too.

Morgan le Fay did have her revenge on King Arthur, by sending him no Grail, but a horn of betrayal. If any woman were false to her husband, she spilt all the drink in it. So Guinevere did, and thus her husband knew of her love of Lancelot. The same happened to La Beale Isoud, who had to confess her love for Tristram to her husband, King Mark. She was sentenced to be burned alive, but Tristram saved her.

They had originally fallen in love by drinking out of a golden flask on their voyage an aphrodisiac meant for her and King Mark: 'they thought never drink that ever they drank to each other was so sweet nor so good'. Later, in his madness in the Forest Perilous, Tristram saved Arthur with the help of the Lady of the Lake, who rode off with a false woman's head on her saddle-bow, severed by the King's sword. Eventually, Tristram was accepted as a Knight of the Round Table in the company of his great friend Lancelot, who lodged him with Isoud at his castle, Joyous Gard. Lancelot, too, first heard of the Sangreal or Holy Grail in the foreign country of King Pelles, the cousin of Joseph of Arimathea. After rescuing from a tower a naked maiden boiling in scalding water and after slaying a dragon, Lancelot was sat down in the Castle of Corbenic by Pelles:

> There came in a dove at a window, and in her mouth there seemed a little censer of gold. And there was such a savour as all the spicery of the world had been there. And forthwith there was upon the table all manner of meats and drinks that they could imagine. So came in a fair and young maiden, and she bore a vessel of gold between her hands; and the king kneeled devoutly, and said his prayers, and so did all that were there.
>
> 'O Jesu,' said Sir Lancelot, 'what may this mean?'
> 'This is,' said the king, 'the richest thing that any man has living. And when this thing goes about, the Round Table shall be broken. And know you well,' said the king, 'this is the Holy Sangreal that you have here seen.'

This original sight of the Sangreal by Lancelot was different to other visions in the previous Arthurian romances. First seen by the adulterer with Arthur's Queen, it was foretold by the golden flask that bound La Beale Isoud and Tristram forever in love. It appeared in two forms: the censer in the dove's beak with its heavenly perfumes; and the vessel born by the Grail maiden. It had the property of providing manna and ambrosia for all. It stimulated King Pelles into an art of trickery worthy of Merlin. He went to an enchantress, who gave Lancelot some drugged wine, which so besotted him that he thought that Elaine, the daughter of Pelles, was his beloved Guinevere. So he fulfilled a prophecy and made Elaine pregnant with Galahad, whom Pelles knew would deliver his country from danger and would achieve the Sangreal, as Perceval had done in the previous Arthurian romances.

Lancelot rode away, for he could not come closer to the Grail, but Sir Bors followed him to Corbenic, where he saw the infant Galahad in his mother's arms. He wept for joy and prayed. Again the white dove appeared with the golden censer; again the miraculous meal, the sweet smells and the Grail maiden, who said before she disappeared with the Holy Vessel: 'This child is Galahad, who shall sit in the Siege Perilous and achieve the Sangreal, and he shall be much better than ever was his father Sir Lancelot of the Lake.' Sir Bors took confession, although he had little to confess; he was a virgin except for one night with another king's daughter. And so Malory granted him that night some visions of the other sacred objects of the Grail quest and of the future with Arthur.

A long and great spear of light with a burning point wounded his shoulder. As Bors lay back in pain, he was accosted by a knight, who fought him before being cut down. Then a hail of arrows and crossbow bolts wounded him all over. Next he was attacked by a lion and had to cut off its head. Then a dragon entered with gold letters on its forehead that signified something to do with King Arthur: it fought an old leopard and spat from its mouth a hundred small dragons that tore it to pieces – a prophecy of the dissension that would break apart the Round Table.

An old harper now entered with the two adders of wisdom round his neck and sang a song of Joseph of Arimathea coming to the foreign country. Bors was told to leave the next day, for he was not worthy of the Grail Castle. Four children appeared with four candles, and another old man with a censer in one hand and the Spear of Vengeance in the other. Four women came to kneel at a silver altar with four pillars. They were joined by a kneeling bishop, but Bors was blinded for a while by a naked silver sword blade hanging over his head. Again he was ordered to depart to Camelot and report the news of Galahad and the Sangreal. Later, Lancelot was tricked for a second time into sleeping with Elaine instead of Guinevere: he went as mad as Tristram had in the woods, when he learnt of the deceit.

The Sangreal began to appear more openly as a healing vessel for wounded virgin knights. It cured them and was identified by Sir Ector, the tutor of King Arthur, as the container of some of the Holy Blood of Jesus. It might only be seen by a perfect man, yet when the wild Lancelot ran out of the forest back to Corbenic, he was laid by force close to the Sangreal, 'so by miracle and by virtue of that Holy Vessel Sir Lancelot was healed and recovered'. Banished from Camelot, he was given a castle on the Joyous Isle and called himself the Knight of the Trespass. After many jousts, he was recalled to Arthur's court for the feast of Pentecost, and here Malory claimed to have created himself 'the noble tale of the Sangreal', although much of his material was still scrambled together from previous sources, particularly *Mort d'Artu* and *The Quest of the Holy Grail*.

Twelve nuns now brought the grown Galahad to the court, and fresh golden letters on the seats of the Round Table declared: *Here ought he to sit, and he ought to sit here*. On the Siege Perilous or Judas Seat which hurled sinners into hell was written that it would be filled four hundred and fifty-four winters after the Passion of Christ. Once more, a sword in a stone appeared floating on the river; dressed in red, without a sword, Galahad sat safely in the Siege Perilous and drew the blade from the rock on the water. At the end of a tournament the Sangreal appeared after evensong at Camelot to the Knights of the Round Table in the cracking and crying of thunder and the flames of Pentecostal fire:

In the midst of this blast a sunbeam entered clearer by seven times more than ever they saw day, and they were all enlightened of the grace of the Holy Ghost. Then every knight began to behold each other apparently fairer than they ever saw before. There was no knight who might speak one word for a great while, so they looked every man on the other as if they had been dumb. Then covered with white samite, the Holy Grail entered into the hall, but there was no one who might see it, nor who bore it. And good odours fulfilled all the hall, and every knight had such meat and drink as he best loved in this world. And when the Sangreal had been borne through the hall, then the Holy Vessel departed suddenly, but they did not know where it went. Then they all had the breath to speak. And then the king yielded thanks to God, of His good grace which He had sent them.

The coming of this Christian Grail would break up the Round Table. For Malory had lived during the decline of medieval chivalry in the fratricidal Wars of the Roses. All the knights vowed to leave on their individual quests after the vision of God's grace, and King Arthur knew that he had lost the feudal loyalty that had kept Britain together. His warriors were now pledged to God. 'You have bereft me,' he told Gawain, 'of the fairest fellowship and the truest of knighthood that ever were seen together in any realm of the world; for when they depart from here I am sure they all shall never meet more in this world, for they shall die many in the quest.' Almost as prophetical as Merlin, Malory was describing how the pursuit of individual excellence and salvation would rend apart the unity of the Catholic faith and feudal ties of obligation. As for the searchers for the Sangreal, they departed with weeping and mourning among rich and poor, and every knight took the way that he liked best.

Galahad was soon given a shield with a cross made with the blood of Joseph of Arimathea after his arrival in Britain.

In a vision by a ruined chapel, Lancelot saw a sick knight cured by a floating silver altar with six candlesticks and the Sangreal; but he was too heavy with sin to kiss the Holy Vessel. And Merlin came back into the story in an account given to Perceval by his aunt, the Queen of the Waste Land. She told him that the Welsh wizard had created the Round Table to represent the world. Those who became knights of it could be heathen as well as Christian. The quest for the Sangreal had broken up this ungodly fellowship, which ignored family and kin.

A vision came to Perceval of the old and wounded Joseph of Arimathea, begging to be cured by the Holy Blood and Body. He was then tricked into lying down with a naked woman, who disappeared into a black cloud after Perceval had seen his drawn sword and its pommel containing a red cross and the sign of the crucifix. He stabbed himself in expiation for his sin and sailed away on the magic Ship of Solomon, which drifted to shore for his use.

So the quests of the knights seeking the Sangreal were recorded. They were made to listen to many sermons, prophecies and Christian allegories; but clearly only three of them would achieve their goal. These were the three wise virgins, Galahad, Perceval and the once-spotted Bors, who would all meet on the magic ship. As in *The Quest of the Holy Grail*, they found on board a bed made from the Tree of Good and Evil in Eden, another magic sword with a serpent and a fish on its pommel of many colours, and a snakeskin scabbard. King Pelles had been maimed incurably through both of his thighs by the Spear of Vengeance because he had half drawn the sword, now identified as the weapon of King David. Only Galahad could cure Pelles and revive the Waste Land of Logres with the touch of the sword, before the three knights might finally seek the apotheosis of the Grail in the Land of Sarras.

Again Lancelot achieved a vision of the Holy Vessel at Corbenic, this time at the ceremony of the Mass, where a priest held up the youngest of three men by the body to show to the people. This vision of the Trinity at the mystery of the sacrament caused Lancelot to be struck down with fire and left in a coma for nearly a month. His recovery was due to the care of King Pelles, who told him that Elaine was dead: and so Lancelot returned to Camelot with the news that more than half of the members of the Round Table were slain. He was followed to Corbenic by the three pure knights on the Ship of Solomon, and these were granted the full vision of the Sangreal, heralded by Joseph of Arimathea, who had been the first Bishop of Christendom in Sarras. 'They saw angels; and two bore candles of wax, and the third a towel, and the fourth a spear that bled marvellously, so that three drops fell within a box which he held with his other hand.' The sacred spear was set upright on the Holy Vessel on its silver table. Then Joseph took up a piece of bread which was transformed into the 'likeness of a child, and the visage as red and bright as any fire'. Later, when Joseph had disappeared, the three knights saw a man come out of the Holy Vessel bearing all the signs and wounds of the Passion. He took the Grail and gave Himself through it to the kneeling knights and identified it as the dish of the Paschal Lamb at the Last Supper. They must take the Grail back to Sarras; also the blood of the sacred spear to cure the maimed King of Logres. Galahad healed Pelles with the Holy Blood, then left with his fellows to sail away on the Ship of Solomon, where the Grail was already translated. They were imprisoned on arrival with their precious gift, but they were fed as Joseph had been in confinement by manna and divine grace, and Galahad was chosen to be King of Sarras. He built a shrine of gold and gems for the Sangreal, before the Hand of God came down to take up his sword. 'And then it came right to the Vessel, and took it and the spear, and so bore them up to heaven. Since then, no man has been so brave as to say that he has seen the Sangreal.'

If this was Malory's ending of the quest for divine grace, taken so largely from the earlier *Quest of the Holy Grail*, he could not conclude his book. For he had to deal with the death of King Arthur. He defined the legend that still persists: the enduring love of Lancelot for Guinevere, their betrayal to Arthur by Mordred, the siege of Joyous Gard by the royal forces and the following civil war abroad, the treason of Mordred and the final battle of Camlann, with the taking of the King's body to the Vale of Avalon. To this requiem of the Grail legend of the Middle Ages, Malory even promised a sequel:

Yet some men say in many parts of England that King Arthur is not dead, but taken by the will of our Lord Jesus into another place; and men say that he shall come again, and he shall win the Holy Cross. I will not say it shall be so, but rather I will say: here in this world he changed his life. But many men say that there is written upon his tomb this verse: Hic jacet Arthurus Rex, quondam Rex, que futurus. [Here lies King Arthur, past King, and future.]

Malory's re-creation and definition of the legend of Camelot was a boon for Tudor propaganda. King Henry VII's newborn son – who was born in Winchester, now identified as Camelot – was christened Arthur. The heir of the Houses of both Lancaster and York, he would unite Britain as his royal ancestor had done through the Round Table. He might also repeat Arthur's conquests in Europe as far as Rome. Merlin's prophecies remained popular. In 1510, Wynkyn de Worde published *A Little Treatise of the Birth and Prophecies of Merlin*, which ran into several editions. Later books claimed that Merlin had predicted the Reformation, while *The Mirror for Magistrates* of 1559 wrote of the Welsh bard as 'learned Merlin whom God gave the spirit to know and utter princes' acts to come'. The astrologer Lilly named his almanac *Merlinus Anglicus*, and by Stuart times, Thomas Heywood's *Life of Merlin* claimed him as a Protestant as well as a prophet. And that he was, in the sense that the Grail quest was the individual search for grace without benefit of clergy.

In his breach with Rome, Henry VIII used the defiance and heresy of the Arthurian legend to justify his institution of an independent Church of England under his authority. Most significantly, a Round Table was created at Winchester in memory of the tables of Arthur and Charlemagne. It represented an allegory of the whole world, which was now open to the dominion of the new dynasty, occupied in building the first significant British navy, the force for rebuilding an empire overseas after the loss of France. John Dee and Richard Hakluyt, the chronicler of the voyages of the Elizabethan captains, would use the myth of Arthur's conquests to legitimise expansion abroad. And as Cervantes and Ariosto had sublimated the medieval romances for modern times, so Edmund Spenser would in *The Faerie Queene*.

> *Then Merlin thus: Indeed the fates are firm,*
> *And may not shrink, though all the world do shake.*
> *Yet ought men's good endeavours them confirm,*
> *And guide the heavenly causes to their constant term.*

The Faerie Queene

Edmund Spenser tried to follow Ariosto and so become the Virgil of England. To his friend Sir Walter Raleigh he also confessed the influence of Homer and Tasso. But he used the legend of Arthur in a new manner. The quest of the 'Briton prince' was the love of the Faerie Queen. Through this desire, Spenser could lavish praise on Elizabeth I; as Gloriana, she took the place of the Grail. 'In that Faerie Queene,' he wrote to Raleigh, 'I mean *Glory* in my general intention, and in my particular I conceive the most excellent and glorious person of our soveraine the Queene, and her kingdom in Faerie Land.' As for Arthur, he was chosen 'as most fit for the excellency of his person, being made famous by many men's former works, and also furthest from the danger of envy, and suspicion of present time.'

Tudor propaganda had already identified Arthur as a royal ancestor of Queen Elizabeth, while *his* ancestor was the Emperor Constantine. His fabulous empire which reached to Rome was re-created to justify Elizabethan ambitions in the Americas. And the long poem was less an imitation of its predecessors than a weapon in the Protestant cause against the Catholic Church. Arthur did wear a bloody cross on his surcoat and shield as a glorious badge to his 'dying Lord'. But on his first adventure after slaying a dragon he was made to encounter the usual hermit:

> *He told of saints and popes, and evermore*
> *He strew'd an Ave-Mary after and before.*

Instead of blessing the knight's sleep, the Catholic priest went to his cell to consult his 'magic books, and arts of sundry kinds'. With these charms, he conjured up devils and nightmares to disturb Arthur's conscience and peace of mind. The holy man was changed into a magician and alchemist in the holy war between England and Spain. He tried to direct Arthur away from the new Grail, the praise of Gloriana, the ruler of his heart and her enchanted realm.

Later in this epic, the cup of bounty that led the questing knights to an earthly paradise was also altered into a savage Puritan reaction. The noble Guyon rode into a Bower of Bliss: his name appeared to derive from the river Gehon in the Garden of Eden, from Gawain and from Guyana, the American Eldorado sought by Raleigh. He met the half-naked lady Excess who offered him a golden cup of wine:

> *Thereof she us'd to give to drink to each,*
> *Whom passing by she happened to meet:*
> *It was her guise all strangers goodly so to greet.*
>
> *So she to Guyon offered it to taste;*
> *Who, taking it out of her tender hand,*
> *The cup to ground did violently cast,*

> *That all in pieces it was broken found,*
> *And with the liquor stained all the land.*

Spurning the false wine in the cup, Guyon rode on through 'the most dainty paradise', where all pleasures were in plenty, and nobody envied another's happiness. Art and nature had agreed 'through sweet adversity, this garden to adorn with all variety'. In a fountain of silver water, paved with jasper, two nymphs were bathing, almost fairer than the owner, Acrasia, who was then trapped with a young knight, Verdant, under a net. Guyon broke down the paradise and its palace, considering the late medieval world of romance and luxury a wicked delusion.

> *Their groves he fell'd; their gardens did deface;*
> *Their arbours spoil; their cabinets suppress;*
> *Their banquet-houses burn; their buildings raze;*
> *And, of the fairest late, now made the foulest place.*

This wanton destruction, or destruction of wantonness, was a cruel commentary on what the Elizabethans held against Portugal and Spain in their conquests in the New World. They had destroyed a natural paradise over there. Guyon's worst encounter was with two knights, Pyrochles, or Portugal, and Cymochles, or Spain, directed by Archimago, the Supreme Magus or Pontiff. King Arthur himself rescued Guyon from his terrible combat with these two Paynims, or Pagans, who wanted to despoil him of his gold. Although wounded with his blood flowing as red as the Rose of Lancaster, Arthur was victorious in honour of the Faerie Queene, whose ancestor Elfin 'all India obey'd, and all that men America now call'. The English magus John Dee had already given Queen Elizabeth a map of the Americas, claiming that King Arthur had colonised it; later, the Lord Madoc of Wales, another of the royal ancestors, was said to have reached Florida. On other occasions in the adventures, Arthur was attacked by poisoned arrows, such as the Indians used, and he avoided the foul evil 'that rots the marrow, and consumes the brain', the new strain of syphilis in Europe. So Virginia, or the land of the Faerie Queene, was saved. In his dedication to Elizabeth, Spenser already referred to her as Queene of Virginia as well as France and Ireland.

In a chronicle of the kings of Britain, Spenser exhorted his countrymen to take up the cause of empire for their Gloriana, as the ancient Britons had done for Arthur – and as later Englishmen would do in the name of Queen Victoria. In particular, he wanted them to espouse the cause and dream of Raleigh. He ended a long list of the renowned rivers of the world with the newly found Orinoco, where the warlike Amazons were held to live:

> *Joy on those warlike women, which so long*
> *Can from all men so rich a kingdom hold!*
> *And shame on you, O men, which boast your strong*
> *And violent hearts, in thoughts less hard and bold,*
> *Yet quail in conquest of that land of gold!*
> *But this to you, O Britons, most pertains,*
> *To whom the right hereof itself hath sold;*
> *The which, for sparing little cost or pains,*
> *Lose so immortal glory, and so endless gains.*

So with the discovery of a New World of Nature, apparently inviting its own destruction, the quest for the Grail would be translated to the search for glory, gold and imperial rule across the Atlantic and Pacific oceans.

Chapter Thirteen

The Grail Across the Oceans

The world was all before them, where to choose
Their place of rest, and Providence their guide:
They hand in hand with wand'ring steps and slow,
Through Eden took their solitary way.

John Milton, *Paradise Lost* (Adam and Eve)

Nothing is proven about the discovery of the Americas by the Egyptians, the Phoenicians or the Greeks. To admit that pyramids were built in different continents separated by the Atlantic is not to say that they knew one another. Recent discoveries of cocaine and tobacco in Egyptian mummies only infer the later loss of ancient narcotic plants used at the time of the pharaohs, who were known to achieve ecstasy by dropping lotus in their wine, as well as trying opium and hemp. Platonic accounts of Atlantis have no credible geography. Only the blessed voyage of Saint Brendan, given the far sea crossings of the Irish evangelical monks after the seventh century, has some shreds and patches of plausibility.

In the *Navigatio*, a Latin work written in the early tenth century, Brendan was described as spending seven years on a search for a paradise over the western ocean. The voyage was considered a part of the Matter of Britain and was translated into most of the European languages, including Provençal. This Celtic *Odyssey* was begun by a monk named Barinthus, who told Brendan of a huge land towards the sunset that contained the early Eden. Sailing away, Brendan and his companions passed a Paradise of Birds who told him that they were spirits in disguise, neither angels nor devils as in the legends of Dante and Wolfram von Eschenbach. Later, Brendan reached a Land of Promise; under an autumn sun, its rich fields and fruits fed the Irish monks for forty days as they progressed on foot. Then a Shining One met them to say that God had kept them on their quest for the seven years only to reveal to them the mysteries of the immense ocean; but now that Brendan had reached the frontiers of paradise, his search was over. Like many a Grail knight, he could not achieve his quest. So he returned with his fellows and sailed home.

This Atlantic voyage, recorded before the Vikings actually reached North America, had its believers. Even the great Arab geographer and historian of the twelfth century, al-Idrisi, called the land mass to the west of Iceland 'Ireland-the-Great'. The very name 'Brasil', which figures on medieval Venetian maps before the Portuguese reached it, may well derive from Brendan's voyage and the Irish *breas-ail*, or 'blessed'. In another fable, the *Voyage of Bran*, an adventurer named Máeldúin visited twenty-nine western islands larger than Ireland, with many more to go. And Richard Hakluyt, wanting to base Elizabethan claims to Virginia on history, claimed that America was reached not only by Hanno from Carthage, but by Britons 'long before Columbus led any Spaniards thither'.

Because of necessary Tudor propaganda, Hakluyt and the astrologer John Dee also emphasised the legend of the voyage across the Atlantic of the Welsh prince Madoc. The mythical large island Frisland, which appeared on the Venetian Zeno map and influenced cartographers for two hundred years, was claimed as a colony of King Arthur. Madoc, however, was said to have reached North America or the West Indies in the twelfth century with a band of national colonists, never to be sighted again. He had existed and became a legend in his own country, the pioneer of Welsh emigrants as far away as Patagonia.

Among the supposed voyagers was Herzog Ernst, the subject of a popular romantic poem in medieval German, its fourth Gotha manuscript probably written by Ulrich von Eschenbach in the late thirteenth century. Ernst quarrelled with his stepfather, the Holy Roman Emperor, and set off with a companion towards Jerusalem, only to be driven across the ocean by storms. Menaced by sea beasts and monsters, passing like Sinbad the Sailor a coagulated sea and a magnetic mountain, he reached the otherworld paradise of the one-eyed Arimaspians, only to steal away in order to defeat the infidels who beset the Holy City. He endowed and prayed at the Church of the Holy Sepulchre as the Teutonic Knights had, before returning to a reconciliation with his Emperor in his native land. Most interesting was the fact that Ernst kept one thing from his Eastern travels: the *weise* or gemstone of the imperial crown, found in a journey along a subterranean river.

Possibly the earliest version of *Herzog Ernst* was an inspiration for the identification in *Parzival* of the Grail as a stone, as was the *Chanson d'Esclarmonde*, in which Charlemagne was the Emperor. That poem declared of the hero Huon and his talisman:

> *A man who keeps such a stone with him*
> *Cannot die in his flesh in a struggle grim,*
> *Nor be brought down in battle or by a charm,*
> *Nor hated by anyone under the sun,*
> *Nor put in prison for any old crime.*

The *weise* of *Herzog Ernst*, brought back from the underground water, was turned into the Philosopher's Stone in Ulrich von Eschenbach's version. The two heroes saw a brilliant stone called a unity, or 'something unique'; there was nothing like it in form or nature anywhere else in the world.

The first European colonists of the New World, who have left their traces at L'Anse aux Meadows in Newfoundland, were the Vikings. They slowly crossed the Atlantic, hopping from Orkney to Iceland, then on to Greenland and Markland, probably Labrador. In the year 1000, Lief the Lucky was held by the sagas to have reached Vinland; grapes do not grow north of Massachusetts. For four hundred years, a small string of Norse colonies held together a trade in furs, timber, resin and salt fish across the northern ocean, before the last settlements died out in Greenland, as Columbus opened the southern route. Their stories inspired the family of the Holy Light, the Sancto Claros or St Clairs, to undertake a mission of imperial evangelism to the New World.

The refugee Knights Templar wanted to create another paradise and Temple of Solomon beyond the reach of papal authority. Their example was the Teutonic Knights, whose crusade from their headquarters at Marienburg against the pagan Slavs had created an empire on the eastern Baltic Sea. With the accession of Margaret to the thrones of Norway and Sweden and the regency of Denmark, a Commonwealth was created that might engender a trading bloc across the high Atlantic. Third in precedence to the Queen was Prince Henry St Clair of Rosslyn, which had housed the fugitive Templars. He was also the Lord of Orkney and the Shetlands, the axis of transatlantic trade. When two Venetian captains were shipwrecked there, Prince Henry pressed them into his service. They were the Zeno brothers, whose explorations with their master produced the definitive map of Greenland for the next two centuries; also much later speculation about the truth of their narrative.

Exhaustive research in a previous work of mine, *The Sword and the Grail*, has proved beyond reasonable doubt that in 1398 Prince Henry St Clair set out with a large expedition of soldiers and monks to establish two colonies in the New World: one at Louisburg in Nova Scotia, where a contemporary primitive Venetian ship's cannon has been found; and another at Newport, Rhode Island. The notorious round tower on a hill there, with its eight arches in the manner of the original Church of the Holy Sepulchre and of Charlemagne's chapel at Aachen, could never have served as the colonial windmill that some claim it to be. It was designed as a church and a lighthouse; the fireplace on its first floor directed through a window towards the bay still demonstrates that use. Its construction is identical to the base of the round tower at Charroux, which used the same Templar models and now has the two doves drinking from the Grail in its crypt.

Prince Henry did not take the Grail to the New World, although the two 'Grails' of the Templars – the containers of the Holy Shroud and the Holy Veil from Constantinople – may have reached the vaults of Rosslyn with the flight of the French knights to Scotland with their treasures and their records. He took across the Atlantic the idea of the Grail as the civilising mission of the European knight to pagan countries, an ideal that would inspire the Portuguese, the Spaniards and even the later British Empire. Although he was killed by an English raid shortly after his return to Orkney, and although his two colonies were lost, he set an example for other European nations to follow. The first were the sailors of Portugal, already probing towards the west. The disappearance of the expeditions of the Cortereal brothers argues for another traceless colony. The signature of 'Miguel' on the Dighton Rock, along with a possible Shield of Portugal, suggests an arrival in Massachusetts well before the Pilgrim Fathers.

Portugal was the first founder of the European empires over the oceans. Yet it lost its independence on a last crusade against the Muslims. It confused imperial designs with a holy mission. Led by Henry the Navigator and his refugee Templars, the Knights of Christ, a scientific, religious, diplomatic and commercial offensive was launched against Africa, Asia and America. Reinforcements with guns were sent to 'Prester John', the Christian Emperor of Ethiopia. Ships reached Persia, India, the spice islands of Indonesia, China and Japan. And Brazil fell into Portuguese hands, although the rest of the Americas went to Spain by papal decree. The greatest of the Pacific discoverers and empire-builders, Vasco da Gama, was equally fortunate in finding his Virgil, Luis Vaz de Camõens, who made da Gama's expedition to India a reflection of the voyage of Aeneas to found Rome and its empire under the direction of the classical gods, and so celebrated for ever the global enterprises of Lisbon, which Ulysses himself was said to have built.

As Geoffrey of Monmouth had claimed Brutus of Troy as the coloniser of ancient Britain, so Camões claimed Lusus, the friend of Bacchus, as the father of Portugal, because he discovered the Elysian Fields off the Douro river and thought them too pleasant to leave. Camões wrote *The Lusiads*, the epic poem of his nation's mythology leading on to its claims to possess new territories around the globe. Ancient history sanctified the Portuguese destiny to spread the true faith all over the world. The Germans and the English were denounced for splitting Christendom, the French for their attacks on the papacy, and Italy for its divisions and vices. Only the people of small Portugal had realised their duty in conquering the lands of the infidel.

> *Death you must face wherever he may lead,*
> *To spread the Word that brings eternal life.*
> *You may be few, but Heaven has decreed*
> *You shall exalt your faith by valiant strife.*

The theme of *The Lusiads* was explicit. This was the story of a regal line which extended the frontiers of faith and empire among the infidels of Africa and Asia. These exploits were greater than those of Ulysses, Aeneas, Alexander and Trajan and their famous victories; even of Orlando in Ariosto's work. The ancient heroes and poets were finished. Another higher courage had appeared. The new King Sebastian would lead his Argonauts and make the whole world tremble more than Julius Caesar or Charlemagne had done. Taking Vasco da Gama's expedition through the wiles of Muslim treachery, instigated by Bacchus, Camões told stories of the heroic past of Portugal, the tragic love of Inês de Castro, and the twelve who went to England to defend the honour of the ladies of that court.

Defying all the plots of the gods and the infidels, da Gama and his men reached the Island of Love of the sea goddess Tethys and her Nereid nymphs, a paradise of the otherworld. Gemstones littered the meadows. The sailors trod on emeralds and rubies. Suspended in the air was a marvel of alchemy, a transparent globe showing the motion of the heavens, started by the Primum Mobile, which started all. The golden belt of the zodiac was there, and the seven planets including the Sun and the Moon revolving round the Earth with its centre in Christian Europe, which was so restless that it left the sufferings of dry land for the dangerous seas. Tethys prophesied what Camões already knew: that the new regions of the East would fall under Portuguese dominion; also Brazil in the West with its forests of red wood.

The epic poem concluded with another sad invocation of King Sebastian. The work was published six years before his catastrophic crusade against Islam in North Africa, where he and his army of twenty-five thousand were wiped out at Alcácer-Kebir in 1578, leaving Philip II of Spain to march unopposed across the frontier and unite the Iberian peninsula and the overseas empires. Camões was already dead in despair; his hopes of a worldwide mission and conquest were spilt on the bloody desert sand. How could he do what he had promised his dead ruler, who had failed to level the fortifications of Morocco? Wanting a sequel to *The Lusiads*, he had decided that he would sing to all mankind of his king, a second Alexander, who would not even envy Achilles his good fortune, because Homer had made him immortal. It was too late.

The Lusiads included elements of the medieval romances, particularly the travels of Mandeville, who had approached paradise from the east. He had also found it a mountain, so high that it almost touched the circle of the moon, but its mossy wall had only one entrance, barred by fire so that no mortal could enter. Camões was also influenced by other medieval legends of a material Grail peak, where precious metals and stones were scattered. For the Spanish conquest of the New World had brought back so much silver and gold that the whole economy of Europe was transformed. Originally, Columbus had set out on a crusade to discover paradise, as the Portuguese had. He made this clear in his entry in his log on Boxing Day 1492, after reaching Hispaniola. He hoped to God that he would find enough gold and spices so that the rulers of Spain would undertake the capture of the Holy Land. He wanted all the profits of his enterprise spent on the conquest of Jerusalem, whatever was done in his New World.

In his letter back to Spain, Columbus described his discovery as another Garden of Eden. Among the nightingales, green fields and metal mines, the natives were naked and innocent. 'They are so guileless and generous with all they possess, that no one would believe it who has not seen it.' They even knelt down at the time of the Ave Maria, as the Spaniards did. At the Azores on his voyage home, he declared that the theologians and the philosophers were correct: the earthly paradise was at the end of the temperate Orient, and he had discovered it. If on his later voyages, Columbus found that the West Indians could retaliate and that some of them were cannibals, this revelation never dispelled his illusion that he had found another natural heaven on earth, with gold mines too. His purpose was to spread the Word of God among the pagans. As his original biographer, Antonio de Herrara, declared, the sending of his mission and the papal donation which gave the Americas, except for Brazil, to Spain was justified. 'Because it was not in prejudice of any man, and because their Catholic Majesties had acquired a just title by temporal power for the promulgation of the Gospel.' Even the fourth – and last – and failed voyage of Columbus to the Americas ended with his Biblical prophecy in a letter to his sovereigns:

The Indies are part of the world, so rich, and He gave them to You as Yours. You gave them to those who

251

*pleased You and He gave You power to do so. The fet-
ters of the Ocean, bound with such strong chains, these
keys He gave to You. And You were obeyed in many
lands and won such honour and fame among
Christians. What more did He do for the people of Israel
when He led them out of Egypt?*

Just as there had been material Grails in the hanging ornamental bowls of the sixth century at the time of King Arthur,
so there were in Mexico and Peru, when the conquistadors
reached those American empires. The colonists were looking
for silver and gold. They found the precious metals in trea-
suries and mines. When Cortés and his four hundred invaders
took the Aztec state, they sent home to the Emperor in
Brussels 'a whole golden sun, a fathom wide, and a whole
silver moon of the same size' and armouries of gilded
weapons, valued at a hundred thousand gulden. The artist
Albrecht Dürer had never seen anything that so filled his
heart with joy. When Pizarro and his small force ransomed
the Inca emperor, the booty was a large room filled with
exquisite works in gold and silver, valued at four and a half
million ducats. Most of these treasures were melted down.
The few that survive argue their quality, as the Celtic bowls
do; flasks as golden gourds, chalices of grinning faces, dishes
on tripods ornamented with scrolls, skulls and beasts. These
works of art had also given offerings of blood and food to the
gods of other cultures.

The New World was seen as a cornucopia of riches, a vast
Grail. Contemporary drawings show semi-naked Indian
women with feathered head-dresses offering platters dripping with pearls to carracks offshore. 'How much the richest
empire in the world,' Oviedo wrote, 'is that of the Indies.'
Dominion and motive were symbolised as a whole by the
frontispiece of a Spanish captain's book of 1599, *Military
Occupation and Description of the Indies*. This showed the
conquistador Vargas Machuca with one hand on the hilt of
his sword and the other on top of a pair of open compasses

measuring the span of the globe. The motto was:

> *By the compass and the sword*
> *More and more and more and more.*

The Pilgrim's Progress?

Puritan colonists to Massachusetts in 1630 did not emigrate in search of riches or tobacco plantations to be worked by slaves, as in Virginia. They wanted to set up a model society. Its example might serve to reform the abuses of Christendom. 'For we must consider,' their governor John Winthrop declared, 'that we shall be as a City upon a Hill, the eyes of all people are upon us.' In America, they would find more of the wisdom, power and truth of God than from their former acquaintance with Him in royal England. Their mission was not dissimilar to that of the Knights of the Round Table, for they sought divine grace at the end of a terrible journey, leaving temptation behind them. As Cotton Mather declared in his work on faith in the New World, 'I write the Wonders of the Christian Religion, flying from the Depravations of Europe, to the American Strand.'

By the irony of history, their search for liberty led to them institute a state of repression. They were cruel to their own dissenters and to the local Indian tribes, almost as bloody as Perceval enforcing the New Law in the place of the Old in the land of Logres. In a sense, the 'errand into the wilderness' of the Pilgrim Fathers was another crusade towards the unknown. Too terrified of the licence they found in the savage country as well as within themselves, they preferred self-restraint to the enlightenment of the free spirit. They had not fulfilled the mission of *The Pilgrim's Progress*, the achievement of the Celestial City, although it was written by their contemporary, John Bunyan. He turned the romances of the Grail into Protestant propaganda, but only in allegory, not in fact. Yet paradoxically, *The Pilgrim's Progress* confirmed the hidden message of the Holy Vessel – the direct path of the individual to the Heavenly City – while condemning the previous Catholic signs and pointers on the path. As Bunyan promised in his apology for his work:

> *This book will make a traveller of thee,*
> *If by its counsels thou wilt ruled be:*
> *It will direct thee to the Holy Land*
> *If thou wilt its directions understand.*

In the author's dream, a ragged pilgrim called Christian set out, as had similarly the Perceval of Chrétien de Troyes, to reach the City of Zion and find salvation for the City of Destruction. In his trials on his way through the Slough of Despond, he was met by three Shining Ones, who forgave him his sins, changed his clothes, and gave him a pass for the celestial gate. His way lay through the Delectable Mountains, before he encountered the fiend Apollyon. Suddenly armoured, he smote the devil with his two-edged sword, as Arthur so often did in the romances.

> *Then there came to him a hand with some of the leaves of the Tree of Life; the which Christian took, and applied to the wounds that he had received in the battle, and was healed immediately. He also sat down in that place to eat bread, and to drink of the bottle that was given to him a little before.*

Surviving the Valley of the Shadow of Death, he passed to its end, where lay the blood, bones, ashes and mangled bodies of former pilgrims. The cause of the horror, in Bunyan's words, was two giants, named Pope and Pagan, whose power and tyranny had put so many men cruelly to death:

> *I have learnt since, that Pagan has been dead many a day; and, as for the other, though he be yet alive, he is, by reason of age, also of the many shrewd brushes that*

> *he met with in his younger days, grown so crazy and stiff*
> *in his joints, that he can now do little more than sit in*
> *his cave's mouth, grinning at pilgrims as they go by,*
> *and biting his nails because he cannot come at them.*

Another jibe at the papacy occurred when Christian and
Faithful passed through Vanity Fair, where there were
British, French, Italian, Spanish and German Rows. Their
chief promotion was of the merchandise of Rome: only
England and some other nations took a dislike to that. There
pilgrims were killed, because they only wanted to buy the
truth. Christian's companion Faithful died rather as Christ
had, before being carried up to heaven.

> *They therefore brought him out, to do with him accord-*
> *ing to their law: and first they scourged him, then they*
> *buffeted him, then they lanced his flesh with knives;*
> *after that they stoned him with stones, then pricked him*
> *with their swords, and, last of all, they burned him to*
> *ashes at the stake. Thus came Faithful to his end.*

Christian carried on, now accompanied by Hopeful.
Escaping from Doubting Castle kept by Giant Despair, they
reached their goal. At the entrance, they were informed by
two more Shining Ones of what they would achieve at the
end of their quest.

> *There is the Mount Zion, the heavenly Jerusalem, the*
> *innumerable company of angels, and the spirits of just*
> *men made perfect. You are going now to the Paradise of*
> *God, wherein you shall see the Tree of Life, and eat of*
> *the never-fading fruits thereof . . .*

The pilgrims would receive comfort for their toil and joy for
their sorrow. 'You must reap what you have sown, even the
fruit of all your prayers, and tears, and sufferings for the king
by the way.' And in the Celestial City, they would enjoy

perpetual visions of the Holy One. 'For there you shall see Him as He is.'

This was an exact description of the discovery of the Grail. Each knight was rewarded for his trials on his journey by the vision of the grace of God, according to what he had done to reach it. Only the few, such as Perceval or Galahad, would see 'Him as He is'. No Catholic Church stood between the pilgrim or the knight and his search for the divine. It was a personal path towards salvation, which meant abandoning city, home and family. Bunyan mocked any institution that stood between the individual and his pursuit of heaven. The flight there of a Christian lay through his own deeds and sufferings.

Far more subtle than Bunyan, with his Puritan allegories, John Milton long searched for an epic subject worthy of his greater genius. While travelling to Rome as a young man, he met a flatterer called Salzilli, who ranked him above Homer, Virgil and Tasso. Meaning to rival those heroic and epic poets, Milton wrote in a Latin poem, *Manso*, of his aspirations 'if ever I recall in song our native kings, and Arthur waging war even beneath the earth, or if ever I proclaim the great spirit of the heroes of the Round Table . . .' Returning to England on the eve of the Civil War, he began his *Arthuriad*, but he soon suspended the attempt in order to finish his superb elegy *Lycidas*. To his friend Diodati, he declared that he would still write of 'Igraine pregnant with Arthur by a fatal treachery, of the counterfeit face and arms of Gorlöis, Merlin's wizardry'.

Milton abandoned the project when he began collecting materials for a prose *History of Britain*, which he would never complete. He even doubted the authenticity of Arthur and sneered at the monks and Welsh historians who had believed songs and romances about the British king rather than the truth. 'He who can accept of legends for good story may quickly swell a volume with trash.' His reading for these projects went into his stark and ironic *Samson Agonistes*, when his growing blindness was clarifying his inner vision.

And the quest for the Grail was transmuted in *Paradise Lost* into the pride of Satan fallen from heaven for daring to challenge God rather than seek his grace. No longer for Milton's muse:

> *Wars, hitherto the only argument*
> *Heroic deem'd; chief mastery to dissect,*
> *With long and tedious havoc, fabled knights,*
> *In battles feign'd; the better fortitude*
> *Of patience and heroic martyrdom*
> *Unsung; or to describe races and games,*
> *Or tilting furniture, emblazon'd shields,*
> *Impresses quaint, caparisons and steeds,*
> *Bases and tinsel trappings, gorgeous knights*
> *At joust and tournament; then marshall'd feast*
> *Served up in hall with sewers and seneschals;*
> *The skill of artifice or office mean,*
> *Not that which justly gives heroic name*
> *To person or to poem.*

Because of the Puritan success in the Civil War, Milton even turned against the pilgrims of the Middle Ages, searching for their Heavenly City. They lived in a Paradise of Fools, a Limbo of Vanities, all the hermits and the white, black and grey friars:

> *Here Pilgrims roam, that stray'd so far to seek*
> *In Golgotha Him dead, who lives in Heav'n;*
> *And they who to be sure of Paradise*
> *Dying put on the weeds of Dominic,*
> *Or in Franciscan think to pass disguis'd . . .*
> *Cowls, Hoods and Habits with their wearers toss'd*
> *And flutter'd into Rags, then Relics, Beads,*
> *Indulgences, Dispenses, Pardons, Bulls,*
> *The sport of winds . . .*

For Milton, the quest for the Grail was both individual and interior. Turning to his own soul, by his own acts, the pilgrim should travel towards the divine. The public performances of the past, the ritual journeys to Jerusalem, Rome, Vézelay and Compostela, these were the pageants of the past. Now spiritual analysis should provide the clues to the ultimate experience of God. Public shows of faith were worth little. The rigorous examination of one's blind self might point the prickly path forward from one's pride and disobedience to divine will. This was a reformed faith, but also the dawn of the Age of Reason, when pilgrimages and legends of Arthur and the Grail would be discounted. Few would take the way forward of a Milton or a Bunyan, who sought the truth of the Word of God in verses or parables. As Bunyan declared in his Apology to *The Pilgrim's Progress*:

> Were not God's laws,
> His Gospel laws, in olden time held forth
> By types, shadows, and metaphors? Yet loth
> Will any sober man be to find fault
> With them, lest he be found for to assault
> The highest wisdom. No, he rather stoops,
> And seeks to find out by what pins and loops,
> By calves and sheep, by heifer and by rams,
> By birds and herbs, and by the blood of lambs,
> God speaketh to him; and happy is he
> That finds the light and grace that in them be.

Chapter Fourteen

Destruction and Revival

> I thought ten thousand swords must have leaped from their
> scabbards to avenge even a look that threatened her with
> insult. But the age of chivalry is gone. That of sophisters,
> economists, and calculators, has succeeded; and the glory
> of England is extinguished for ever.

> Edmund Burke, *Reflections on the Revolution in France*
> (on the fall of Marie Antoinette)

The building of Pandaemonium, the high Capital of Satan,
was the perversion of the Grail. In *Paradise Lost*, the fallen
angels no longer sought the grace of God; they mined, forged
and moulded base metals in the smithies of hell. Unlike the
alchemists, who sought materially and spiritually to trans-
mute lead into gold, Milton's devils debased the Holy Spirit
into minerals.

> *Mammon led them on,*
> *Mammon, the least erected Spirit that fell*
> *From Heaven, for even in Heaven his looks and thoughts*
> *Were always downward bent, admiring more*
> *The riches of Heaven's pavement, trodden gold,*
> *Than aught divine or holy else enjoyed*
> *In vision beatific: by him first*
> *Men also and by his suggestion taught,*
> *Ransacked the Centre, and with impious hands*
> *Rifled the bowels of their mother Earth*
> *For treasures better hid.*

The Industrial Revolution, not the age of chivalry, brought Britain to greatness and empire. Pollution was no longer confined only to the capital, as John Evelyn had complained in his *Fumifugium*: 'The City of London resembles the face rather of Mount Ætna, the Court of Vulcan, Stromboli, or the Suburbs of Hell rather than an Assembly of Rational Creatures.' Swathes of the peaks, saddles and valleys of the north of England were reduced in the eyes of their visitors to scenes that Dante had viewed in his 'Inferno'. The Swan of Lichfield, the poet Anna Seward, lamented that her local Eden was turned from a green idyll into a black hell:

> *O, violated COLEBROOK! . . . Their pondr' ous engines*
> *   clang*
> *Through thy coy dales; while red the countless fires*
> *With umber' d flames, bicker on all thy hills,*
> *Darken' ning the summer' s sun with columns large*
> *Of thick, sulphureous smoke, which spread, like palls*
> *That screen the dead, upon the sylvan robe*
> *Of thy aspiring rocks; pollute thy gales,*
> *And stain thy glassy waters.*

To travellers, this damaged region was also the forge of a new economy. The full purse or the new job was the goal, no longer the search for the divine or the riches of nature. Riding from Birmingham to Wolverhampton, a distance of thirteen miles, John Britton found vats of molten metal rather than cornucopias.

> *The country was curious and amusing; though not very pleasing to eyes, ears, or taste; for part of it seemed a sort of pandaemonium on earth – a region of smoke and fire filling the whole area between earth and heaven; amongst which certain figures of human shape – if shape they had – were seen occasionally to glide from one cauldron of curling flame to another . . . The surface of the earth is covered and loaded with its own entrails,*

*which afford employment and livelihood for thousands
of the human race.*

The same impression was given to the engineer James
Nasmyth, who 'lingered among the blast furnaces, seeing the
flood of molten iron run out from time to time . . . The workmen within seemed to be running about amidst the flames or
in a pandaemonium; while around and outside the horizon
was a glowing belt of fire, making even the stars look pale
and feeble.'

In the works of Joseph Wright of Derby, the best of the
industrial painters of the age, we can see the transformation
of a concept of a holy vessel of birth and regeneration,
bounty and spirit, into a crucible of gain. In his *The
Blacksmith's Shop* of 1771, the figures of the group bend
over a fiery bucket, while the smith plunges his ladle into the
molten iron, and shadows all around menace their endeavours. Men stoop over the entrance to *An Iron Forge*, as if following the inscription over Dante's Inferno: 'Abandon Hope
All Ye That Enter Here'. Grouped as in a Holy Family, children watch in wonder as a scientific experiment suffocates a
bird in an air pump.

Certainly the mechanical horrors of the time inspired John
Martin's apocalyptic paintings, particularly *The End of the
World*, later entitled *The Great Day of His Wrath*. As his son
wrote of his father's journey through the Black Country by
night, 'The glow of the furnaces, the red blaze of light,
together with the liquid fire, seemed to his mind truly sublime and awful. He could not imagine anything more terrible
even in the regions of everlasting punishment.' And so
Martin turned to the Book of Revelations as the Gnostics and
Dürer had, to imprint his vision with the opening of the sixth
seal of prophecy, when there was an earthquake and the sun
became as black as sackcloth and the moon as red as blood:

*And the kings of the earth, and the princes, and the chief
captains, and the rich, and the strong, and every bondman*

*and freeman, hid themselves in the caves and in the rocks
of the mountains . . .*

*For the great Day of their Wrath is come, and who is
able to stand?*

A romantic reaction from the Age of Reason and profit
would lead to a revival of the cult of the Grail. At the end of
the eighteenth century, the Economic Man of Adam Smith
seemed to have extinguished any champion of the Round
Table. As the poet Samuel Taylor Coleridge declared in his
despair: 'In a few years we shall either be governed by an
aristocracy, or, what is still more likely, by a contemptible
democratical oligarchy of glib economists, compared to
which the worst form of aristocracy would be a blessing.'

The restoration of the Grail would be achieved in spite of
Economic Man through a new interest in medieval studies;
also through Scots and German Romanticism, and the coronation of a nostalgic British king, although his nature was rather
far from Arthur's. Macpherson's three epics, translated from
fictional Gaelic poetry in *Ossian*, were widely popular; and
before his suicide Chesterton fabricated verses from earlier
times. A vogue was beginning again for bardic poems and
gothic romances, as a refuge from the new age of machines.
Sir Walter Scott became its advocate and its apologist across
the Western world, but its ironic gravedigger was Thomas
Love Peacock, in his novel *The Misfortunes of Elphin*. If the
Lemuel Gulliver of Swift and Defoe's ultimate survivor
Robinson Crusoe had put to rest any transcendental notions
such as finding divine cups or extracting sunbeams from
cucumbers, Prince Elphin and the bard Taliesin in Peacock's
mocking romance put paid to any Arthurian visions.

The first of many poems in *The Misfortunes of Elphin* was
called 'The Circling of the Mead Horns' and was taken from
an ancient Welsh poem about a Prince Owain, feasting after
his victory. For Peacock, the ceremony was farce, merely a
prelude to the Lord Seithenyn drinking everybody under the
table from his personal golden goblet, while the bard sang:

Fill the blue horn, the blue buffalo horn:
Natural is mead in the buffalo horn:
As the cuckoo in spring, as the lark in the morn,
So natural is mead in the buffalo horn.

Although deriding the legends, Peacock had read his Welsh history. He stated that the religion of King Arthur's time was Christianity grafted on to Druidism. He knew of the antagonism of the Celtic clergy to Rome, for they had been converted from Ireland with its Greek rite. His hero Taliesin 'had been with the cherubim at the fall of Lucifer, in Paradise at the fall of man, and with Alexander at the fall of Babylon', the matter of many of the medieval romances. But for Peacock, 'names are changed more readily than doctrines, and doctrines more readily than ceremonies'.

He was hardly a historian of King Arthur, whom Taliesin went to meet at Caerleon. On the way, the magic minstrel was made drunk again by Seithenyn with the memorable phrase about his drinking cup: 'Horn is well; silver is better; gold is best.' At Arthur's court, however, the Druids were still in charge of the ancient feast called Yule:

The Druids, at this festival, made, in a capacious
cauldron, a mystical brewage of carefully-selected
ingredients, full of occult virtues, which they kept from
the profane, and which was typical of the new year and
of the transmigration of the soul. The profane, in hum-
ble imitation, brewed a bowl of spiced ale, or wine,
throwing therein roasted crabs; the hissing of which, as
they plunged, piping hot, into the liquor, was heard with
much unction at midwinter, as typical of the conjunct
benignant influences of fire and strong drink. The
Saxons called this the Wassail-bowl . . . King Arthur
kept his Christmas so merrily, that the memory of it
passed into a proverb: 'As merry as Christmas in
Caerleon.'

So Peacock reduced the quest for the Grail into a Nordic saturnalia. Avallon, the island of apples afterwards called Glastonbury, was made into a castle of the church militant under King Melvas, the Scourge of the Pelagians, the original British heretics. He had stolen Arthur's wife, but was persuaded to restore the Queen without a fight. And so the novel ended in a bardic contest rather than a battle or a joust, with Merlin chanting about his apple trees at Avallon, while Taliesin sang a lay derived from the recent *Mabinogion*, the translations of ancient Welsh literature by Lady Charlotte Guest. This poem, 'The Cauldron of Ceridwen', was named after one of the six legendary Welsh Grails. Taliesin asserted that it had given birth to him, after his mother had made an extraordinary brew:

> She placed the gifted plants to steep
> Within the magic cauldron deep,
> Where they a year and day must boil,
> 'Till three drops crown the matron's toil.

These were not the three drops of Holy Blood on the Spear of Vengeance, which could heal and regenerate. But they did enable the birth of Taliesin, by his account, in place of his mother's misshapen child. And he was protected from all harm by Ceridwen, which also gave him the gifts of prophecy:

> She has for me Time's veil withdrawn:
> The images of things long gone,
> The shadows of the coming days,
> Are present to my visioned gaze.

The truth of Taliesin's song about his coming from the magic cauldron of Wales was not authenticated by Peacock, who washed his hands of his own and ancient inventions. Certainly, Taliesin 'told this story to his contemporaries, and none of them contradicted it. It may, therefore, be presumed that they believed it; as any one who pleases is most heartily welcome to do now.' There were quite a few who now did so.

The Revival of the Grail

The Protestant Grail was resurrected by an enigmatic theologian in Tübingen, Johann Valentin Andreae, the probable author of three strange works published in the second decade of the seventeenth century. The first was the *Fama Fraternitatis . . ., The Declaration of the Worthy Order of the Rosy Cross*; the second was the *Confessio Fraternitatis*; and the third, written in German and not Latin, was *Die Chymische Hochzeit . . ., The Chemical Wedding of Christian Rosenkreuz*. Borrowing from *Parzival*, Paracelsus, the German mystics and alchemists, the visions of Meister Eckhart and *De Occulta Philosophia* by Heinrich Cornelius Agrippa, the author of these three works claimed that a secret Order of the Rosy Cross had been founded in the fourteenth century by Christian Rosenkreuz, who had acquired Gnostic wisdom in the Far East. The brothers of the order had healing powers and possessed the Philosopher's Stone and the elixir of life. Christian had also visited a Grail Castle of wonder, where he had witnessed many of the scenes of *Parzival* in an occult setting. The symbolism of the Rosy Cross, the associations of the cult of the Virgin Mary and the Magdalene as the Rose with those of the Passion of Christ restored the esoteric beliefs of the Knights Templar and the Teutonic Knights. These guardians of the Grail, as Wolfram von Eschenbach had called them, were now revived.

The Teutonic Knights were still in existence. In 1683 they provided a whole regiment to defend Vienna against Muslim assault, and they resisted a later attack on Hungary. Yet they were soon reduced to a core of twenty nobles, who were officers in the German army; these men would play important roles in the Napoleonic and First World Wars. In the eighteenth century, however, Charles Gotthelf, Baron von Hund and Alten-grotkare, used his Jacobite connections to resurrect the German Order of the Knights Templar. He claimed that he was anointed in Paris by the Young Pretender, Prince Charles Edward Stuart, who was the Sovereign Grand Master of the original refugee order in Scotland.

By the time of his death, Baron von Hund had recruited twelve reigning German princes to replace the twelve Peers of Charlemagne in his new order. These included the Landgraf of Hesse-Darmstadt, the Markgraf of Brandenburg, the Duke of Brunswick and his three sons. One of these revived Templars, Friedrich Ludwig Werner, produced a poem on the old military order in Cyprus, which defined another version of the Grail:

> *That which was sought, but never found,*
> *But kept hidden from the world,*
> *So that the world did not burn its fingers . . .*
> *The key that opens the future's iron door,*
> *And all the hidden caverns of the past,*
> *And nature's most occult laboratory.*

The Scots Baron von Hund was Alexander Deuchar, who became the Grand Master in 1810 of the *Scotia Militia Templi*. He tried to pass on his position thirteen years later to Sir Walter Scott, the champion of the old traditions across Europe; but Scott turned him down. The poet and novelist, however, had not rejected in their decline the Sancto Claro or St Clair family of Rosslyn, who had been so close to the original Templars and were the guardians of their archives and relics as well as of the sacred medieval treasures of Scotland. Scott wrote of the twenty St Clair knights buried in full armour in the vaults of Rosslyn Chapel, as if they were everlasting Knights of the Grail, on sentry duty over the mysteries entrusted to their keeping. Ruined by loyalty to the Stuart cause and by secret Catholicism, Sir William St Clair, the last of the male bloodline that had been unbroken for seven hundred years, was praised by Scott as the end of a breed, made for war and archery, as had been the giant and 'famous founder of the Douglas race'; he had died on a Spanish crusade, carrying the Heart of Bruce towards Jerusalem with that other William de St Clair of the Templar Grail tombstone at Rosslyn – my first significant discovery.

Reading an old account of the rites and secrets of the Rosicrucians led me to my second crucial finding, the most ancient Grail symbol in England, even more illuminating than the relief in the crypt of the tower at Charroux. The cult of the Black Virgin in Europe reached England in the shape of seven black baptismal fonts. The most Gnostic of these is in Winchester Cathedral. Carved about 1150 from black limestone at Tournai in Flanders, the font dated from the middle period of the kingdom of Jerusalem. After the Second Crusade, Thierry of Alsace, Count of Flanders, had created the Chapel of the Holy Blood at Bruges, not too far from Tournai, while his son and successor Philip had become the last patron of Chrétien de Troyes; he claimed that his first Grail romance, *Perceval*, derived from a book given to him by Count Philip, who was also a crusader and a scholar of Eastern thought. The Winchester font was created from the mysticism of the Levant and the cult of the Holy Blood, which so influenced the maker of the Grail in literature in that same period in Flanders.

On two sides of the black cube was carved the life of Saint Nicholas. One scene of the blessed man reviving three drowned children also depicted the first North Sea boat with a rudder. The other two façades set out pairs of doves, preening under their wings or picking at a bunch of grapes; also a salamander, emblematic of fire, recalling in the Rosicrucian interpretation a passage from Saint Matthew's Gospel: 'He shall baptise you with the Holy Ghost and with fire.' But my revelation was the sight of the reliefs on two of the four corners of the top of the baptismal vessel. On each, as at Charroux, twin doves could be seen drinking from a vase, but now a fiery ragged crucifix rose out of this Grail, with a sun boss in the middle of the flames. These were like the visions of the pure Arthurian knights in the Castle of the Fisher King. The dark colour of the font recalled the sacred meteorite in the Ka'aba at Mecca, while both the dove and the black stone were the Grail symbols in *Parzival*. This mystic cross of fire resembled the flames of the Holy Spirit which descended on the disciples at Pentecost, the feast when the Grail occasionally appeared at Camelot in the romances.

Also recognised by the Rosicrucians for its cosmic significance was the Round Table of King Arthur, which is still mounted on the wall of the Great Hall of Winchester Castle. This late-medieval painted circle was influenced by alchemy and the zodiac, as were many of the porticos of creation over the entrances to French gothic cathedrals. It was divided into twelve green and twelve white sections, with two for the Siege Perilous. King Arthur was shown ruling from his throne over the mystic red rose – its centre the five petals of the white rose of the Virgin Mary containing a yellow sun. The black font with its fiery cross and the Round Table with its central red and white roses were for the Rosicrucians two confirmations of their quests for the Philosopher's Stone, the elixir of life, the perpetual lamp, and the talisman of healing. They interpreted the Arthurian circle as the place where the twenty-six 'Mystic Guards of the Holy Grail' might sit, backed by the Saints in a fusion of the natural and the supernatural, of alchemy, legend and religion in a common search for the universal.

Rather as the original Templars had been destroyed as a dangerous secret society within the body politic, so the Rosicrucians, the revived Templar orders and other Masonic bodies were considered to be threats to the nation state across most of Europe after the French Revolution. In the early nineteenth century, the French followed the Germans by discovering a charter, said to date from 1324, in which a Jean-Mark Larmenius had been appointed as the successor to the last Grand Master of the Knights Templar, Jacques de Molay, before de Molay's execution. The refugee Templars in Scotland were condemned as deserters, and the rift between the Templars of France and Scotland has continued. The sword of de Molay was also thought to have been rediscovered and became a potent symbol. Those against Freemasonry in France saw in the revival of the Templars a long conspiracy that ran forward from the heretic Gnostics through the Essenes, the Assassins, the Cathars, the Templars and the Masons to modern times, an enduring subversion against pope and king, a form of revolutionary anarchism.

Various orders of the Rosy Cross were also developed in France, blending Cabbalistic and Hermetic symbolism with mystic references to the Resurrection of the Saviour and His Mother. There were Rosicrucian Societies in Scotland and in England, which culminated in the Hermetic Order of the Golden Dawn. With a Chief Adept taken from the Sufis and the Cathar *perfecti*, the aspirants were given an address that mixed the processes of alchemy with the Passion:

> *Buried with that light in a mystical death, rising again in a mystical resurrection, cleansed and purified through Him our Master, O Brother of the Cross and the Rose. Like Him, O Adepts of all ages, have ye toiled. Like Him have ye suffered tribulation, Poverty, torture and death have ye passed through. They have been but the purification of Gold.*
>
> *In the alembic of thine heart, through the athanor of affliction, seek thou the true stone of the Wise.*

The true stone of the wise was historically the Philosopher's Stone and the German romantic Grail of bounty and healing. In one of his novels, *The Talisman*, Sir Walter Scott became the heir of Wolfram von Eschenbach. With the scene set in Syria during the Third Crusade, the magic stone was used by Saladin to cure his wounded opponent King Richard the Lionheart, before he sent it as a wedding present to the Prince Royal of Scotland, who bequeathed it in turn to Sir Simon of the Lee. This gave a provenance to a known healing stone in the shape of a heart, set in a groat and called the Lee Penny. Scott also involved a 'most holy elixir' of life in the cures of the talisman, which was a meteorite 'composed under certain aspects of the heavens, when the Divine Intelligences are most propitious'. Only to be used by a sage and hermit, the stone was also connected with the Templars. For Saladin worked its powers on the wounded traitor Conrade, Marquis of Montserrat, who was then stabbed and killed by the Grand Master of the Templars, the guardians of the Grail.

In *Ivanhoe*, his other medieval romance of that period, Scott showed the same appreciation of the Jews as of the Muslims. His villains as well as his heroes were Christians. At her trial, Rebecca was sentenced to death for her medical powers; also the employment of drugs, amulets and Cabbalistic charms. Ambiguous towards the Templars, Scott made their Grand Master a bigot at Rebecca's trial, condemning her as if she were a second Witch of Endor. Yet her would-be champion was another Templar, Brian de Bois-Guilbert, ordered by his Grand Master to fight against her final champion Ivanhoe. Brian became the victim of his internal conflicts and lost to his foe.

However much Scott appreciated the medieval romances of knighthood, he knew their time was long gone. Although he had individually resurrected the feudal, he did not expect it still to rule. Even his paragon, Richard I, appeared out of date in the thirteenth century. 'In the lion-hearted king,' *Ivanhoe* declared, 'the brilliant, but useless character, of a knight of romance, was in a great measure realised and revived; and the personal glory which he acquired by his own deeds of arms, was far more dear to his excited imagination; than that which a course of policy and wisdom would have spread around his government.' And Scott knew the power of nationalism. When his native Templar answered the question of why he was warring on a Christian king at the Battle of Halidon Hill, the reply was: 'I was a Scotsman ere I was a Templar, sworn to my country ere I knew my Order.'

That insight was used by Scott in his greatest political achievement, the reconciliation of the Scottish nationalism of his *Rob Roy* and *Waverley* with the fact of the Union with mercantile England. 'Seriously,' he once wrote to a friend, 'I am very glad I did not live in 1745 for though as a lawyer I could not have pleaded Charles's right and as a clergy man I could not have prayed for him yet as a scholar I would I am sure against the conviction of my better reason have fought for him even to the bottom of the gallows.'

The choice he made was to glorify King George IV's visit to Scotland. During his coronation, the epicene monarch had wanted a show more sumptuous than a Grail procession, with bands of herbswomen scattering rose petals from baskets before His Royal Majesty and his courtiers, dressed in ancient magnificence. Foreigners were, in Scott's words, 'utterly astonished and delighted to see the revival of feudal dresses and feudal grandeur when the occasion demanded it, and that in a degree of splendour which, they averred, they had never seen paralleled in Europe.'

When the British King came north of the border, Scott organised the preparations. The Highland clans turned out in kilts and eagle feathers, and two hundred thousand strangers crowded the streets of Edinburgh. In the novelist Thackeray's opinion in his *Four Georges*, Sir Walter 'was the king's Scottish champion, rallied all Scotland to him, made loyalty the fashion'. So popular were his lyrics and novels that he could sway his countrymen through the heart, if not the head. As Macaulay observed so tartly: 'History commenced among the modern nations in Europe in romance.' What the bards and the troubadours had done for medieval Europe, Scott would do for the nineteenth century, restoring legend and emotion to an Industrial Revolution.

As a child and a young man, Scott was influenced by German romantic literature. He translated *Goetz von Berlichingen*, Goethe's drama about a stern robber-knight, before he became a correspondent of the German poet, who, like most of his nation, was an admirer of *Ivanhoe*. 'Walter

Scott is a great genius, who does not have an equal,' Goethe declared to a friend. 'He gives me much to think about, and I discover in him a wholly new art, which has its own laws.' *Ivanhoe* was even turned into a mediocre opera, *Templer und Juedin*, by Heinrich Marschner, but he was no Wagner to match the genius in *Parzival* with his own and give the Grail a more celestial music.

As a reviewer, Scott mocked other romantic writers, particularly the English Gothic school of Mrs Radcliffe and Teutonic sentimental offerings. If *Waverley* had been a German romance, his readers might have expected 'a secret and mysterious association of Rosicrucian and Illuminati, with all their properties of black cowls, caverns, daggers, electrical machines, trap-doors, and dark-lanterns.' Goethe had actually started a poem on the themes of the Rosicrucians, only to abandon it when they quarrelled with the Illuminati in Bavaria. But Scott himself fell into his own trap-door in a weary novel at the end of his life, *Anne of Geierstein*, which had its orders of the Rosy Cross and the Illuminati with their rituals and dark habits. Anne's father conducted a Secret Tribunal as if it were a supernatural agency, while her grandfather was an alchemist and astrologer. Count Frankenstein would have envied their elaborate research into the nature of mysticism and man.

Scott had himself been influenced by the bardic writers of Italy and Spain, Dante, Tasso, Ariosto and Cervantes. Explaining the plot of *The Heart of Mid-Lothian*, he wrote that he had followed the digressive *Orlando Furioso*, interleaving the adventures of his people until they met one another again: it was a better method than dropping stitches. He took over characters, acknowledging that his solitary in *The Talisman* was modelled on Tasso's Peter the Hermit. And yet only in his earlier poetry had he taken up the Arthurian Matter of Britain.

Trying to rival Byron's *Childe Harold*, Scott used a modern soldier Arthur to tell stories of a medieval border knight, Sir Roland, and of King Arthur, both of whom were taken to an enchanted castle of Saint John, full of maidens. The king was seduced for a summer in order to make the sorceress Guendolen pregnant. And his escape rivalled the emblem on the Winchester font, as it was through a cup of liquid fire, offered to him by necromancy rather than the Holy Spirit. Guendolen held up a 'draught which Genii love'. She drank it herself:

> *And strange unwonted lustres fly*
> *From her flush'd cheek and sparkling eye.*
>
> *The courteous Monarch bent him low,*
> *And, stooping down from saddlebow,*
> *Lifted the cup, in act to drink,*
> *A drop escaped the goblet's brink –*
> *Intense as liquid fire from hell,*
> *Upon the charger's neck it fell.*
> *Screaming with agony and fright,*
> *He bolted twenty feet upright –*
> *– The peasant still can show the dint,*
> *Where his hoofs lighted on the flint. –*
> *From Arthur's hand the goblet flew,*
> *Scattering a shower of fiery dew,*
> *That burn'd and blighted where it fell!*

This goblet of hellfire was more a Cauldron of Death than a Cup of Life, worse than the golden cup held up by Excess, which Guyon broke to pieces in *The Faerie Queene*. Although Scott continued the traditional story of Arthur, ending in the disaster at Camlann, he was reducing the Grail quest to Nordic folklore and magic tales. The Protestant in him rebelled from the idea of a vessel of divine grace, which was to him more of a superstition than a heavenly vision. His Knights of the Round Table fought their battles and endured their trials for the love of Guendolen's daughter Gyneth and her wealth, not for any revelation of God.

The supreme visionary of this time, William Blake, wrote

a long poem entitled *Milton*, using that poet as his guide on a spiritual journey, as Dante had used Virgil. The Pandaemonium built by devils and machines as Satan's capital had become actual in the Black Country of Blake's green and pleasant homeland, where he wanted to build a new Jerusalem. And yet he, as his predecessor, still strove for a Paradise regained. His Grail, as the anthem declared in the preface of *Milton*, was still the spiritual, the Face of God, the original goal of the pilgrims and the Knights of the Round Table.

> *And did the Countenance Divine*
> *Shine forth upon our clouded hills?*
> *And was Jerusalem builded here*
> *Among these dark Satanic Mills?*
>
> *Bring me my Bow of burning gold;*
> *Bring me my Arrows of desire;*
> *Bring me my Spear; O clouds unfold!*
> *Bring me my Chariot of fire!*
>
> *I will not cease from Mental Fight*
> *Nor shall my Sword sleep in my hand . . .*

Chapter Fifteen

The Singing Grail

And in the middle stands a shining temple,
More valuable than any left on earth.
Inside it, a sacred, wonder-working vessel,
Is guarded as the holiest of most worth.
It was – so the purest of the pure
Might keep it safe – brought down by angels.
Once every year, a heavenly dove is sure
To fill it with more power in its walls.
Its name? The Grail. And peace and faith and love
On its close band of knights pour from above.

Richard Wagner, *Lohengrin*

Two sacred places in the Alps on the Swiss-German border particularly claimed to possess the Holy Blood: the ancient abbeys of Reichenau and Weingarten, now one of the larger baroque churches in Germany. The relic of the Body of Christ and a piece of the True Cross at Reichenau are said to have been given to Charlemagne by the diplomatic Islamic prefect of Huesca in Spain, after the German Emperor's incursion there. The Abbey Treasury also asserts that its split urn from the Near East and the Christian era is a vessel from Cana, in which water was turned into wine. It does not resemble any Greek *amphora* of the period, nor the simple pots of the miracle, as were shown on Archbishop Maximian's sixth-century ivory throne in Ravenna. Its provenance is given as from an obscure knight of Charlemagne, while the Holy Blood at Weingarten is said to derive from Saint Longinus and his spear. It was rediscovered twice at Mantua, which also contributed a sacred onyx vessel to Brunswick; there in Italy, indeed, the centurion saint had brought the Blood which was split three ways in Germany after much argument.

The portion at Weingarten derived from a pious Count Baldwin V of Flanders in the eleventh century. Thousands of Bavarians have appeared for hundreds of years at its procession in its precious reliquary. Further, an engraving and a tradition boast of a healing piece of earth soaked with His Blood from Calvary; also fragments of the cup of the Last Supper and the bowl of Joseph of Arimathea at the foot of the Cross. As Weingarten was destroyed in the fifteenth century, these are speculations. Neither the relics there nor those at Reichenau can complete in veracity with those of Charlemagne, most of which are now in Vienna or France, other than those still preserved at Aachen, along with a gold, enamel and amethyst liturgical pitcher in the treasury of Saint Maurice Abbey in Switzerland. The history of the Grail in Germany remains the *Parzival* of Wolfram von Eschenbach; the Marienburg and the deeds of the Teutonic Knights; the castles of Ludwig II and the operas of Wagner. Hitler's exploitation of these written, sung and built legends would be a splendid aberration which would end as a desperate perversion.

Ludwig and Wagner

Wolfram von Eschenbach had designed the story of Lohengrin to be a sequel to *Parzival*. In the last book of his romance, his hero was reunited with his wife and discovered that he had given her twin sons. Surrounded by his Templar Knights of the Grail, he appointed one of his sons, Lohengrin, as his successor to be their king on the Mount of Salvation. As a young man, Lohengrin served the Grail as a true knight, and Wolfram was his prophet. He would arrive in the land of Brabant on a boat drawn by a swan, save the heiress Elsa from false accusation and marry her and have children. But in a contradiction to his father Parzival, who did not ask the question of the maimed Fisher King, Lohengrin would return home to become the Grail King, if Elsa never broke her word and demanded to know his name. She did:

> *And her question broke the spell,*
> *And drove him out unwilling, so shall the story tell.*
> *His friend the swan found him, a small boat its offering.*
> *He sailed away and left his sword, his horn and ring.*

This tale of the Swan Knight was again ascribed to Guiot de Provins, the minstrel, while the master, Chrétien de Troyes, was accused of not setting it down rightly. 'Thus from the land of Provence,' Wolfram insisted, 'the story was brought to Germany.' It would become a prodigal source, as would the other innovations in *Parzival*. The mysterious oriental Grail stone would be retained as the symbol of the Holy Vessel by the poets of the *Wartburgkrieg* – the inspiration for Richard Wagner's opera *Tannhäuser* – and of the full *Lohengrin* and the *Younger Titurel*. Not until the poet Novalis would the Grail be turned from stone to flower, while Wagner would see it as a cornucopia of excess as well as a Christian chalice.

The Grail as the pagan horn of plenty was at its crudest in *Tannhäuser*, which was the weakest of Wagner's operas, not only in his concept of the Sacred Vessel, but in his characterisation of the wandering and satanic minstrel on his pilgrimage to Rome – certainly not as complex as his model Wolfram. In fact, Wagner did say that Tannhäuser was a human being, while Wolfram was a poet. The Grail was said to be on the Hörselberg with Venus, the seductress of the passive Tannhäuser, who declared, 'I boldly approach the fount of delight.' The Grail was thus the sex of the Goddess of Love, the giver of sensual pleasures, and little more, although Wagner joked in the margins of his first draft of the libretto, 'Study the manuscript, otherwise you won't get to heaven.' At the rival Wartburg of the Landgrave Hermann, where the famous Contest of Song was staged, Elisabeth only represented spiritual love, although she saved Tannhäuser from the swords of his jealous rivals. This conflict of the flesh and the spirit turned the Grail into a kind of orgy of sexual perversity, hardly a sacrament.

The tragedy of *Tannhäuser* was its effect on Wagner's patron, King Ludwig II of Bavaria. The Venusberg became his chief inspiration in the erection of his Grail castles. Unlike most fantasists, Ludwig had the resources to make his dreams come true. Even a medieval knight who could read the Arthurian romances did not have his royal wealth or self-indulgence. So Ludwig could have his myths made fact, although the dreadful ostentation and bad taste of the nineteenth century in southern Germany turned these venerations of the fortresses of the Fisher King into gigantic containers for luxury and childishness. They were the results of the romantic effusions of a lonely boyhood. The Bavarian Commission was correct in declaring Ludwig unfit to govern before he finished his last masterwork on the island at the Herrenchiemsee. There, as at Linderhof, he had to have a brute mechanism to lower his golden Grail Table down to the kitchen in order that it might come up with all the fancies of his desires. This iron contraption proved that even industrialisation had forced its way beneath his fairy realm, and Nibelungs of cogs and chains were mining for new riches. If Ludwig's suspicious end by drowning was no repetition of the Lady of the Lake drawing him down like Excalibur under the water, his extravagances still endure, more gilt and replete than William Randolph Hearst's Xanadu or Disneyland in California and outside Paris. Curiously enough, Walt Disney chose Ludwig's castle at Neuschwanstein, the New Stone of the Swan, as his model for the home of the Sleeping Beauty, the princess under the spell of animation.

If Wagner was to ennoble the myths of the Grail in his

Lohengrin and *Parsifal*, Ludwig dressed up the legends so ornately that they ended in a treasury of vulgarity. The room of the Knight of the Swan in his childhood castle of Hohenschwangau, the living room at Neuschwanstein devoted to Lohengrin and the Grail, the golden shell-boat at Linderhof in which the King used to sit, drawn by a swan as was Lohengrin, how wilful and opulent they appear against the actual chapel of the Swan Knights at Ansbach, the home of the Hohenzollern dynasty. That military order was founded in 1440 by the Elector Frederick II of Brandenburg; eleven tombs of the real knights still survive in the rebuilt choir, austere in the style of the Margrave George the Pious, who spread Lutheranism all over the region. Wolfram von Eschenbach himself, the creator of the original *Parzival*, was born ten miles away and was buried at the town named after him. Under the many-coloured church spire and by the old Commandery of the Teutonic Knights, now the Rathaus and the Alte Vogtei Inn, stands a statue to the poet and knight, donated by the Emperor Maximilian II. Four black swans surround its plinth, while Wolfram has his hand on his lyre with its eagle head; also his sword hilt. Dressed in armour, his helmet is crowned by a wreath of laurels. His honour and memory are well preserved in his birthplace, unlike in the gilded dreamlands of the later King of Bavaria.

Ludwig did not approve of Wagner's final conversion to a Christian Grail of redemption in his *Parsifal*, and did not attend its first performance. The hill of steps and terraces opposite the Linderhof palace was crowned by a cupola, under which a white marble Venus took a quiver of arrows from Cupid. Lower down, ranks of urns led to two nymphs pouring their pitchers into an everlasting fountain. To Ludwig, love and giving richly were the dominant symbols of the Wagnerian legends. The Herrenchiemsee with its separate Island of Women also stressed the final chaste reclusion of the King, as if he were a Knight of the Grail. There, in external statues, Venus held up an overflowing vase of plenty, while the huge golden royal bed and table were the luxury of delirium.

Having bankrupted his kingdom, Ludwig with his profligacy now helps to pay for the federal state. His fairy castles draw far more prying visitors than ever the sick in the Middle Ages went to be healed by the Holy Blood and the broken cup of Christ at Weingarten Abbey. Although in his lifetime Ludwig did not appeal to the beggared people of Bavaria, his death has enriched them mightily. For he was a prophet of the imagination of the masses, which coincided with his own. For a modern pilgrimage, the climb up the slope at Neuschwanstein still compares with a struggle up a Mount of Salvation. As Ludwig wrote to Wagner, 'The place is one of the most lovely that can be dreamed of. It is sacred and inaccessible.' Yet once the lifeless and spectacular paintings of German and Grail myths are reached, nobody can receive any sacred message in such a bedlam of sightseers and babble of tongues. On my visit to the Singer's Hall, I was graced by a ray of afternoon sun, which illuminated only the Grail Princess presenting the Holy Vessel on a green cushion to Parsifal. The bad stage design of the glittering room by Jank was based on the Festive Hall of the Wartburg Castle where the Landgrave Hermann of Thuringia had held a famous contest for the Meistersinger. And this sudden light settling on the Grail there did transform the dull set into a precious moment of theatre.

Wagner had made dramatic the legend of the Grail at the end of his opera *Lohengrin*, after which he wrote no more music for five years other than some notes for the greatest of his German myths, the *Ring*. The villainess in the libretto, Ortrud, invoked unsuccessfully the pagan Nordic gods Wotan and Freya, but the perfect Swan Knight Lohengrin was so transcendent that his image was preferred by Ludwig II in his desire to be king of an otherworld as well as of Bavaria. Wagner himself thought that he had met a real Lohengrin, writing after his first meeting with the glorious young ruler that the encounter was a miracle, 'that precious reward of my genius . . . born for me out of the womb of a queen'. Ludwig replied in kind and with influence: 'Since the power is mine, I will use it to sweeten your life.' His nickname in the composer's circle would be Parsifal, although Wagner's wife Cosima thought that her husband's soul belonged forever to the King, rather than the other way round.

In the opera, indeed, Lohengrin's confrontation with reality led to the final tragedy: his return to his Grail kingdom and the death of Elsa of Brabant. Once his name was known, along with the mundane details of his origins, he had to retreat to the spiritual world whence he had come. While Tannhäuser saw in the Grail and the Venusberg the fulfilment of human love, Lohengrin looked to the Mount of Salvation as his faith and his destiny. In that year of revolutions of 1848, Wagner himself had caught the radical fervour, when the German National Assembly came together in May at Frankfurt. Having finished the score of *Lohengrin*, he declared that 'the fate of the monarchs will depend upon their conduct'. This was the fate of the Knights of the Grail; by their deeds, they attained grace. In the third act of the opera, the King of Brabant and his army were made to shout:

> *A German sword for the German land!*
> *So will the Reich's power take command.*

And Lohengrin returned to pledge his sword to the defence of his Grail kingdom.

> *He who is chosen to stand and serve the Grail*
> *Is given by its grace more than mortal force.*
> *Faced with the power of evil, he'll not fail.*
> *The sight of it destroys death at its source.*

Named and known, Lohengrin had to leave Brabant, which wanted him as its heir. By the magic of art, Wagner found a solution in the swan which had brought the knight there. The white bird was transformed into Elsa's brother Gottfried, now released from his feathered spell to take his place beside the throne. The white dove of Wolfram von Eschenbach flew down to pick up the chain of the golden shell-boat in its beak and draw Lohengrin back to his other-world by the power of the Holy Spirit. Bereft of human love by the will of God, Elsa fell lifeless to the ground.

Certainly in *Lohengrin*, Wagner recognised the mystical thrust of the Grail legend, its strength as a judge between the body and the soul. In his final opera, *Parsifal*, he would see it as the vessel of divine blood and redemption. He translated pagan myth into Christian symbol. The Valhalla of the Nordic gods became the Temple of the Grail, which also represented the treasure of the Nibelungs, while the Ring of authority was transformed into the Spear of Destiny and the Holy Lance. Although Wagner's source was Wolfram's medieval poem, he rejected the Grail as an oriental talisman for the chalice of the Eucharist. Using much of Wolfram's plot and many of his characters, he transcended the action in the search for absolution. The character of the sorceress Kundry was his supreme transformation; he saw her as 'this fabulous and wild Grail-herald'. She had seduced the Fisher King Anfortas, so tainting the divine blood in him, and allowing him to lose the Holy Lance to the evil magician Klingsor, who transformed it into the pagan Spear of Destiny and so gave Anfortas his incurable wound. Yet she appeared in the first expository act of *Parsifal* with an Arabian balsam, which might heal the ever-bleeding sore. While Anfortas despaired with the Knights of the Grail at any cure for himself and the Waste Land of his kingdom, Klingsor created a false bower of bliss, rather modelled on the Garden of Allah, with Flower Maidens to entice any rescuer who might seize the piercing and healing spear from his domain.

The innocent fool and Nordic hero, Parsifal, entered, killing a passing swan with an arrow. He heard from Kundry that his mother had died of grief at his going. This was the beginning of his repentance and his understanding. He asked the wise hermit Gurnemanz what was the Grail, only to hear that there was no saying; yet if he were the chosen one, the knowledge of it would not escape him. The next scene at the Grail castle closely followed Wolfram's *Parzival*. The ailing Anfortas was brought in on a litter to watch the veiled shrine of the Grail carried in front of the waiting brotherhood of its knights, to be placed on an oblong stone table. Anfortas compared Christ's Blood on the Holy Lance to his incurable wound, which was giving him agony because of his sins. The Grail was revealed as a purple crystal goblet, which was illuminated by a brilliant ray of light. With this chalice, Anfortas blessed the pitchers of wine and baskets of bread for the meal of the knights, who sang of changing the Holy Body and Blood into strength and power to fight for the Christian cause. Parsifal remained mute and transfixed, never asking the question that could cure the Grail King.

The second act at Klingsor's magic castle dealt with the efforts of the wizard to entrap Parsifal through Kundry and the Flower Maidens, whom he escaped with ease. And when Kundry gave Parsifal the first kiss of love, he clutched at his heart, thinking that the wound of Anfortas was burning there like a torch. His vision was suddenly concentrated upon the purple Grail. Kundry was overwhelmed. Did her kiss give him the vision of the divine? If he must be a redeemer, let him redeem her or damn her forever. The thwarted Klingsor, who had castrated himself, hurled the phallic Spear at Parsifal, but it hovered above him. He plucked it from the air to describe the sign of the Cross. The castle collapsed, the magic garden of pleasure and corruption became a desert, the flowers withered. Parsifal left with the lethal and curative weapon for the hermit's cell.

There Kundry was waiting for him with Gurnemanz, who enlightened Parsifal on his stupidity and ignorance. Yet he was the chosen redeemer, and Kundry now played the role of the Magdalene, bathing his feet, anointing them from a golden phial kept between her breasts and drying them with her hair. Transformed into another Christ, Parsifal accepted his role and was baptised by Gurnemanz in the nearby sacred spring. He was told that this was Good Friday. Prepared to die in front of his despondent knights, Anfortas was touched on his wound by Parsifal with the head of the Spear, now changed back to the Holy Lance. 'One wound is enough,' he declared. 'The wound is only healed by the Spear that gave it.' The Lance now ran again with the Holy Blood. Parsifal took the purple cup from its shrine and sank to his knees in prayer. The Grail glowed with radiance, the dove of the Spirit descended on the pure knight, and Kundry sank down as Elsa did in *Lohengrin*, forgiven, but dead. The Grail was held over all by its new king.

Although a last work of personal resignation, *Parsifal* was criticised by the philosopher Nietzsche as the relapse of an old man from a bold confrontation with the truth into a weak and sentimental Catholic faith. 'More Liszt than Wagner,' he told a friend, 'the spirit of the Counter-Reformation; it is too Christian and narrow for me.' The novelist Thomas Mann also judged the opera, reckoning that the Christian element was false. The theme of the 'Dresden Amen' with its assurance of redemption was a trick to deceive an audience into believing that the Brotherhood of the Knights of the Grail was not another order of Teutonic or Templar Knights – or early Storm Troopers – ready to lead a racial crusade against evil Eastern forces, as they had done from Marienburg against the pagan Slavs, Mongols and Russians. For by now, Wagner had met and read Count Arthur de Gobineau's notorious works on an elite Aryan race.

Yet the facts are that Wagner identified his Grail Castle most probably with Montserrat and the early Spanish crusades against the Moors, while the inspiration for Klingsor's flower garden derived less from his anti-Semitism than from the enchanted gothic greenery of the Villa Ruffolo at Ravello, where the precious blood of the alchemist Saint Pantaleon liquified each year by some miracle, a testament to the healing power of the Catholic faith. In his 'Religion and Art', Wagner had already declared: 'Where religion becomes artificial, it remains for art to salvage the essence of it.' The literal belief in the mythical symbol of the Grail had to be recreated by song and music in an ideal representation, to recover the profound and hidden truth concealed in the ancient allegory. For him, the noblest heritage of the Christian Church was the soul of its music, which soared out of temple walls, gave life and freedom, and taught 'a new language in which the infinite and the incomprehensible can be perfectly expressed'.

In that desire, the legend of the Grail was the ultimate vehicle for Richard Wagner. Wolfram von Eschenbach had performed a miracle almost as complex as transubstantiation in his masterpiece *Parzival* by blending Oriental faiths and Nordic myths into a Christian occurrence. So Wagner transcended the Faustian *Tannhäuser* to reach the otherworldly *Lohengrin* and an apotheosis in *Parsifal*. There, his anti-Semitism, racialism and crude propaganda for German mastery were transmuted through the genius of his music, which he wanted to 'consist of the elements', into a spiritual drama of the possibility of redemption and the vision of God. If the rituals of the Knights of the Grail and their fierce chastity seemed to smack of earth ceremonies and even Black Masses, the blessed music, often derived from the liturgy, and the Christian imagery overlaid Wagner's bigotry and contradicted the misuse of his work by the Third Reich. No more than Christ was responsible for the cruelty of the crusades was Wagner guilty of being a cause of German propaganda in the First and Second World Wars. If he was committed to a philosophy, it was Schopenhauer's belief in the primacy of the will. In terms of the Grail, that was its old heresy, that the divine could only be seen by those who deserved to see it. God came to those who fought to Him. Understanding and compassion were the keys as much as trial and pain. Yet by good acts did Parsifal reach his goal.

Postscript on Nuremberg

The great irony in Germany was that the Church of Saint Lawrence in Nuremberg was the centre of the themes of the Grail in the late Middle Ages, although the city became the focus of fervent patriotism, Hitler's processions, and, finally, the trial of the Nazi leaders. Nowhere in Europe were the symbols of the Christian Holy Vessel shown in such beautiful profusion, except perhaps in Lukas Moser's *The Sea Voyage* on the silver and gilt altarpiece of Saint Mary Magdalene Church in Tiefenbrohn. Saint Lawrence, of course, had been given a Grail by the Pope, but he sent it west to Spain, not north to Germany. He appears twice in his church, carrying the gridiron on his shoulder like an oblong tennis racket. The Oriental version of the Grail in Wolfram's *Parzival* is celebrated in the painting over the Krell'scher high altar in the apse, the stone dropping into the chalice and being presented to the Christ child.

Other significances abound. A whole altarpiece of 1517 to Saint Martha puts her sister Mary Magdalene in a minor role; she reprimands the dragon of Tarascon and is buried by the first two bishops of France, her brother Lazarus and Saint Maximin, who sprinkles the water of absolution over her from a sponge on a rod, dipped in the sacred vessel in the shape of a bucket. A carved Saint Veronica displays Christ's face on her veil, and many Last Suppers, both painted and in relief, show the beloved apostle John asleep at table in front of the Lamb on a platter and the wine in a cup. The best of them is the simple scene painted in 1437 for the Diocarus altar. Yet one rare unattributed altarpiece of the Risen Christ, created at the waning of the Middle Ages when Catholicism was about to be broken in Middle Germany by the Protestant Reformation, is a parting tribute to the decline of the Grail cult. At the base, there is a carving of the dead Jesus, with three women above His Body, one holding a jar of spices, and Nicodemus and Joseph of Arimathea at His Head and Feet. In the pictures, He appears as Christ the Gardener, holding his spade by a golden Grail bucket with a lid, while the Magdalene kneels alone before Him. The medieval closed garden is depicted here as the Garden of Eden; surrounded by a fence, it is all grass except for the two trees from Genesis: the Tree of Life and the Tree of Knowledge of Good and Evil.

The Church of Saint Lawrence would be bombed during the Second World War, as if in retribution for the later perversion of its messages. For Hitler would make Nuremberg his place of ceremonies, which in their vast arrangements would surpass even the jousts of King Arthur at Camelot and the rituals of the Fisher King. But the Nazi revival of the Grail myths through the inspiration of Wagner in order to justify another crusade against the East, still godless and now Marxist, had been anticipated by the imperialism of Victorian Britain, which needed a talisman and lamp to illuminate its occupation of a quarter of the globe in the greatest overseas empire yet seen on earth. In painting, poetry and national ideology, King Arthur and his knights were revived to ride again, winning battle and far lands in the search not only for the good and the true, but for the markets of the world.

Chapter Sixteen

The Empire of the Grail

> I am a part of all that I have met;
> Yet all experience is an arch where thro'
> Gleams that untravell'd world, whose margin fades
> For ever and for ever when I move.

Alfred Lord Tennyson, 'Ulysses'

The ultimate heresy of the Grail – that the individual might try a direct approach to God – and of the Romantic revolution – that man might seek to replace God the Creator – was realised in Mary Shelley's *Frankenstein*. While a novel of horror, *Frankenstein* was also a penetrating analysis of the outer limits of freedom and the need for the restraints of society. The hero Victor Frankenstein was himself a compound between two poets: the author's husband, Percy Bysshe Shelley, and Lord Byron. On her way to spend the summer with them in 1816 on the shores of Lake Geneva, Mary had visited a Castle Frankenstein near Mannheim, where an alchemist and physician, Dippel, had conducted experiments on corpses to 'engender life in the dead'. Her Count also sought the origins of life and human nature. He put together a monstrous image of himself that was a foul caricature of his desires.

> *His limbs were in proportion, and I had selected his features as beautiful. Beautiful! – Great God! His yellow skin scarcely covered the work of muscles and arteries beneath; his hair was of a lustrous black, and*

288

flowing; his teeth of a pearly whiteness; but these luxu-
ries only formed a more horrid contrast with his watery
eyes; that seemed almost of the same colour as the dun
white sockets in which they were set, his shrivelled com-
plexion and straight black lips.

In fact, Frankenstein had created the savage and distorted version of himself, the fiend of the inward dream. This monster raged away, and yet he was innocent. He had not chosen to be deformed. He was created as someone horrible to other people. When he later confronted Frankenstein on the wild summit of a Swiss mountain, he was full of bitter anguish, disdain and malignity. His unearthly ugliness was almost too obscure for human eyes, and yet he rightly complained to his master: 'Remember, that I am thy creature; I ought to be thy Adam; but I am rather the fallen angel, whom thou drivest from joy for no misdeed. I was benevolent and good; misery made me a fiend. Make me happy, and I shall again be virtuous.'

Rejection warped the behaviour of the monster into malice and revenge. He had heard of the discovery of the Americas and had wept 'over the hapless fate of its original inhabitants'. In his own case he was no Adam, but an outcast demon, rather like those neutral fallen angels who brought down from heaven the stone Grail of Wolfram von Eschenbach in *Parzival*. 'God, in pity,' the monster said, 'made man beautiful and alluring, after his own image; but my form is a filthy type of yours, more horrid even from the very resemblance. Satan had his companions, fellow-devils to admire and encourage him; but I am solitary and abhorred.'

So the monster put the case of those who were doubly deformed, the first time by creation, the second time by society. He forced the German Count to make him a mate in desolate Orkney. Her resurrection would breed a race of devils which might make 'the very existence of the species of man a condition precarious and full of terror'. If science might create the damned of the earth, they would revolt and destroy the society that damned them. At the last moment, Frankenstein cut up the female monster, and in revenge, the monster destroyed Frankenstein's own wife and his best friend. The Count was then compelled to hunt down his murderous other self through the Arctic wastes to destroy it. His Promethean urge to discover the secrets of life ended in self-destruction. He could only replace the arrogance of trying to be God by the slaughter of himself and all that he had done. The end of the search for the elixir of living, the Grail itself, would culminate in a being who saw himself as another Adam, but was turned into a destroyer like Cain. *Frankenstein* was a romantic Book of Genesis, with its hero repeating the sin of the alchemists: the creation of humanity without the benefit of the Almighty.

In her subtext, Mary Shelley was also joining her husband and Lord Byron in warning her readers of how the power of the Industrial Revolution might deform its controllers and, through them, the whole of nature. Before he fled his homeland, Byron's maiden speech in the House of Lords had been in defence of the Luddites, who were smashing the new 'spider-work' machines, which were putting them out of a job and leaving them to starve. 'The rejected workmen,' Byron said with some irony, 'in the blindness of their ignorance, instead of rejoicing at these improvements in arts so beneficial to mankind, conceived themselves to be sacrificed to improvements in mechanism. In the foolishness of their hearts they imagined that the maintenance and well-doing of the industrous poor were objects of greater importance than the enrichment of a few individuals by any improvement, in the implements of trade.'

Another noble lord, the Earl of Eglington, was so inspired by the novels of Sir Walter Scott and so disgusted by Victorian commerce that he held in 1838 at his Ayrshire castle an Arthurian tournament. There the Knight of the Red Lion jousted in full medieval armour against the Knights of the Burning Tower and of the White Rose, while Eglington himself wore golden mail. Torrential rain and mud spoiled the presentation of the prizes by the Queen of Beauty and her maids of honour, and the tourney was almost washed out. Yet it fired a national interest in medieval history with its creeds and codes. As one critic, Lycion, pointed out, even if the proceedings in Scotland were a sham, the real point about the revival of chivalry was an attitude to life, not a charade in fancy dress.

The popular poet Alfred Tennyson, later ennobled himself, followed the tournament with long poems on Merlin and Lancelot, Percivale and Galahad, and King Arthur and 'The Holy Grail'. In that poem, the monk Ambrosius met the wandering knight Sir Percivale in a Victorian version of the character invented by Chrétien de Troyes. The reason for his solitary quest was this:

> *The sweet vision of the Holy Grail*
> *Drove me from all vainglories, rivalries,*
> *And earthly heats that spring and sparkle out*
> *Among us in the jousts, while women watch*
> *Who wins, who falls; and waste the spiritual strength*
> *Within us, better offer'd up to Heaven.*

The monk asked whether the Grail was a phantom of a cup that came and went. But Percivale identified it as a material thing, the cup from which 'Our Lord drank at the last sad supper with his own'. Joseph of Arimathea had brought it to Glastonbury, where the winter thorn tree blossomed at Christmas. Abiding there for a while, it was taken back to heaven because of evil times. Through fasting and prayer, the sister of Percivale saw 'the Holy Thing' again in a vision, and spoke of it:

> *And down the long beam stole the Holy Grail,*
> *Rose-red with beatings in it, as if alive,*
> *Till all the white walls of my cell were dyed*
> *With rosy colours leaping on the wall;*

> *And then the music faded, and the Grail*
> *Past, and the beam decay'd, and from the walls*
> *The rosy quiverings died into the night.*

When Galahad, perhaps the son of Lancelot, heard of this vision at Arthur's court, he was transfigured. He wore a sword-belt with the device of the crimson Grail embroidered within a silver ray, made from the long yellow hair of Percivale's sister. 'He believed in her belief. Then came a year of miracle.' Galahad sat and survived in Merlin's chair of serpents, the Siege Perilous, which had swallowed up its wizard creator. This act of daring produced the collective vision of the Grail to all the Knights of the Round Table.

> *And in the blast there smote along the hall*
> *A beam of light seven times more clear than day:*
> *And down the long beam stole the Holy Grail*
> *All over cover'd with a luminous cloud,*
> *And none might see who bare it, and it past.*

Many of the knights then swore to leave the sacred mount of soaring Camelot to seek the blessed cup, wherever it had gone from them. King Arthur hated their going, and declared that the Grail hidden within its shining fog was 'a sign to maim this Order which I made'. His knights had won his twelve great battles. How could he fight the forces of evil without them? Meeting mirages and nightmares, Percivale rode out alone. All turned to dust before him, so he thought that if he touched the Grail, it would also crumble into dust. A hermit gave him the sacrament, and Galahad appeared in silver armour, seeing what his fellow knight could not see:

> *Saw ye no more? I, Galahad, saw the Grail,*
> *The Holy Grail, descend upon the shrine:*
> *I saw the fiery face as of a child*
> *That smote itself into the bread, and went:*
> *And hither am I come; and never yet*

Hath what thy sister taught me first to see,
This Holy Thing, fail'd from my side, nor come
Cover'd but moving with me night and day,
Fainter by day, but always in the night
Blood-red, and sliding down the blacken'd marsh
Blood-red, and on the naked mountain top
Blood-red, and in the sleeping mere below
Blood-red. And in the strength of this I rode,
Shattering all evil customs everywhere,
And past thro' Pagan realms, and made them mine,
And clashed with Pagan hordes, and bore them down,
And broke thro' all, and in the strength of this
Come victor. But my time is hard at hand,
And hence I go; and one will crown me king
Far in the spiritual city; and come thou, too,
For thou shalt see the vision when I go.

Alfred Tennyson would become the Poet Laureate of the Victorian empire. He was repeating for his expanding nation what Geoffrey of Monmouth had done for the Norman kings and Malory for the Tudor rulers: the equation of seeking dominions overseas with a divine mission. In his quest for the Grail, Galahad was presented as the victor over pagan hordes and realms. He would be crowned finally in a spiritual city, which, as that of Saint Augustine, would also be represented on earth – in the case of Tennyson by the port city of London. There Queen Victoria, uniquely in Europe, played the ancient role of Melchizedek in Israel; she was the future Empress of India as well as the Queen of Britain; also the religious ruler of the Church of England.

The poem concluded Tennyson's revival of the responsibilities of the global Grail kingdom. Sir Percivale saw Galahad 'far on the great sea, in silver-shining armour stormy-clear'. The Holy Vessel hung over his head, shrouded in white samite or a shining cloud. On a winged boat, Galahad passed to the spiritual city of the Book of Revelation, its spires and gateways made of one great pearl.

The Grail hung above his head 'redder than any rose', then fell into the floods of heaven, never more to be seen by human eyes. Returning to Camelot, Percivale asked the other questing knights if they had viewed the Grail. Only Lancelot declared that in his insanity he had seen it, fainting in a furnace blast of heat, an ecstatic vision:

> *All pall'd in crimson samite, and around*
> *Great angels, awful shapes, and wings and eyes.*
> *And but for all my madness and my sin,*
> *And then my swooning, I had sworn I saw*
> *That which I saw; but what I saw was veil'd*
> *And cover'd; and this Quest was not for me.*

That was exactly what the bitter King Arthur said when his surviving knights returned to the misty spires of Camelot. He had not gone on the quest, for he had to guard what he ruled. He could not leave the throne of power, nor indeed should they, who had only seen dreams, except for Galahad, now the transfigured ruler of the Grail kingdom of the otherworld. 'Let visions of the night or of the day,' Arthur said, 'come as they will.' These might be induced by the self or by God. The knights had merely seen what they had seen. Their duty was to defend with him the realms which they had won.

So Tennyson preached the mission and the duties of empire in his legend of the Grail. And in 1851 at the Great Exhibition, the new technology built the supreme Grail Castle of the industrial age. This Crystal Palace included the machines, cylinders and metal vats that produced the new riches and bounty; but within its walls of iron and glass, trees grew and nature survived among the clanging of the engines. So inspiring was this extraordinary creation that Britain's temporary dominance in the manufacture of goods rather than the pursuit of the good was confirmed. The Poet Laureate wrote an ode to be sung at the opening ceremony, emphasising the benefits of the Great Exhibition as a divine cornucopia:

Uplift a thousand voices full and sweet
  In this wide hall with earth's invention stored,
  And praise the invisible universal Lord,
Who lets once more in peace the nations meet,
  Where Science, Art, and Labour have outpour'd
  Their myriad horns of plenty at our feet.

Lady Charlotte Guest, the young wife of the self-made master of the Dowlais Ironworks in South Wales, had translated the Celtic legends of King Arthur in the *Mabinogion*. These helped to spread the cult of the resurrected myths into architecture and art. A gothic revival influenced the style of the reconstructed House of Commons and many cathedral restorations – such as at Ely – while the pre-Raphaelite painters depicted lush romantic versions of the adventures of the Knights of the Round Table, not seen since the medieval illuminations to the *Roman de la Rose*. The artist Edward Burne-Jones wrote to a friend about founding a brotherhood. He should learn Tennyson's poem on Sir Galahad by heart: 'He is to be the patron of our order.' In many sumptuous and sexually disturbing pictures, Burne-Jones, Dante Gabriel Rossetti and William Morris would re-create the loves of Lancelot for Guinevere and Tristram for Iseult. Rossetti dwelt on the Holy Grail as well as on the adulterous lovers, illustrating, for an edition of Tennyson's poems of 1859, 'Sir Galahad at the Ruined Chapel' drinking holy water from a sacred horn cup. Burne-Jones even attended a performance of Wagner's *Parsifal* in the Albert Hall, and was gratified that the German composer had struck the 'Celtic vein' in the Grail legends, as he was trying to do in his art. This cult of imagery would end with the perversity of Aubrey Beardsley at the turn of the century. His illustrations of Malory's ever-popular *Morte D'Arthur* turned even 'The achieving of the Sangreal' into an ambiguous rite, with Galahad and Perceval as two willowy figures at worship before a hermaphrodite of a winged angel, carrying a spiky vase and veil above the open five petals of the Virgin's rose, a trinity of shoots growing from its stamen.

More indicative of imperial art celebrating the divine mission of Victorian Britain were such works as Thomas Jones Barker's picture of 1864, *The Bible: The Secret of England's Greatness*, now in the National Portrait Gallery in London. Carved into the bottom of the gilded frame was an open book, named as HOLY BIBLE. One page read: 'Thy world is a lamp unto my feet, and a light unto my path.' On the facing page, the text was: 'I love thy commandments above gold; yea, above fine gold.' The painting showed the young Queen Victoria with her consort Prince Albert behind her, presenting a gilt Bible as the Word of God to a kneeling Moorish Sultan dressed in splendid robes. Two of her statesmen lurked in the background, the Lords Palmerston and Russell. The Victorian empire in Africa and Asia was represented as the Portuguese had done – a Christian crusade with the purpose of converting mercenary Islam. Broadcasting the Good Book worldwide appeared to be more important than acquiring wealth and new markets. And the Grail quest was a splendid lamp and light to direct the Victorian navy on its way.

Perhaps the finest poem by Tennyson on the never-ending wanderings of British merchants and adventurers over the seven seas was his recall of the last voyage of Ulysses, also the subject of Dante in his 'Inferno'. The aged king would not rot and die on his Greek island, but still was yearning 'to follow knowledge like a sinking star, beyond the utmost bound of human thought'. His search for the ultimate vision of wisdom was worthy of a Knight of the Round Table. It was not too late to seek a newer world. And so he set forth with his old companions across the water to the ends of the earth, 'strong in will/To strive, to seek, to find, and not to yield'.

Such exhortations on Britain's imperial mission did not endear the Poet Laureate to all of his friends. The translator of Oriental mysticism to the west, the poet Edward Fitzgerald, in his *Omar Khayyám*, hardly enjoyed the *Idylls of the King*, which he bought at Lowestoft. In a letter he declared that Tennyson had gone even further than him into the clouds.

> *The whole myth of Arthur's Round Table Dynasty in Britain presents itself before me with a sort of cloudy, Stonehenge grandeur. I am not sure if the old knights' adventures do not tell upon me better, touched in some lyrical way (like your own 'Lady of Shalott') than when elaborated into epic form. I never could care for Spenser, Tasso, or even Ariosto, whose epic has a ballad ring about it. But then I never could care much for the old prose romances much either, except* Don Quixote. *So, as this was always the case with me, I suppose my brain is wanting in this bit of its dissected map.*
>
> *Anyhow, Alfred, while I feel how pure, noble and holy your work is, and whole phrases, lines and sentences of it will abide with me, and I am sure with men after me, I read on till the 'Lincolnshire Farmer' drew tears to my eyes. I was got back to the substantial rough-spun Nature I knew; and the old brute, invested by you with the solemn humour of Humanity, like Shakespeare's* Shallow, *became a more pathetic phenomenon than the knights who revisit the world in your other verse.*

Queen Victoria even discerned an Arthurian figure in her prime minister, Disraeli. 'He is full of poetry, romance and chivalry,' she wrote to her daughter. 'When he knelt down to kiss my hand which he took in both of his – he said: "In loving loyalty and faith".' He called Her Majesty 'the Faery' after Spenser's praise of Gloriana and Queen Elizabeth in his *Faerie Queene.* She certainly revelled in her role as the *belle dame* and ideal of Christian civilisation across the globe. She created knights in her service across her dominions; the numbers of those dubbed with the honour increased sixfold in her reign to some two thousand baronets. The suppressors of the Indian Mutiny were seen as the paladins and Rolands of their time. 'What knight of the Round Table,' asked the historian

J.A. Froude, 'beat Havelock and Sir John Lawrence?' Tennyson, after all, ended the twelve books of his *Idylls of the King* – the resurrection of King Arthur and the Grail – with an ode to his Queen and her faithful subjects across a quarter of the land mass of the earth.

> *O loyal to the royal in thyself,*
> *And loyal to thy land, as this to thee . . .*
> *Thee and thy Prince! the loyal to their crown*
> *Are loyal to their own far sons, who love*
> *Our ocean-empire with her boundless homes*
> *For ever-broadening England, and her throne*
> *Is our vast Orient, and one isle,*
> *That knows not her own greatness.*

The *Idylls of the King* had ended after the battle with Modred, the loss of the realm of Lyonesse and the passing of Arthur to Avallon. Such an end for the Victorian empire was not the prediction of its Poet Laureate, although he did identify his sovereign with her supposed everlasting ancestor:

> *He passes to be King among the dead,*
> *But after healing of his grievous wound*
> *He comes again.*

Prelude to Massacre

The chivalry and code of honour to those who would be Christian gentlemen and dedicate their lives in the imperial service created a series of petty Camelots in the clubs and officers' messes of Britain, its dominions, its colonies and its garrisons. Being Masons was an important element in these brotherhoods of service; but military pride was almost more demanding. In his strange poem of 1875, John Addington Symonds, the historian of Renaissance Italy, linked the various Victorian strands of a certain male communion, as if in the Order of the Grail:

O nobler peerage than thou ancient vaunt
Of Arthur or of Roland! Chivalry
Long sought, last found! Knight of the Holy Ghost!
Phalanx Immortal! True Freemasonry!

As Mark Girouard has pointed out in his illuminating book, *The Return to Camelot*, certain military and political leaders used the ancient myths to develop a cult of personality. The imperial and intellectual group named the 'Souls' referred to their leading member, who was to become prime minister, as 'King Arthur' Balfour.

Wolseley had his 'ring' in India; Kitchener had his
'cubs' in Egypt and the Sudan; Milner had his 'kinder-
garten' to help him with the reorganisation of the
Transvaal after the Boer War; back in England the
kindergarten developed into a closely knit group of
imperialists known as the Round Table.

This return to feudal attitudes opposed the making of too much money. Duty was the clarion call, to be carried out by noble and muscular Christians who modelled themselves on Lancelot, Perceval and Galahad.

Contemporary Americans were not immune to this contagion of antique idealism. Ralph Waldo Emerson wrote four Merlin poems: in one of them, the Harp praised the Wizard who played it:

> *But my minstrel knows and tells*
> *The counsel of the gods,*
> *Knows of the Holy Book the spells,*
> *Knows the law of Night and Day*
> *And the heart of girl and boy,*
> *The tragic and the gay,*
> *And what is writ on Table Round*
> *Of Arthur and his peers.*

Meanwhile, the Anglophile Edwin Austen Abbey even played cricket and painted large canvases of the *Quest for the San Graal* for the Boston Public Library. And Camelot would become the name given to the White House in Washington during the presidency of John Fitzgerald Kennedy, although its source would not spring from Tennyson's poems, but from the lyrics of an American musical, as if the troubadours of the Grail had crossed the Atlantic Ocean.

Curiously enough, a Congregational minister from Vermont, William Byron Forbush, was the chief influence on Robert Baden-Powell when he formed the Boy Scouts, that extraordinary child training scheme which even the Nazis were to fear as a precedent and rival to their Hitler Youth. The American Knights of King Arthur were guided by adult Merlins at Round Tables. Their sports were changed into quests; their goals were chivalry, courtesy and Christian daring. After his experiences in the Boer War, when he became the hero of the siege of Mafeking, Baden-Powell combined his experiences as a bush reconnaissance expert with the legends of the Grail. The Boy Scouts were brought up between the camp fire and Camelot on a 'Knight's Code' with nine rules, said to date from the reign of King Arthur. These involved self-discipline, honour and helping women and children in distress. The ideal was to bring up Young Knights of the Empire on the model of Saint George of England and the Round Table.

The First World War put these trainees out of imperial service on to the Western Front. To fight there as an officer meant probable death, mutilation or a nasty injury. There was only one cavalry charge by the British, which ended as disastrously as the Charge of the Light Brigade in the Crimea. The slaughter was the massacre of a class that expected to rule. At one time in the war, the survival time of a second lieutenant in the front line was estimated at six weeks. He was meant to lead over the top, reconnoitre between the trenches at night, bring in the casualties from the barbed wire and expose himself first to every risk. Small wonder that he died at three times the rate of his soldiers. A privilege in birth and education seemed a privilege in death and extinction. 'Our generation becomes history,' Duff Cooper wrote to Lady Diana Manners, 'instead of growing up.'

The war poetry from Flanders was bleak and terse, although the propaganda of knightly duty continued from the women at home, even though they knew of the horrors of the mud, the machine-guns and the mustard gas. The millions of volunteers, so Mildred Huxley declared in 'A Song of Oxford', were the Knights of God, who 'shall see His glory and find the Grail even in the fire of hell'. And if the war on the ground resembled the circles of Dante's Inferno, the aerial battles in single-seater fighters still seemed to be jousts or tournaments. Maurice Baring wrote a memorial poem to Auberon Herbert, Lord Lucas, who died in the Royal Flying Corps. He was sure that Herbert had met fit companions in that high place above.

> *Knights of the Table Round*
> *And all the very brave, the very true*
> *With chivalry crowned.*

The combats, indeed, against the great German ace, the Red Baron von Richthofen, were described as duels, while his impersonation by Erich von Stroheim in Renoir's film *The Grand Illusion* depicted an old-fashioned aristocrat of scrupulous honour.

The Germany of Kaiser Wilhelm II, indeed, had approached the conflict as something of a crusade, if not a Wagnerian opera. One of the chief preachers of an aggressive and racialistic foreign policy, Houston Stewart Chamberlain, with his very popular *Foundations of the Nineteenth Century*, chose Wagner as his passion and his ennoblement, a prophet of his own mystic nationalism, which in turn inspired the Kaiser. A return to the primitive and the worship of the body beautiful; a stress on the uniquely German spiritual *Kultur* as opposed to Latin and Anglo-Saxon material cultures; an obsession with the elemental purity of the Aryan race free from alien taints: these national traits were being allied to a pride in German techniques and industrialisation as well as in military prowess. Soul, body and skill appeared to prove God's choice of the Germans as the master people of Europe. 'In Germany, there is a single will in everyone,' even the liberal Conrad Haussmann wrote, 'the will to assert oneself.'

For Germany, the outbreak of war was also an apocalypse, a millennial and cleansing process. *Kultur* had to be defended from the barbarians of the East and the materialism of the West. Only so could German freedom and values be preserved. Yet the foul experiences of the years of trench fighting destroyed the myths that had sent the Germans to suffer and die. By July of 1918, Rudolf Binding recorded in his diary, later published as *A Fatalist at War*: 'We are finished. My thoughts oppress me. How are we to recover ourselves? *Kultur*, as it will be known after the war, will be of no use; mankind itself will probably be of still less use.' And chivalry of the least use of all.

The ending of the war brought the loss home. There would be no replacement of those who had gone. 'One will at last fully recognise,' wrote Lady Cynthia Asquith in her diary, 'that the dead are not only dead for the duration of the war.' The young 'Souls' from Oxford were nearly all fallen: Raymond Asquith and Aubrey Herbert and the Grenfell brothers. Not since the Napoleonic Wars a century before had there been such a decimation of fighting men and future leaders. Those who did survive had almost a sense of guilt about their continuing existence. They exaggerated the number and the quality of the dead, for not all of the bravest and the best had been exterminated. The methods of killing by artillery bombardment, machine-gun fire, mine, bomb and gas were random. There was little discrimination by character in that wayward slaughter. Statistically, 700,000 British combatants died, of which 37,500 were officers, a proportion of some nineteen to one. There had been five million British males between the ages of twenty and forty before the First World War, but there was the same number alive three years after its end. A generation had certainly not been killed: some of its more brilliant members had, and, most certainly, the ideal of imperial service. The story was the same among the some ten million other European males who perished by combat. An élite with its codes was mostly destroyed in many nations, along with the Habsburg Empire.

Tennyson had forecast this grand finale of chivalry when he put this lament into the mouth of the dying King Arthur after his final battle:

> *Such a sleep*
> *They sleep – the men I loved. I think that we*
> *Shall never more, at any future time,*
> *Delight our souls with talk of knightly deeds,*
> *Walking about the gardens and the halls*
> *Of Camelot, as in the days that were.*
> *I perish by this people which I made.*

Chapter Seventeen

The Perversion of the Grail

> As I went homeward
> At dusk by the shore,
> *'What is that crimson?'*
> Said Merlin once more.
> 'Only the sun,' I said,
> 'Sinking to rest' –
> *'Sunset for East,'* he said,
> *'Sunrise for West.'*
>
> Alfred Noyes, *The Riddles of Merlin*

The massacres of the First World War were followed by an epidemic of influenza, which killed tens of millions more people in Europe. The coming of peace led to a great disillusionment about the value of fighting. John Maynard Keynes, the chief representative of the British Treasury at the post-war negotiations in Paris, denounced the terms reached at the Treaty of Versailles in a polemic called *The Economic Consequences of the Peace*. It condemned the punitive reparations exacted from Germany and the self-interested land exchanges of the victorious powers. He foresaw that the consequences of the peace would be the financial ruin of Europe and another world war. 'Vengeance,' he predicted, 'will not limp.' Nothing would delay a final civil war between the forces of reaction and revolution. In that conflict, the horrors of the late German combat would fade into nothing. It would destroy 'whoever is the victor, the civilisation and the progress of our generation'.

This was to become the prevailing attitude of many of the

generation of 1914 who had gone to the trenches so readily and were discomfited by the peace. Their feeling of betrayal by the old men governing them had led to revolutions in Europe, suppressed outside Soviet Russia, and to the rise of Fascist movements, particularly in Italy. Extreme solutions advocating social change of the left or of the right promised a catharsis as violent as the recent European conflict, itself welcomed originally by a host of young men as an answer to the political turmoil of the pre-war years. The myth of a lost generation produced in its survivors a revulsion and a determination never to repeat the horrors of the slaughter. Its legacy was a certain pacifism that would abhor self-sacrifice in the name of any cause or modern Grail. Self-fulfilment was a better goal in the face of mass cynicism and disbelief.

So the Americans, who were called the Lost Generation, believed when they fled the prohibition of liquor in America for the freedoms of Paris. They were following the creed of Hemingway's Lieutenant Frederick Henry. 'I was not made to think. I was made to eat. My God, yes. Eat and drink and sleep with Catherine.' The trinity of food, alcohol and sex; the directness of action, thought and word which is the last refuge of sophistication; the search for the simple life and the American Adam, which had once been the mythological right of the frontiersman and the Indian: these were what the Yankee refugees sought in the Select and the Ritz Bar. They were looking for an escape from that Puritan morality which they could never escape. In their flight, they created great works, which they thought sprang from nihilism and Dada, but which really sprang from their dream of the lost youth of a great nation, now corrupted in their minds by the materialism of easy money and the caricature of idiotic reforms. Yet the expatriates, in their prohibition of the mentality of Prohibition, did not give up the code of the reformers at home. The drinking and the girls were taken less for themselves than for the cult of taking them. Liquor was drunk not only for enjoyment, but as the liquid food of emancipation. For, as William Carlos Williams wrote, '. . . whisky was to the imagination of the Paris of that time like milk to a baby'. In this desperate reaction from Prohibition, the Lost Generation prohibited itself from the need to understand complex humanity and its urgent problems. The escape to France was the escape into egocentricity, the blindness of the self-styled American expatriates to everything but the satisfaction of their own despair.

Contemporary Germany, particularly Berlin, saw just such a heady hedonism. These were the years of 'that strange Indian summer – the Weimar Republic', as the English poet Stephen Spender wrote in his preface to his homosexual novel, *The Temple*. 'Germany seemed a paradise where there was no censorship and young Germans enjoyed extraordinary freedom in their lives.' As fugitive American writers and painters went to France to escape Prohibition, so their English rivals were fleeing repression by going to Germany. 'For them, drink; for us, sex,' Spender's friend Christopher Isherwood boasted. He was 'doing what Henry James would have done, if he had had the guts . . . *My* will is to live according to my nature, and to find a place where I can be what I am.'

The Great Depression, which caused a reaction from escapism along with the return home of the intellectual refugees, unleashed in Germany a reaction towards a revolution. For that was the paradox of Nazism, which aimed to create a new world and a new race by reviving ancient myths and the German spirit. More a dream than a reality, the message preached by Nazi propaganda was of strong and eternal youth with a will to power. The members of the nation could all aspire to being Parsifals and Siegfrieds. The National Socialist German Workers' Party was a method of carrying out by other means the war experiences of its leader Adolf Hitler in the front line. He wanted another total mobilisation of Germany to avenge the losses of the Treaty of Versailles and to revive the German Empire to the east and the south. The Nazis claimed to be the heirs of that dynamic *Kultur* which had so inspired the First World War. They promised action on the theme of a lost grandeur, to be regained by the thousand years of the rule of the Third Reich.

Their great annual September dramas over seven days were promoted at the Grail centre of Nuremberg. There the parades were staged with tens of thousands of uniformed members of the Party. The choreography of the gymnasts and the dancers, evoked by Leni Riefenstahl in *The Triumph of the Will*, almost put to shame the Hollywood extravaganzas of Busby Berkeley. Cathedrals of ice, created by Albert Speer, crowned the massive processions with aerial cones of hundreds of searchlights. Forests of banners recalled the crusades and the imperial Iberian fleets setting off towards the conquest of Asia, Africa and the Americas. All would culminate in a speech by Hitler, high on his podium, the White Knight of the Swastika, as he was so often painted. He called himself the anonymous warrior and the unknown soldier, who had been gassed and decorated three times with Iron Crosses for courage in the front line. Yet his notoriety and power would affect the whole earth.

The imagery of Fascism, in both Germany and Italy, was an aphrodisiac to the masses. Even when the bombing of Berlin by the Allies would cause despondency, Hitler would insist on great shows. 'Theatrical performances are needed,' he said, 'precisely because the morale of the people must be maintained.' His newsreels and those of Mussolini showed interminable ranks of aeroplanes, tanks and guns; also smiling parades of troops and tractors, villagers and harvests and even religious festivals. Instead of Jesus hanging upon the Cross, a bare German youth was draped over the four prongs of the Nazi emblem. Horst Wessel took the place of Christ as the Party martyr in the propaganda of the sacred corpse. The mental pictures of pagan myths and Wagnerian operas, the Nordic themes of godlike battles and intransigent heroes, were evoked in a panoply of nostalgic reverence and imminent action. As Hitler declared, Nazism was a doctrine of conflict.

A streak of perverse mysticism ran through Nazi ideology.

After the defeat of the First World War, the mercenary bands of the *Freikorps* had put down radical risings in Berlin, Bavaria and Latvia. They saw themselves as new Teutonic Knights, sworn to suppress the heresy of Bolshevism in the East. Their other inspiration was a secret organisation, attributed to Charlemagne, named the *Vehm*, which for many centuries had tyrannised the conquered lands of Saxony with its vigilant tribunals and judgements. The actual inspiration for the Nazi Party was mythical as well as political through the drug-addicted writer Dietrich Eckart, also a leading member of the Thule Society, which sought a pure Nordic homeland. Eckart's talisman was a piece of black meteorite as in the Ka'aba at Mecca, and when he died, he claimed that Adolf Hitler was his successor and would follow his racist and ancestral teachings. Hitler, however, only used paganism as a theatrical device and psychological scalpel into the national subconscious. He left the doctrines of the primitive and the occult to his ringmaster, Alfred Rosenberg, to his deputy, Rudolf Hess, and to his chief of propaganda, Heinrich Himmler. Although a lover of Wagner, Hitler wanted no return to the religion of Odin and Wotan. He wanted a new religion based on earth ceremonies and blood rituals.

During Hitler's term in prison in 1924 after the Munich uprising, Rosenberg had been the temporary leader of the nascent Nazi Party. Unlike the Bible of the movement, Hitler's vainglorious *Mein Kampf*, Rosenberg's book, *The Myth of the Twentieth Century*, was a weird evocation of an Aryan race from a lost Atlantis which sailed on dragon and swan ships like Lohengrin to found all ancient civilisations, including the Indian one. From there, that master people overran Asia, returning through Iran and the worship of Zoroaster, or the Zarathustra of Nietzsche's Superman. This noble élite joined the Nordic gods in their struggle for light and life against the forces of darkness, such as the Serpent of the Middle Earth. Rosenberg wanted the suppression of the Bible so that it could be replaced by *Mein Kampf*; for the ultimate Triumph of the Will had arrived in the person of Adolf

Hitler. But the later Führer was too polite to discard Christianity wholly, however much he wished to become the Messiah of his New Order. He officially remained a Roman Catholic until his suicide, whatever pagan rituals and sacrifices were enacted in his name.

Heinrich Himmler enthused about the legends of King Arthur, who had, after all, finally been defeated by the invading Anglo-Saxons when they crossed the Rhine and the Channel. He aimed to re-create the medieval *Ordenstaat* of the Teutonic Knights in Poland and Lithuania, where the Jews and the undesirable Slavs were to be totally exterminated. He encouraged Hitler to see himself as a superior reincarnation of previous Holy Roman Emperors from Charlemagne to the Habsburgs. The coronation regalia of past dynasties was looted from Prague, Reims, Warsaw and Vienna, including the crusaders' Holy Lance, now confused with the Nordic Spear of Destiny. These sacred signs of power were transported to Nuremberg, the site of the great Nazi processionals, where they might be held to confer on the Führer a mystical and traditional sovereignty over Europe.

The deputy Nazi leader, Rudolf Hess, was particularly affected by the legends of the Grail. He had fallen under the influence of General Karl Haushoffer, who was responsible for two mystic pagan brotherhoods, *Vril* and the Society of the Green Dragon. Rather as in the later *Star Wars* trilogy of films, the secret energy of these groups was an esoteric 'Force', which had its origins in Lord Edward Bulwer-Lytton's book, *The Coming Race*, 1871 as well as in Nietzsche's theories of Superman and the will. Bulwer-Lytton had been the head of the British Colonial Office as well as writing a romance on King Arthur. His biographer was a member of the Scottish Theosophical Society, which was visited by Dr Karl Hans Fuchs of the Nazi Thule Society, an organisation particularly patronised by Hess and Rosenberg with its rituals based on the *Ring* cycle of Wagner and the past of the Grail.

As that Holy Vessel was said to be concealed within the curious Apprentice Pillar of Rosslyn Chapel near Edinburgh, Fuchs inspected the place in 1930, accompanied by somebody who signed the visitors' book as D. Hamilton. Later, at the Theosophical Society in Edinburgh, Fuchs declared that Hess claimed to have Hamilton blood in his veins and was particularly interested in the 10th duke, a close friend of Bulwer-Lytton, as well as in the contemporary duke, who graced the Nazi leaders with his presence at the Olympic Games in Berlin. Fuchs added that Hess was known as 'Parsifal' in the inner circles of the Third Reich, and that he believed Rosslyn was the Grail chapel 'where the black hand snuffed out the candle'.

The extraordinary flight of Hess in a Messerschmitt to Scotland during the Second World War may well have had something to do with his obsession with the ducal Hamilton family and the cult of the Holy Vessel. Hitler's fury at his defection led to terms in concentration camps for many German Freemasons and astrologers. The Ancestral Heritage Organisation, or *Ahnenherbe*, however, was spared. Some of its fifty departments were connected to the SS secret police, whose head, Himmler, was called 'my Loyola' by Hitler as though he led a society of lethal Jesuits. At Sachsenhain, Himmler imitated Avebury, Carnac and Stonehenge in creating avenues of 4,500 standing stones to commemorate the Saxon victims of Charlemagne, who had them slaughtered before destroying the pagan oak grove and temple at the Irminsul, now reconstructed at the rocky outcrop of the Externsteine, where the German chief Herrmann had once destroyed two Roman legions. To the mystic philosopher Rudolf Steiner and his follower Walter Johannes Stein, the Externsteine rather than Nuremberg was the centre of the energy and the cult of the Grail in Germany. A medieval rock carving of the twelfth century still shows the Descent from the Cross set between the sun and the moon, with Nicodemus and Joseph of Arimathea carrying the body of Christ while a headless Mary Magdalene holds His head in her hands.

Above them, God the Father bears a triple emblem crowned by the cross of the Teutonic Knights.

At these sacred stones and the monoliths of Sachsenhain, Himmler conducted Mithraic and winter solstice ceremonies of sun worship for some ten thousand members of the SS and the *Ahnenherbe*. And at the triangular castle of Wewelsburg in Westphalia, he developed a monastic college and mausoleum for his secret police. In its great hall stood his oak Round Table, modelled on that of King Arthur; it was placed upon a floor with mosaics of swastikas and the patterns of the zodiac. Thirteen high chairs stood around it for Himmler and his twelve paladins among the *Obergruppenführers*, who followed his orders with total devotion. In the crypt beneath, a 'Realm of the Dead' had twelve niches and plinths to hold the urns for the ashes of the bones and coats of arms of the chosen SS paladins, after their deaths had been purified by fire. If he ever died, Hitler was expected by Himmler to be buried there as well.

The search for the Grail was another task for the *Ahnenherbe*. Hitler's interest in Wagner's *Parsifal* was well known, with its Nordic figure of Christ and its secret male order of Grail knights, modelled on their Teutonic and Templar predecessors. Hitler was painted wearing the silver mail of these literary guardians of the Castle of the Fisher King. And although Hess believed the actual Grail was in Scotland, Otto Rahn, an SS officer, had written a book in 1933 called *The Crusade for the Grail*, which was followed by *The Heart of Lucifer*. He revived the traditions of the Cathar chalice, buried in the nearby caves after the fall of Montségur at the end of the Albigensian Crusade. His version of the Grail was taken from the Oriental influences on Wolfram von Eschenbach in his *Parzival*. Rahn believed that Montségur was besieged by the troops of Lucifer, who wanted to recover the emerald which had fallen from Satan's crown at his battle with the angels of heaven. This sacred green stone had been rescued by a white dove and hidden in a black chasm at the fall of the Cathar stronghold. Rahn then used geomancy and sacred geography to locate the places where the Grail of the heretics might be hidden, spawning a succession of books overlaying the maps of the mountain peaks of the south of France with triangles and trapezoids to created 'the Hermetic Star of the Templars' or the 'Sacred Rectangle of the Gauls', one of the three 'Grail tables' set upon the earth. In his investigations in the grottos of Lombrives, Bethlehem, l'Ermite, Ornolac and other caverns near the Cathar castles, Rahn became obsessional in his examinations of them, declaring that he did not know which was the more marvellous or beautiful. Within them, 'the inscriptions represent a Ship of the Dead which has for a sail the sun, the sun which gives out life and is reborn each winter . . . Also a tree I saw, "The Tree of Life", drawn in charcoal.'

Rahn declared that the sacred geometry of the walls of Montségur proclaimed that it was a sun temple, based on the summer solstice, an interpretation which enthused Himmler with his SS ceremonies. In 1937, he was sent by Rahn a consignment of the objects which had been excavated from the French caves. Without clear proof, writers have claimed that this consignment included the Cathar sacred vessel, which was then placed on one of the plinths in the 'Realm of the Dead' in Wewelsburg Castle. Later happenings did not support such a theory. On his return to Germany, Rahn was probably sent to the concentration camps, along with the other mystics, after the defection of Hess; certainly, he did not survive the Second World War. And the *Ahnenherbe* sent teams of secret policemen and prehistorians, linguists and archaeologists into Vichy France in order to follow up Rahn's digging around Montségur. This appeared to be a last effort to locate the Holy Vessel as a talisman to prevent the reconquest of France by the Allies on a second front and thus alleviate the German pressure and crusade into Russia.

The specialists of the *Ahnenherbe* were located in the forest of Basqui at a camp which was called the Place of the Aurochs. In the grotto of Causson, they discovered some inscribed stones, which were again transported to Germany.

Yet whatever was found by Rahn and by this later expedition disappeared in the fall of the Third Reich, which so much resembled the Gotterdammerung of Nordic and Wagnerian legend. If Hitler's bunker in Berlin was hardly the Valhalla of the gods, its destruction with the mass suicide of its inhabitants was as total an ending as any millennial New Order might have desired.

Curiously, the apotheosis of the Grail as the Celtic cauldron of destruction was not in the fire-bombing of Berlin and Dresden, but in the atomic destruction of Hiroshima and Nagasaki, two cities of imperial Japan. A vast incendiary chalice, miscalled a mushroom cloud, intervened as the mythical Nordic world tree Yggdrasil between earth and heaven. Instant and slow dying was its only giving. The ideal of divine bounty and life being distributed by a cup or a dish, a dove or a stone from the sky was undermined into a darker Nordic and Biblical past, where the hidden hand of God bestowed retribution and the plague. Out of the classical *krater* or mixing-bowl of creation had spurted the volcano rather than the seed. Yet the legend of the Grail would not be lost in this immeasurable snuffing-out. Its message – the personal quest for transcendence and the individual vision of the divine – would be revived on the couches of psychiatrists and in the preparations of a New Age.

313

Chapter Eighteen

The Vision of the Grail

What else can we see in the Grail but a bundle of paradoxes?

It is visible and invisible; an object – cup, vessel, or stone – and not an object; a person and not a person – neither male nor female; it dispenses earthly food or celestial; it inspires love, it inspires terror; it embodies predestination, but requires, nevertheless, individual effort. These, of course, are the paradoxes of the Divine, and they have found in the Grail symbol a perfect representation – so perfect, indeed, that the Grail, like the Divine, baffles description, remaining an imageless image.

Helen Adolf, *Visio Pacis*

In the December before the outbreak of the First World War, Jung first used what he later called active imagination. The technique was based on the visionary practices of ancient Oriental and Western mystics, a system of exercises designed to eliminate the critical faculties and so produce a vacuum in consciousness. Then the repressed fantasies of the unconscious might appear. Jung was sitting at his desk in the winter of 1913 when he took the decisive steps. He let himself drop. The ground gave way, he landed in a sticky mess. Before him was the entrance to a cave guarded by a leathery dwarf. Slipping by, he saw on a hollowed rock a glowing red crystal. Beneath, in a river, a dead blond youth with a wound in his head floated past, followed by a giant scarab beetle and the blazing red sun. Blinded by the light, Jung wanted to cover the well stone, but he was sickened by a jet of blood leaping from it, which blotted his active vision.

This intense view of some of the signs of the Grail had been induced by reading the alchemical text of the *Emerald Table* of Hermes Trismegistus: Jung had a long obsession with the paranormal and the occult. Despite his analytic psychology, he remained a psychic and a romantic. He was using mystic devices to reach his own desires. In an explanation of his methods, he wrote that each of us should concentrate on a mental picture until it began to move and develop. Consciously, we might distrust that process. It could be our own invention. Yet that doubt was untrue. We were overestimating our intention and Nietzsche's power of the will. If we concentrated on the inner picture, our unconscious would unlock 'a series of images which make a complete story'.

Jung had long had an interest in Gnosticism and the Grail. He thought that the metaphysical terms of the Oriental sages matched his psychological terms. He was particularly fascinated by alchemy, which seemed to prophesy the modern examination of the unconscious. 'The experiences of the alchemists were, in a sense, my experiences, and their world was my world . . . The uninterrupted intellectual chain back to Gnosticism gave substance to my psychology.' He thought that the procedures of his active imagination closely resembled the methods of the alchemists, who had tried to control and interpret what the Greeks had called hypnagogia or the waking dream. In fact, the directed reverie was a way of attaining visions of the divine. As Jung's wife Emma defined it in her work with Marie-Louise von Franz on *The Grail Legend*, 'the individual became like a vessel for the inflowing contents of the unconscious'. Her husband had agreed with the legendary writer of antiquity, Maria Prophetissa, that 'the whole secret lies in knowing about the Hermetic vessel'. Maria was called the sister of Moses and was connected with the *Sophia* of Wisdom of Gnostic tradition. Jung also quoted the teachings of Herakleon that a dying man should pray to the demiurgic powers: 'I am a vessel more precious than the feminine being who made you. Whereas your mother knew not her own roots, I know of myself, and I know whence I have come.'

So Jung used the language of alchemy and the classical origins of the Grail as the mixing-bowl of wisdom and self-knowledge to create a process of depth psychology. The mysterious vessel was a fiery womb, which transformed the being within it. Although it might enlighten the spirit, it could also destroy the unworthy viewer, as when Lancelot was scorched and fell into a deathly coma in *The Quest of the Holy Grail*. The Holy Ghost had been interpreted by the Gnostics as the female *Sophia*, for the Spirit of God was the mediator of the birth in the flesh, bringing out Christ to illuminate the darkness of this world.

Furthermore, Jung linked the ancient healing horn cups with the chalice of the Eucharist. He quoted Hippolytus on the Greek cup of Anacreon, which was dumb.

Yet Anacreon affirms that it tells him in mute language what he must become, that is, spiritual and not carnal, if he will hear the secret hidden in silence. And this secret is the water which Jesus, at that fair marriage, changed into wine. That was the great and true beginning of the miracles which Jesus wrought in Cana in Galilee, and thus he showed forth the kingdom of heaven.

That cup was also an alchemical retort as well as the lower half of the world, made of water and earth. It gave out life and healing, as did the sacred vessels of gold and silver taken from the Temple of Jerusalem to Babylon and returned to the second Temple built by Zerubbabel, described in the Book of Ezra and the Apocryphal Ezra:

Then I opened my mouth, and lo! there was reached unto me a full cup, which was full as it were with water, but the colour of it was like fire.

And I took it and drank: and when I had drunk,
My heart poured forth understanding.
Wisdom grew in my breast,
And my spirit retained its memory.

Jung emphasised the interpretation of the Holy Vessel as
the womb. He cited Saint Ambrose, declaring that God
'chose for himself this vessel, through which he should
descend to sanctify the temple of shame.' He continued: 'In
the womb of the virgin, grace increased like a heap of wheat
and the flowers of the lily.' In Gnostic literature, the 'vase of
sins' was contrasted with the 'vessel of virtue' of the Mother
of God. When Jung considered how strongly the Fathers of
the Church were influenced by Gnostic and heretical ideas,
he conceived that the symbolism of the vessel might be a
pagan relic which was adapted by Christianity. The worship
of Mary secured for Rome the heritage of the Earth Mother,
Isis and other ancient goddesses. 'The image of the *vas
Sapientiae*, vessel of wisdom, likewise recalls its Gnostic
prototype, Sophia.'

What Jung wanted to do was to elucidate the psychological relations between the veneration of woman and the
legend of the Grail, so characteristic of the early Middle
Ages. The central Holy Vessel seemed to Jung to be a 'thoroughly non-Christian image . . . a genuine relic of
Gnosticism'. The feminine principle, as in the demonstrated
cult of Saint Mary Magdalene, was strengthened in the masculine psychology of that time. 'Its symbolisation in an enigmatic image must be interpreted as a spiritualisation of the
eroticism aroused by the worship of woman.' Yet an effective symbol had to be by its very nature unassailable. The
Grail symbol fulfilled these requirements, and as the operas
of Wagner showed, its vitality lasted until modern times,
'even though our age and psychology strive unceasingly for
its dissolution'.

For Jung, Wagner's *Parsifal* was remarkable in uniting the
Spear of Destiny and the Grail, and so solving a sexual

problem. Yet the lance that harmed was also the thing that healed Anfortas. Such a paradox became true when vision saw the opposites of male and female united on a higher plane. On the threshold of modern times, triple thinkers had influenced the future of Germany: Goethe; Wagner, the prophet of incestuous and spiritual love; and Nietzsche, the prophet of power and the significant will for individuality. At the end, Wagner resurrected the Grail legend as Goethe brought back Dante, but Nietzsche seized on the idea of a blond master caste of Nordic knights. That three of the greater minds of Germany should revive early medieval psychology convinced Jung that the Grail legend, which had inspired the Templars, might have been 'the germ of a new orientation to life'. The Gnostic basis of the Grail took him back to the early Christian heresies, in which the unconscious psychology of man was in the full and luxuriant flower of its perversity. For it strongly resisted the rules of the Church and society. It represented 'that Promethean and creative spirit which will bow only to the individual soul and to no collective ruling . . . a belief in the efficacy of individual revelation and individual knowledge. This belief was rooted in the proud feeling of man's affinity with the gods, subject to no human law, and so overmastering that it may even subdue the gods by the sheer power of Gnosis.'

The genius of Jung wedded early-medieval heresy and the quest for the Grail to modern depth psychology and the analysis of self. He also related the sacred vessel to nascent feminism. 'It is always the knight,' one guardian of her sex wrote, 'the masculine representative of the Quest, who goes in search of the divine vessel – perhaps because it is a feminine symbol to begin with, but also because women do not *need* the quest, are already vessels of the Holy Blood, their archetype the Virgin, and are therefore Grail *bearers* rather than seekers. Each may give birth, therefore, to the new Grail Lord.'

Such stimulating works of cultural history as Riane Eisler's *The Chalice and the Blade* stressed that much of human history was essentially a male domination over producing women. The Garden of Eden was an allegory of Neolithic times, when women cultivated the soil with men. In Mesopotamian legends the supreme deity was the Queen of Heaven. The Earth Goddess had been worshipped since the beginnings of civilisation. But the blade or the phallus, the Holy Lance or Spear or Sword of Destiny, these had become the nuclear warheads, the supreme weapons of destruction. Against them in Marian and psychological terms stood the chalice and the womb, the Grail and rebirth, the Spirit and regeneration. Jung, indeed, also quoted the Cistercian prior of Châlis, Guillaume de Digulleville, on the alchemical colour of the Holy Ghost, which was green because 'it sprang forth and gave comfort'. So should future societies be for the feminist social scientists, looking for places 'where the power to give and nurture, which the Chalice symbolises, was supreme'.

This was not so in the medieval legends of the Grail. There the male knight by bloody deeds had looked for the divine. In a sense, if the Grail was the feminine symbol of the womb which gave birth to all men, then the Galahad and Perceval who achieved that goal were returning to their source. Yet such an interpretation was no longer the Matter of Britain nor of France, but the psychology of Jung and the feminists. The search for the Grail had always been a heresy, a personal inquiry after God; but only now was it reduced to self-analysis or a version of cultural history, indoctrinated with modern perceptions. Hermes Trismegistus may have been percipient in his *Rosarium* when he declared: 'And thus the Philosopher is not the Master of the Stone, but rather its Minister.' The Grail and its symbols cannot be used for contemporary causes. They are what they appear to be, and they may declare what is done with them.

Beatific States

'The Being of all beings is a wrestling power.' So wrote

Jakob Boehme, a mystic of the early seventeenth century, about the conflicts which led him to the insight of the divine. He might have been describing the hallucinogenic states of Lancelot and his cousin Yvain, when their dreadful adventures towards the Grail were interrupted by visions of boiling fountains, ravening lions and incinerating fires. They strove towards God, and yet they were denied the final sight of Him, because their strife was their unseeing. Unlike the hermits who directed them on their paths to the Castle of the Fisher King, the Knights of Camelot had no knowledge of the spiritual exercises which were the conditions of a final joust with the Holy Ghost. These rules were necessary, if a seeker were to engage beatitude.

Again Jung was the master guide towards a view of the transcendental. To him, prophets and seers were poets as well as mystics. They could glimpse the primordial experience of myths and translate these into our world of forms. They could give a shape to the Grail within 'the strange paradoxes of their vision'. Jung particularly cited the phantasmagoric world of India, the Old Testament and the Apocalypse; also of Dante's *Divine Comedy*, the otherworld in Goethe's *Faust* and the poetry of William Blake. Such records of archetypes had the power to stimulate the imagination, when the receiver was in an induced trance. 'Formation, transformation' was Jung's definition, 'Eternal Mind's eternal recreation.'

The Grail itself in its apparitions was everything to everyone – magic cauldron, cup, dish, stone, or pentecostal tongues of fire – or wrapped in samite or clouds to hide itself from the unfit. Its shape depended on the state of mind of the viewer after reaching the sight of it. Its original romancers knew of the severe practices endured by hermits and holy people if they wanted to reach an ecstatic experience by the exclusion of all the world of the senses. Saint John of the Cross would negate everything except the vision of fiery love, while Jan Van Ruysbroek had to consider sunlight. Julia of Norwich prayed for the bodily sight of Christ on the

Cross and the receipt of His Blood from His three wounds. The price she would pay was a terrible trial by disease. She was granted all her desires. As she lay dying at the age of thirty, a priest held a crucifix before her eyes. In her dark chamber, she beheld a light on the image of the Cross. She could hardly breathe and thought that she was expiring, then suddenly 'all my pain was taken away from me, and I was as whole as ever I was before'. In her hypnotic concentration on the death of Christ, she was restored to her own life and granted her wants, seeing the red blood trickle down His Body from his Crown of Thorns, 'hot and freshly and right plenteously'.

Such mystic perceptions were the matter of the Grail; but they could only be perceived by trial and rigour in the West, and in the East by religious rituals such as the Buddhist tantra. In these, the novices were taught to chant and to concentrate on six syllables signifying six colours – as in alchemy – and six beings. *Aum* was white and denoted the gods. *Ma* was blue and dealt with those who were not gods. *Ni* was yellow and human. *Pad* was green and animal. *Me* was red and subhuman, while *Hum* was black and connected with sinners in the underworld. The repetition of these syllables while meditating upon them resulted in the six transitory realms of being on their passing into the acceptance of the One. Other mystical traditions had their own series of negations and contemplations, but the aim was the same – the final understanding of and looking at the Creator and the Whole.

This ultimate vision of the divine might be an illusion. 'From my own unforgettable experience,' wrote Martin Buber, 'I know well that there is a state in which the bonds of the personal nature of life seem to have fallen away from us and we experience an undivided unity. But I do not know – what the soul willingly imagines and indeed is bound to imagine (mine too once did it) – that in this I had attained to a union with the primal being or the godhead. That is an exaggeration no longer permitted to the responsible understanding.' The short cuts to the experience of the Whole, particularly by drugs rather than penances, did not guarantee the value of the deep insight.

That was especially the way of the American 'Flower Children' of the 1960s, from the Beats to the Yippies. They paid for their trips towards a union with the divine with magic mushrooms and other sacerdotal drugs. Timothy Leary was to preach that his League for Spiritual Discovery was a religion. 'The sacraments marijuana and LSD should only be used by initiates and priests of our religion and only used in shrines.' These were the bread and wine, the Holy Body and Blood of his new cult. 'LSD is ecumenical. God is not Christian. He doesn't speak Greek or Latin. When you contact God as we have you realise that His energy and His blueprint were going on long before man worked out these verbal formulas.' The psychedelic revolution was a spiritual revival, which would change American culture. Leary's revelation was not original. The genetic code, which he considered to be the main instrument of God, had been telling us the same message for thousands of years. Each of us must search inside the self. That was his primary conclusion. 'Nothing you do outside is important unless you're centred within.'

Just such a radical insight had been a message of the quest for the Grail. Yet its trials and tests were no part of the new counter-culture in which each seeker after truth was, in a sense, his or her own work of art. Narcissus rather than Galahad was the ideal of this new generation, which rejected any heritage in favour of instant creation. Among the drug abusers, the Holy Lance became the needle of the hypodermic syringe, and the Crown of Thorns was the tourniquet used to find a vein; all this pain in the quest for the Grail of selfish beatific vision. A dependence on stimulants and a sexual free-for-all pitted this alternative culture against the old moralists and traditions. As that troubadour of the New Age, Allen Ginsberg, chanted in 'Howl', the best minds of his generation were destroyed by madness. 'Looking for an angry fix, angelheaded hipsters burning for the ancient heavenly connection to the starry dynamo in the machinery of night.'

The psychologists of 'psychedelic therapy' found that their subjects did achieve a universal central perception. Behind the huge diversity of things in the world of science and the everyday, there was a single reality, which appeared to be infinite and eternal. All beings were united in one Being. Any sense of the separate individual was merged in the pervading Spirit. As with those few knights who saw the Grail, the lives of the drug-users who glimpsed the totality of existence were forever changed by that knowledge. Even if chemical substances rather than actual pilgrimages had been their trips, their minds were altered by an insight into the universal.

The privations suffered by the medieval knights and pilgrims had also given them visions. Fatigue and hunger were their hallucinogens. Fasting and sleeping affected their senses and induced sacred fantasies and encounters of a weird kind. Confused by the imbalances caused by hardships along the way, the travellers saw what they saw at the end of their road because of their concentration on their goal and their faith in their illuminations. We do see, indeed, what we believe we see. A mirage is real enough at a distance, unless we choose to examine it too closely.

The Grail was, after all, invisible as the Holy Spirit and the blessing of God. The forms in which it appeared in the beatific states of its followers were the shapes which they were directed to see. In the eyes of the Celts and the Nordic folk, the Grail was the cauldron and the spear; in classical times, the cosmic bowl and the horn of plenty; for the Jews, the Ark and the Tabernacle; for Christians, the chalice and the dish; for Muslims, the Ka'aba with its black stone; for the dissenters, the fire, the serpent and the dove. Yet the Grail was not all things to all men, but only one – a symbol of each person's direct approach to the divine light. Many have sought it, few have found it – or it has found them. In

Tennyson's poem, Sir Percivale travelled with the Grail which he was seeking. Under its many aspects, it had sustained his journey towards its final grace. Never did this blood-red 'Holy Thing' fail from the side of the Arthurian knight, but moved with him all the way to crown him in the spiritual city of his quest.

Epilogue

> To know that any revelation is from God, it is necessary to know that the messenger that delivers it is sent from God, and that cannot be known but by credentials given by God himself.
>
> John Locke, *A Discourse of Miracles*

Some great works on the Grail still emerged from the slaughter and cynicism of the two World Wars. David Jones painted a Mass in a blasted chapel with the no man's land between the trenches depicted as the Waste Land of the Fisher King. *In Parenthesis* and *The Anathemata* showed the Knights of Camelot fighting beside the Tommies. T. H. White published a quartet entitled *The Once and Future King*, in which he traced the old legends from Arthur's education as a boy to his dark ending after the Battle of Camlann. A posthumous sequel, *The Story of Merlyn*, told of the British King's journey to an otherworld and the divine light. And Charles Williams, one of the group of Inklings at Oxford around C. S. Lewis and J. R. R. Tolkien, wrote two volumes of bardic poems on Arthurian themes, culminating in a vision of the spiritual intellect, 'the building of Logres and the coming of the land of the Trinity which is called Sarras in maps of the soul'.

As the twentieth century declined towards the millennium, the Grail was translated into science fiction, film and musical, to end in derision. Of course, mockery had been a part of the Passion. Jeered as the King of the Jews, Jesus was crowned with a circlet of thorns for the amusement of the mob. His clothes were won at dice. The cup of wine and the dish at the Last Supper, the lance point or the bowl which caught His Blood on the Cross, these became part and parcel of the demeaning of the divine. The quest for the Grail and the Ark was turned into parody and special effects by Spielberg in his Indiana Jones films, which surpassed even the mischievous tricks of the wizard Merlin. The life of Christ was filmed as a practical joke by the Monty Python team as the romp of a nobody who got it all wrong. The sense of the sacred legend was moribund, although John Boorman's film *Excalibur* did confuse Arthur with the wounded Grail King in a rich evocation of the myth. And the trite romantic musical of *Camelot* was moving enough to inspire Jacqueline Bouvier Kennedy to try and re-create a cultural court around her and the martyr President in the White House.

This book essays to be the history of the Grail as well as the story of its discovery in many places. It endeavours, as the Knights of King Arthur did, to take each reader a little closer to the vision of the grace of God by the cautious description of the signs and symbols on the way. At present, we are beset by false prophets. They claim what they cannot show or prove. Their names are as innumerable and inconsiderable as the angels counted as standing on a pinhead. If Jonathan Swift were still with us, he would call them the What-if Facticides. After some research, which is usually taken from the original and serious work of other people and rarely acknowledged, these fantasists put forward a hypothesis. Was Christ or the Grail buried under a mountain in the south of France? We will prove it by mystic graphs spread over the Massif Central and the Pyrenees. Did Jesus marry Mary Magdalene and provide the blood line of the Merovingians? We will show it by a spurious Priory of Zion and a wealthy priest from an obscure mountain village. Diagrams on Poussin paintings demonstrate where the Holy Blood is and how the Grail crossed the Atlantic. What if, as

Swift suggested, we seek to make sunshine out of cucumbers?

Each speculation by these writers of historical fiction is supported by an array of glittering and separate facts curiously linked together, rather like the little jade plates covering the corpses of ancient Chinese princesses. Within a few pages, the assertion becomes the actual, the idea is changed into the proof. These authors are less historians than alchemists. They seek to find the Holy Vessel and the Holy Blood in a Philosopher's Stone of their imagination, although that only produced brass and no gold.

Yet the search for the Grail remains a personal voyage. The question is the choice of a guide. My own journey was begun in Rosslyn Chapel with the discovery of the Templar tombstone with its chalice containing the rosy cross and the crusading blade. And yet many months passed before I noticed that the whole building was a Grail chapel, that its roof was the stone fallen from heaven of the Ka'aba and *Parzival*. Looking above me, I saw that the ceiling was divided into five sections stretching from east to west. In the first four segments, the flowers of creation opened in all their glory, particularly the rose of the Virgin Mary. Then in the west, the stars of the sky clustered on high. To the south, I could see the sun that gives light and life, then the head of Jesus Christ, and then the dove flying down with the host in its beak. Below this sign of the Holy Spirit was carved the symbol of the Grail. It looked like the bowl of a cup or a crescent moon, the emblem of Islam. From it poured God's grace and bounty, seen as waves or flow. Frozen in stone with algae on the heaven behind it, this Grail seemed to let fall all the green things of the Third Day of Creation. As I solved the mystery of this sacred place by finding the Grail among the constellations above, I heard Marlowe's Doctor Faustus plead in my ear:

See, see how Christ's blood streams from the firmament!
One drop would save my soul!

As the Grail legends declared, each of us may only attain a holy vision if we already know what we should see and are fit to do so. By research and circumstance, I discovered the Grail trails, places, shapes and signs which are the matter of this book. There are many more to be found, particularly by those who follow in the steps of the cult of Saint Mary Magdalene. But every person may discern the Holy Vessel only in the form which each of us is able to perceive. As the old command went: 'Seek, and you shall find.'

Living in this sceptical age I found it difficult to believe that all of the intense faith of the Middle Ages came from nothing and went into oblivion. I have studied some of the remains. The crypts and the spires, the blazing glass windows and the stone reliefs, all reflect the secrets and the aspirations of the Grail. If we have souls, then each of us will continue to reach for a kind of transcendence. As a millennium approaches, we will join in a search which may become a frenzy for the perennial. If there is a life after death, the Grail persists as our goal. We do not wish to see the Holy Spirit through a glass darkly, but in fire, face to face.

I may only sketch a few of the ways there. I have tried to describe my guides on that path, and what they have said. I have told you of the signs and the symbols on my road to the Holy Vessel. All I can hope is that I may have spoken occasionally according to the words of Robert de Boron in his *Joseph of Arimathea*:

> *He spoke the blessed words,*
> *So sweet and precious,*
> *Gracious and merciful,*
> *That are rightly called and named*
> *The secret of the Grail.*

Chapter Notes

Chapter One

I acknowledge gratefully the book by Jeremy Black and Anthony Green, with illustrations by Tessa Rickards, *Gods, Demons and Symbols of Ancient Mesopotamia* (The British Museum Press, 1992) for the insights in this book; the drawing of the fish man-god is by Sir Austen Henry Layard. I have used the text of *The Histories* by Herodotus translated by Baehr and Henry Cary (The Folio Society, 1992). Robert Graves, *Greek Myths* (London, 1955) is still incisive on the ancient Greek myths of creation. The illustrations of Manto, the daughter of Tiresias, consulting the priestess and the oracle with the bowl on his tripod at Delphi, and of the Eleusinian mysteries were drawn by Kirk in *Outlines from the Figures and Compositions upon the Greek, Roman, and Etruscan Vases of the Late Sir William Hamilton* (London, 1804).

George St Clair, *Myths of Greece Explained and Dated* (2 vols., London, 1901) and C.H. Moore, *The Religious Thought of the Greeks* (Harvard University Press, 1916) have been helpful on the Orphic and Mithraic cults. Charles Bertram Lewis, *Classical Mythology and Arthurian Romance* (Oxford University Press, 1932) stresses the Greek origins of the Arthurian cycle, while G.R. Levy, *The Sword from the Rock: An Investigation into the Origins of Epic Literature and the Development of the Hero* (London, 1953) is original and compelling.

Inspirational in his treatment of the origins of alchemy and ecstasy is Dan Merkur, *Gnosis: An Esoteric Tradition of Mystical Visions and Unions* (State University of New York Press, 1993). The translation of Zosimos, *The Visions*, is taken from that book. I am indebted to Piero Boitani, *The Shadow of Ulysses: Figures of a Myth* (Oxford, 1994) for his brilliant interpretation of Ulysses as hero. The essays collected in *Perceptions of the Ancient Greeks* (K. J. Dover ed., Oxford, 1992) are perceptive on the attitudes of the Jews and Muslims of the Middle Ages towards the ancient Greeks, particularly Alexander. The quotation from the Koran is from Surah 18 ('The Cave'), and may also refer to Moses.

I have used John Dryden's translation of the *Aeneid*, first published in London in 1697. Brian Branston's *The Lost Gods of England* (London, 1957) and *Gods of the North* (London, 1955) are stimulating and essential reading, particularly on *The Dream of the Rood*. Twelve Arthurian Norse works including the Merlínusspá are listed in 'Scandinavian Literature', an essay by Phillip M. Mitchell in *Arthurian Literature in the Middle Ages* (R.S. Loomis ed., Oxford, 1959). Useful on Celtic sacred cauldrons is Stuart Piggott, *The Druids* (London, 1968). Peter Berresford Ellis, *The Druids* (London, 1994) is excellent on the religion of the Druids. The quotation from Roger Sherman Loomis derives from his *Wales and the Arthurian Legend* (Oxford, 1956).

Chapter Two

John Passmore's excellent work on *The Perfectability of Man* (London, 1970) suggested the connection between the Pelagian heresy and Arthurian literature and Protestantism. Saint Augustine's *Confessions* showed that he was a heretic and a Manichean before his conversion to Christianity and the doctrine of original sin. Essential in studies of the historical truth of Arthur are John Morris, *The Age of Arthur: A History of the British Isles from 350 to 650* (London, 1973), and Leslie Alcock, *Arthur's Britain: History and Archaeology, AD 367–634* (London, 1971), which is particularly significant on excavations at Iron Age hill forts and hanging bowls of the sixth century.

In his cited works, Roger Sherman Loomis is the authority on the Irish and Welsh origins of the Grail theme. There is a fine Penguin Books edition of Geoffrey of Monmouth, *The History of the Kings of Britain* (tr. and intro. by Lewis Thorpe, London, 1966). There was even an Anglo-Saxon version of Geoffrey's Latin *History* and of Wace's French *Brut*, written by a priest in Worcestershire named Layamon. It was brutal but poetic, particularly about slaughter. Strangely, it supported the Celtic resistance to the Anglo-Saxons, as though the enemies had become one British people by the time of the Norman Conquest. For the West Country traditions of the visit of Jesus I am indebted to the Reverend C.C. Dobson, *Did Our Lord visit Britain as they say in Cornwall and Somerset?* (rev. ed., Glastonbury, 1947).

I am again grateful to Roger Sherman Loomis, 'The Oral Diffusion of the Arthurian Legend', in the book edited by him, *Arthurian Literature in the Middle Ages: A Collaborative History* (Oxford University Press, 1959). His magisterial treatment of this subject and of the Celtic roots of Arthurian literature leave all scholars in his debt. Also admirable on its subject is James P. Carley, *Glastonbury Abbey* (rev. ed., Glastonbury, 1996).

Chapter Three

I am indebted to the excellent translation of *Perceval* or *The Story of the Grail* by Ruth Harwood Clive with introduction and notes (University of Georgia Press, 1985). Jean Frappier's works on *Perceval* are most important, particularly his *Chrétien de Troyes et le Mythe du Graal* (Paris, 1972). William A. Nitze, *Perceval and the Holy Grail: An Essay on the Romance of Chrétien de Troyes* (University of California Press, 1949) emphasises the importance of the Byzantine ritual of Chrysostomos in the Grail procession, while Eugene J. Weinraub, *Chrétien's Jewish Grail: A New Investigation of the Imagery and Significance of Chrétien de Troyes's Grail Episode Based upon Medieval Hebraic Sources* (University of North Carolina Press, 1976) is also significant.

A brilliant pamphlet by Leonardo Olschki, 'The Grail Castle and its Mysteries' (Manchester University Press, 1966), alone stresses the power of the Grail as representing the Light of God, deriving from the Gospel of Saint John and Gnostic heresies in the twelfth century. The remarkable *Visio Pacis: Holy City and Grail* (Pennsylvania State University Press, 1960) by Helen Adolf relates the Grail quest to the loss of Jerusalem and the search for a heavenly city. I deal with the connection between the Cistercians and the Knights Templar in *Jerusalem: The Endless Crusade* (New York, 1995) and in *The Sword and the Grail* (New York, 1992), which also emphasises the St Clairs as the family of the Holy Light (Sancto Claro). I have quoted from J.A. MacCulloch, *Medieval Faith and Fable* (London, 1932) on the importance of relics as well as the host in the Middle Ages. The brilliant book by the librarian at Montségur, Raimonde Reznikov, *Cathares et Templiers* (Toulouse, 1993), proves that the Knights Templar both attacked and supported the Cathars in the Langue d'Oc. Michel Roquebert, in *Les Cathares et le Graal* (Toulouse, 1995), considers the Grail texts as orthodox and Catholic, and so he denies the title of his book, stating that the Cathars as heretics had nothing to do with the Holy Vessel. Zoé Oldenbourg, *Massacre at Montségur: A History of the Albigensian Crusade* (New York, 1961), remains magisterial on the subject.

Information on the early history of the St Clair family and of their patron saint may be found in Roland William Saint-Clair, *The Saint-Clairs of the Isles* (Auckland, New Zealand, 1898). He suggested another possible patron saint from Kent. In her book, *The Holy Grail* (New York, 1992), Norma Lorre Goodrich strongly asserts the Scottish provenance of King Arthur and his Knights, including Lancelot. Louis

Charpentier discovered the Templar Commanderies beside the forest lakes near Troyes in his *Les Mystères Templiers* (Paris, 1967).

Chapter Four

The authority on the Lancelot or Vulgate cycle is Jean Frappier, who wrote an article on the subject in *Arthurian Literature in the Middle Ages*, op. cit. I have used the Penguin edition of Gerald of Wales's works, edited and translated by Lewis Thorpe (London, 1978). Helen Adolf, in her *Visio Pacis*, op. cit., is stimulating on the subject of the *Joseph* of Robert de Boron. *The Grail Legend* by Emma Jung and Marie-Louise von Franz was published in Boston, Mass., in 1986. I have used the Penguin edition of *The Quest of the Holy Grail* (London, 1969). It was edited and translated by P. M. Matarosso, whose introduction is illuminating, and who particularly quotes the works of Jean Marx, *La légende arthurienne et le Graal* (Paris, 1952) and Albert Pauphilet, *Etudes sur la Queste del Saint Graal* (Paris, 1921). Matarosso's *The Redemption of Chivalry: A Study of the Queste del Saint Graal* (Geneva, 1979) is also excellent.

Etienne Gilson, in *La Théologie mystique de Saint Bernard* (Paris, 1947), stresses the mysticism and divine grace in *The Quest of the Holy Grail*. P.M. Matarosso, op. cit., is quoted on the grave ambivalence between primitive belief and Christian faith in the text. Norma Lorre Goodrich, *The Holy Grail*, already cited, was particularly struck by *The History of the Grail*, which she preferred to call the *Grand-Saint-Graal*. I have used the King James Bible for the Gospel according to Saint John, Ch. 3, vv. 14–16, Ch. 6, vv. 48–50 and 53, Ch. 19, vv. 40–41, and Ch. 21, vv. 5, 6, 9 and 12. The leading French critic quoted on the *Lancelot* cycle was Ferdinand Lot, *Etude sur le 'Lancelot en Prose'* (Paris, 1918).

Chapter Five

Le Haut Livre du Graal Perlesvaus was edited by William A. Nitze and collaborators in a definitive text and commentary, published by the University of Chicago Press in 1937. For the translations, I have also used *The High History of the Holy Graal*, translated from the old text by Sebastian Evans (London, 1910). I am again indebted to Robert Sherman Loomis for his original and brilliant *Celtic Myth and Arthurian Romance* (Columbia University Press, New York, 1927). The article on 'Gereint, Owein, and Peredur' by Idris Llewelyn Foster in *Arthurian Literature in the Middle Ages* is also excellent. The leading Welsh commentator on *Peredur*, from whom I have quoted, is the admirable Glenys Goetinck, *Peredur: A Study of Welsh Tradition in the Grail Legend* (University of Wales Press, Cardiff, 1975).

Chapter Six

Richard Barber, *The Knight & Chivalry* (London, 1970), is penetrating on the actual effect of the Grail romances on knightly behaviour. The quotation is taken from the translation of Gottfried von Strassburg's *Tristan* by A.T. Hatto, printed in London in 1960. W.H. Jackson deals with *Chivalry in Twelfth-Century Germany: The Works of Hartmann von Aue* (London, 1994). The text of *Parzival* is analysed in my own *The Sword and the Grail*, op. cit., also in David Blamires, *Characterization and Individuality in Wolfram's 'Parzival'* (Cambridge University Press, 1966), and in Margaret F. Richey, *Studies of Wolfram von Eschenbach* (London, 1957). The translations from the original are largely mine.

I am indebted to Walter Johannes Stein, *The Ninth Century and the Holy Grail* (Temple Lodge Press, 1988), for the quotation from the Twelve Keys of Basilius Valentinus. Hugh Sacker, *An Introduction to Wolfram's 'Parzival'* (Cambridge University Press, 1963), is excellent on the subject of the Grail. There is a good comparison in Linda B. Parshall, *The Art of Narration in Wolfram's Parzival and Albrecht's Jüngerer Titurel* (Cambridge University Press, 1981), while Otto Springer's essay 'Wolfram's *Parzival*' is important in *Arthurian Literature in the Middle Ages*, op. cit., an important compendium.

All scholars are indebted to *The Middle High German Poems of WILLEHALM by Wolfram of Eschenbach* (tr. and intro. by Charles E. Passage, New York, 1977). *Wolfram von Eschenbach, Titurel and the Songs* (tr. and intro. by Marion E. Gibbs and Sidney M. Johnson, New York, 1988) is also essential. As always, Helen Adolf in her *Visio Pacis*, op. cit., has striking insights, while Roger Sherman Loomis, *The Grail: From Celtic Myth to Christian Symbol* (Columbia University Press, 1963), identifies the *Alexanderlied* as a source for the stone Grail in *Parzival*.

Chapter Seven

The quotations about the endeavour to destroy the host and other examples of miracles come from the admirable J.A. MacCulloch, *Medieval Faith and Fable*, op. cit., Manly P. Hall, *The Adepts in the Eastern Esoteric Tradition: The Mystics of Islam* (The Philosophical Research Society, Los Angeles, 1994), and Dan Merkur, *Gnosis*, op. cit. (from whom the quotations of the Koranic verses are taken), are penetrating on oriental mysticism. J. D. Anderson and E. T. Kennan translated Saint Bernard's *Advice to a Pope, De Consideratione Libri Quinque Ad Eugenium Tertium* (Kalamazoo, 1976). F. Bogdanow made an excellent comparison in his essay, 'The mystical theology of Bernard de Clairvaux and the meaning of Chrétien de Troyes' *Conte du Graal*' in *Essays in memory of the late Leslie Topsfield* (Peter S. Noble and Linda M. Paterson eds., Cambridge, 1984).

The best assessment of the Templar escape to Scotland is to be found in Michael Baigent and Richard Leigh, *The Temple and the Lodge* (London, 1989). They first noticed the

Templar graves in Argyll. The rule of the Templars is published in Henri de Curzon, *La Règle du Temple* (Paris, 1886). In my *The Sword and the Grail*, op. cit., I have previously written of my first discoveries of the Grail carved upon Templar tombstones. Most useful was Benedicta Ward, *Miracles and the Medieval Mind: Theory, Record and Event, 1000–1215* (London, 1982). And most illuminating and scholarly and original was Susan Hoskins, Mary Magdalene: *Myth and Metaphor* (London, 1993). Yet this admirable work has one strange omission, hardly a mention of the Magdalene and the Grail.

Chapter Eight

Illuminating analysis and the modernised translation from William Wey come from H.N. Wethered, *The Four Paths of Pilgrimage* (London, 1947), J.A. MacCulloch, *Medieval Faith and Fable*, op. cit., is again invaluable on the subject of miracles and provided the quotations from Theodoret, Saint Columba and Pope Gregory. On the subject of the relics in Constantinople and in Rome, Ian Wilson provides expert advice in *Holy Faces, Secret Places: The Quest for Jesus' True Likeness* (New York, 1991). An original Travellers' Guide by Ean and Deike Begg, *In Search of the Holy Grail and the Precious Blood* (London, 1995), provides unique research into the sites of the sacred relics of Europe. The translation from Dante's 'Paradiso', Book 31, lines 103–108, is my own. Teddy Kollek and Moshe Pearlman, *Pilgrims to the Holy Land* (London, 1970) is most useful on its theme, while a recent fine work on the subject is Simon Coleman and John Elsner, *Pilgrimage: Past and Present* (British Museum Press, 1995). I am indebted to the brilliant essay, 'Le Trésor au temps de Suger', by Danielle Gaborit-Chopin, in *Le Trésor de Saint-Denis* (Dijon, 1992); also to Pierre-Marie Auzas, *Eugène Viollet le Duc: 1814–1879* (Caisse Nationale des Monuments Historiques et des Sites, 1979).

Chapter Nine

The two classic works by J. Huizinga, *The Waning of the Middle Ages* (London, 1924) and *Homo Ludens* (London, 1949), were my inspiration for this chapter, and the quotations are from these works. Norman Housley, *The Later Crusades: From Lyons to Alcazar, 1274–1580* (Oxford University Press, 1992), is excellent on the requiems of the movement. M. Keen, in *Chivalry* (Yale University Press, 1984), translated the passage on the Teutonic Knights from Jean Cabaret d'Orville, *La Chronique du bon duc Loys de Bourbon* (Paris, 1876). On pilgrimage, I am again indebted to *The Four Paths of Pilgrimage*, op. cit., and to *Pilgrimage: Past and Present*, op. cit., as well as to Donald R. Howard, *Writers and Pilgrims: Medieval Pilgrimage, Narratives and Their Posterity* (University of California Press, 1980).

Chapter Ten

The most important recent book on frontier conflicts is *Medieval Frontier Societies* (Robert Bartlett and Angus MacKay eds., Oxford, 1989): the work is particularly fine on the *reconquista*. Always useful for the geography of the Grail situation are *The Atlas of the Crusades* (Jonathan Riley-Smith ed., London, 1991) and *In Search of the Holy Grail and the Precious Blood*, op. cit., the only Baedeker on the subject. The quotation about the Christian conversion of Aragon comes from the Rev. Professor Robert Burns, *The Crusader Kingdom of Valencia* (2 vols., Cambridge, Mass., 1967). There is an excellent article on 'Arthurian Literature in Spain and Portugal' by Maria Rosa Lida de Malkiel in *Arthurian Literature in the Middle Ages*, op. cit. And Walter Stein wrote an intriguing appendix on the legend of Saint Lawrence and the Roman Grail in his cited *The Ninth Century and the Holy Grail*. The quotation from Fernand Braudel comes from his seminal work, *The Mediterranean and the Mediterranean World in the Age of Philip II* (2 vols., London, 1972).

I have generally used the Modern Library translation of *Don Quixote* by Samuel Putnam after the Castilian of Miguel de Cervantes (New York, 1949). Yet as Cervantes himself wrote about the problems of translation: 'Translating from one language into another, unless it be from one of those two queenly tongues, Greek and Latin, is like gazing at a Flemish tapestry with the wrong side out: even though the figures are visible, they are full of threads that obscure the view and are not bright and smooth as when seen from the other side.'

Chapter Eleven

Norman Housley, *The Later Crusades: From Lyons to Alcazar*, op. cit., is excellent on the papal misuse of pardon money collected for crusades. The quotations from Erasmus are from *Opus epistolarum Desiderii Erasmi Roterodami* (P.S. Allen *et al.* eds., 12 vols., Oxford University Press, 1906–58). E.C. Gardner, *Arthurian Legend in Italian Literature* (London, 1930), is essential reading, as is Antonio Viscardi, 'Arthurian Influences on Italian Literature from 1200 to 1500', in *Arthurian Literature in the Middle Ages*, previously cited, and Ian Wilson, *Holy Faces, Secret Places*, op. cit., who is stimulating on the Sack of Rome and quoted the letters on the catastrophe.

On the subject of Italian patronage in that period, Sergio Bertelli, *The Courts of the Italian Renaissance* (Milan, 1985), is helpful; and on the Medici, Edward L. Goldberg, *Patterns in Late Medici Art Patronage* (Princeton, New Jersey, 1983), is important. Vasari's *Lives of the Artists* and Cellini's *Autobiography* contain remarkable revelations, while W.L. Gurdesheimer, *Ferrara – The Style of a Renaissance Despotism* (Princeton, New Jersey, 1973), is informative. Harold Acton, 'Medicean Florence' in *Cities of Destiny* (Arnold Toynbee ed., London, 1967), wrote an elegant essay on the subject, while Bernard Berenson, *The Italian Painters of the Renaissance* (London, 1952), remains seminal. The translations from the 'Purgatorio' of Dante and

L'Orlando Innamorato by Boiardo are my own. The critic quoted on *Orlando Furioso* by Ludovico Ariosto is Barbara Reynolds, whose superb translation of the Italian poem is quoted from her rendition of that classic work for Penguin Books (London, 1975). John Hale refers to the Instruction of Emperor Charles V in his definitive *The Civilization of Europe in the Renaissance* (London, 1993). On the subject of the Virgin Mary and the Grail, John Matthews is stimulating in his *The Holy Grail: The Quest for the Eternal* (London, 1981).

Chapter Twelve

I have used Walter Scott's translation and edition of the *Hermetica* by Hermes Trismegistus, published in 1924 in London. Vital for an understanding of alchemy in the Middle Ages is the seminal work by Keith Thomas, *Religion and the Decline of Magic* (London, 1971); also Richard Kieckhefer, *Magic in the Middle Ages* (Cambridge University Press, 1989). The theory of the woundsalve comes from Sir Kenelm Digby, *A Late Discourse . . . touching the Cure of Wounds by the Powder of Sympathy* (London, 1658). I have slightly adapted the text of Malory's *Morte D'Arthur*, as edited by Israel Gollancz for the Temple Classics (4 vols., London, 1901). There is an imaginative essay by Adam McLean, 'Alchemical Transmutation in History and Symbol', in *At The Table of The Grail* (John Matthews ed., London, 1984).

Jung's work on *Psychology and Alchemy* and on *Alchemical Studies* may be found in *The Collected Works of C.G. Jung* (Vols. 12 and 13, London, New York and Princeton, 1953 and 1967). Martin Luther's hatred of the Pope is chronicled in Bernard McGinn, *Anti-Christ* (London, 1994). Nikolai Tolstoy is particularly good on the political value of Merlin's prophecies in his *The Quest for Merlin* (London, 1985), and he does much to establish Myrddin as a true Welsh bard.

Chapter Thirteen

Useful on the early legends of voyages to America is *The Quest for America* (Geoffrey Ashe ed., New York, 1971). David Blamires, *Herzog Ernst and the otherworld voyage: a comparative study* (Manchester University Press, 1979), is excellent on his subject. My own *The Sword and the Grail*, op. cit., establishes the probability and accuracy of the Zeno Narrative. The account of the expedition of Prince Henry St Clair to Canada in Michael Bradley's *Holy Grail across the Atlantic* (Toronto, 1988) is highly speculative. Well researched and convincing on the Cortereal voyages is E.B. Delabarre, *Dighton Rock* (New York, 1928). The translations from *The Lusiads*, Herrara and the letters of Columbus are mine.

Perry Miller, *Errand into the Wilderness* (Harvard University Press, 1956), is seminal on the mission of the Pilgrim Fathers, while J.H. Elliott, *The Old World and the New, 1492–1650* (Cambridge University Press, 1972), is most stimulating. Essential reading on John Milton is his biography by William Riley Parker, published in two volumes by the Oxford University Press in 1968.

Chapter Fourteen

My inspiration for this chapter was the remarkable anthology *Pandaemonium: 1660–1886*, conceived and compiled by the documentary film-maker Humphrey Jennings and edited by Mary-Lou Jennings and Charles Madge (London, 1985). The *Fumifugium* of John Evelyn was published in 1661 in London. Also admirable is Francis D. Klingender, *Art and the Industrial Revolution* (rev. ed. by Arthur Elton, London, 1968). Anna Seward's poem comes from *The Poetical Works*, edited by Sir Walter Scott in two volumes in Edinburgh in 1810. John Britton's *Autobiography* was also published in two volumes in London in 1850, while James Nasmyth's *Autobiography* was edited by Samuel Smiles and published in London in 1883. T. Ashe edited *The Table Talk and Omnia of S. T. Coleridge*, published in 1884 in London. A superb edition of *The Novels of Thomas Love Peacock* was edited by David Garnett and published in 1948 by Rupert Hart-Davis in London.

There is an erudite survey of *The Rosicrucians* by Christopher McIntosh (Wellingborough, 1987), which tells of the Hermetic Order of the Golden Dawn. The Rosicrucian version of the Round Table at Winchester derives from *The Rosicrucians: Their Rites and Mysteries* by Hargrave Jennings (London, 1907). Chevalier Robert Brydon KCT wrote an illuminating article, 'The Germanic Tradition, The Scottish Knights Templar and the Mystery of the Holy Grail', for the magazine *The Scottish Knights Templar*, Winter 1984/5. The end of the St Clairs of Rosslyn is covered in my book, *The Sword and the Grail*. On Sir Walter Scott, I have found particularly interesting the book by Coleman O. Parsons, *Witchcraft and Demonology in Scott's Fiction* (Edinburgh, 1964); the essays by Paul M. Ochojski and R.D.S. Jack in *Scott Bicentenary Essays* (Alan Bell ed., Edinburgh, 1973); Albert Canning, *History in Scott's Novels* (London, 1905); James Anderson, *Sir Walter Scott and History* (Edinburgh, 1981); and Donald Davie on 'Waverley' in *Walter Scott* (D.D. Devlin ed., London, 1968). Scott's Jacobite feelings come from Volume Three of *The Letters of Sir Walter Scott* (H. Grierson ed., 12 vols., London 1932–37), while Kay and Roger Easson have edited an admirable edition of *Milton* by William Blake for the American Blake Foundation (London, 1978).

Chapter Fifteen

In their original and cited book, *In Search of the Holy Grail and the Precious Blood*, the Beggs are strong supporters of the claims of Reichenau and Weingarten to many blessed relics. I am indebted to Bernard Levin for his advice and loan to me of the librettos of *Lohengrin* and *Parsifal*. Of the many recent books on Wagner, I have found most useful Ernest Newman, *The Wagner Operas* (New York, 1949); John Chancellor, *Wagner* (London, 1978); Martin Gregor-Dellin, *Richard Wagner: His Life, His Work, His Century* (London, 1983); and Michael Tanner, *Wagner* (London, 1996).

Chapter Sixteen

I have used the excellent edition of Mary Shelley's *Frankenstein* by M.K. Joseph (Oxford University Press, 1969). Lord Byron gave his maiden speech in the House of Lords in the debate on the Frame-Work Bill on 27 February 1812. Mark Girouard is superb and original in his nineteenth-century analysis, *The Return to Camelot: Chivalry and the English Gentleman* (Yale University Press, New Haven, 1981). For Alfred Lord Tennyson, I have used *The Works*, published by Macmillan in London in 1904. The letter of Edward Fitzgerald to Alfred Tennyson was quoted in Hallam Lord Tennyson's *Tennyson, a Memoir* of 1897. John Addington Symonds's invocation of male brotherhood was privately printed in 1875, while Ralph Waldo Emerson's 'The Harp' was published in 1870. Surprising and evocative, Modris Eksteins' *Rites of Spring: The Great War and the Birth of the Modern Age* (New York, 1989) is essential reading for any true understanding of the wellsprings of the First World War. Rudolf Binding, *A Fatalist at War*, was published in 1929 in London; he was later attracted to Fascism because it made the poet and the soldier one.

Chapter Seventeen

The Economic Consequences of the Peace by John Maynard Keynes was published in 1919 in London. The effects of Prohibition on young expatriate intellectuals have been considered in my *Prohibition: the Era of Excess* (Boston, 1961). Stephen Spender wrote of the Weimar Republic in the preface to his novel, *The Temple* (London, 1988), while

Christopher Isherwood's *Christopher and his Kind, 1929–1939* was published in 1977 in London.

On the occult beliefs of the Nazi leaders, the following books are useful: Jean-Michel Angebert, *Hitler y la Tradición Catara* (Barcelona, 1976); J.H. Brennan, *Occult Reich* (London, 1974); Marcel and Willy Brou, *Les Secrètes des Druides* (Brussels, 1970); Francis King, *Satan and the Swastika* (London, 1976); Roger Manvell, *SS and Gestapo* (London, 1969); W.L. Shirer, *The Rise and Fall of the Third Reich* (London, 1960); and particularly Nigel Pennick, *Hitler's Secret Services* (Sudbury, Suffolk, 1981).

Alfred Rosenberg's *Der Mythus des XX Jahrhunderts* was published in 1930 in Munich, while Edward Bulwer-Lytton's *The Coming Race* appeared in 1871 in London. I am indebted for the account of the visit of Dr Fuchs to the Theosophical Society in Edinburgh to Robert Brydon, the archivist of the Scottish Knights Templar. Otto Rahn's *Kreuzzug gegen den Graal* was published in 1933 in Stuttgart, and his *Luzifers hofgesind* in 1937 in Leipzig and Berlin, while the accounts of his researches near Montségur and those of the *Ahnenherbe* may be found in the works of Gérard de Sède, particularly *Le Secret des Cathars*; of Jean-Paul Bourre, particularly *La Quête du Graal* (Paris, 1993); and of Guy Tarade, particularly *Les derniers gardiens du Graal* (Paris, 1993).

Chapter Eighteen

The *Autobiography* of Carl Gustav Jung talks about his first experiences with active imagination, as does his article of 1916, 'The Transcendent Function', and his Tavistock lectures of 1935. His preoccupation with Gnosticism is curiously revealed in his 'Seven Sermons to the Dead' of 1916, republished in *The Gnostic Jung* (Robert A. Segal ed., London, 1992). Three volumes of his *Collected Works* particularly deal with the Grail: Vol. 6, *Psychological Types*, Vol. 12, *Psychology and Alchemy*, and Vol. 14, *Mysterium*

Coniunctionis (London, 1953–71). The quotation from Hippolytus comes from his *Elenchos*, V, Ch. 8, vv. 5–6. The quotation for the Apocryphal IV Ezra, Ch. 14, vv. 39–40, is taken from *The Apocrypha and Pseudepigrapha of the Old Testament in English* (R.H. Charles ed., 2 vols., Oxford, 1913). The 'guardian of her sex' was Helen Luke, writing on 'The Return of Dindrane' in *At the Table of the Grail* (John Matthews ed.), work already cited. *The Chalice and the Blade* by Riane Eisler was published in 1987 in New York.

For an understanding of prophecy and insight, most useful is Michael Lieb, *The Visionary Mode: Biblical Prophecy, Hermeneutics, and Cultural Change* (Cornell University Press, Ithaca, 1991). Gerald Bullitt is illuminating in *The English Mystics* (London, 1950). Dan Merkur is brilliant in his study of mystical experiences in his *Gnosis*, op. cit., from which the quotation from Martin Buber is taken. Timothy Leary wrote on sacred drugs in *Open City*, 16–22 June, 1967, while Sherwood, Stolaroff and Harman were the authors of the original essay on 'psychedelic therapy'.

Acknowledgements

The sources for quotations are given in the Notes. Where permissions are necessary, every effort has been made to trace copyright holders. Any omissions brought to the attention of the author will be remedied in future editions. The same applies to the illustrations. Their sources are acknowledged in their captions, where their provenance is known. Many of the drawings and photographs are by the author, otherwise in public domain.

Important Grail Texts

(as mentioned in this book)

Virgil	*The Aeneid*
Geoffrey of Monmouth	*The History of the Kings of Britain*
Wace	*Roman de Brut*
Layamon	*Brut*
Chrétien de Troyes	*Perceval* or *The Story of the Grail*
Gautier de Doulens	*First Continuation*
Manassier	*Continuation*
Gerbert de Montreuil	*Continuation*
Anonymous	*Song of Roland*
Anonymous	*Aliscans*
Anonymous	*Didot Perceval*
Jacopus de Voragine	*The Golden Legend*
Anonymous	*Wartburgkrieg*
Hartmann von Aue	*Iwein*
Gottfried von Strassburg	*Tristan*
Wolfram von Eschenbach	*Parzival*
	Willehalm
	Titurel
Albrecht von Scharfenberg	*Jüngerer Titurel*
Heinrich von dem Türlin	*Diû Krône*
Anonymous	*Peredur*
Anonymous	*Perlesvaus*
Anonymous	*The Quest of the Holy Grail*

Important Grail Texts

Anonymous	*The Prose Lancelot*
	Mort d'Artu
	The History of the Grail
Robert de Boron	*Joseph of Arimathea*
	Merlin
Dante	*The Divine Comedy*
Sir John Mandeville	*Travels*
Sir Thomas Malory	*Morte D'Arthur*
Chaucer	*Canterbury Tales*
Camõens	*The Lusiads*
Cervantes	*Don Quixote*
Ariosto	*Orlando Furioso*
Spenser	*The Faerie Queene*
Bunyan	*The Pilgrim's Progress*
Milton	*Paradise Lost*
Peacock	*The Misfortunes of Elphin*
Mary Shelley	*Frankenstein*
Sir Walter Scott	*The Talisman*
Lady Charlotte Guest	*The Mabinogion*
Alfred Lord Tennyson	*Idylls of the King*
Wagner	*Tannhäuser*
	Lohengrin
	Parsifal
C.G. Jung	*Psychology and Alchemy*
T.H. White	*The Once and Future King*
Emma Jung and Marie-Louise von Franz	*The Grail Legend*

Select Additional Bibliography

(of works not mentioned in the notes)

Adorno, Theodor W., *In Search of Wagner* (tr. R. Livingstone, London, 1981).

Anderson, Flavia, *The Ancient Secret* (London, 1953).

Ashe, Geoffrey, *Camelot and the Vision of Albion* (New York, 1971).

Barthélémy, A., *Au XIIᵉ siècle. Le Graal, sa première révélation* (Toulouse, 1987).

Bertrand, M., and Angelini, J., *The Quest and the Third Reich* (New York, 1974).

Bonilla y San Martin (ed.), *La Demanda de Sancto Grial* (Madrid, 1907).

Borst, Arno, *Die Katharer* (Stuttgart, 1953).

Brinkley, R.F., *Arthurian Legend in the Seventeenth Century* (New York, 1967).

Brown, Arthur C.L., *The Origin of the Grail Legend* (Cambridge, 1943).

Bruce, J.D., *The Evolution of Arthurian Romance from the Beginnings Down to the Year 1300* (2 vols., Göttingen, 1923–1924).

Burdach, Konrad, *Der Gral* (Stuttgart, 1938).

Cavendish, Richard, *King Arthur of the Grail: The Arthurian Legends and Their Meaning* (London, 1978).

Currer-Briggs, Noel, *The Shroud and the Grail: A Modern Quest for the True Grail* (London, 1987–88).

Deinert, Wilhelm, *Ritter und Kosmos im Parzival* (Munich, 1960).

Domanig, Karl, *Parzivalstudien* (2 vols., Paderborn, 1880).

Emmel, Hildegard, *Formprobleme des Artusromans und der Graldichtung* (Berne, 1951).

Entwhistle, William J., *The Arthurian Legend in the Literatures of the Spanish Peninsula* (New York, 1925).

Evans, Sebastian, *In Quest of the Holy Grail* (London, 1898).

Evola, Guilio, C.A., *Il Mistero del Graal* (Rome, 1972).

Faral, Edmond, *La Littérature Arthurienne* (3 vols., Paris, 1929).

Fouquet, Jean, *Wolfram d'Eschenbach et le Conte del Graal* (Paris, 1938).

Gadal, A., *Sur le Chemin de Saint-Graal* (Haarlem, 1960).

Gallais, Pierre, *Perceval et l'initiation* (Paris, 1972).

Gilson, Etienne, *Les Idées et les Lettres* (Paris, 1955).

Golther, Wolfgang, *Parzival und der Gral in der Dichtung des Mittelalters und der Neuzeit* (Stuttgart, 1925).

Guyer, Foster E., *Chrétien de Troyes* (Berne, 1958).

Hertz, Wilhelm, *Die Sage vom Parzival und dem Gral* (Breslau, 1882).

Holmes, Urban T., *Chrétien de Troyes* (New York, 1970).

Kahanne, Henri, and Pietrangeli, Renée and A., *The Krater and the Grail, Hermetic Sources of the 'Parzival'* (Urbana, 1965).

Kempe, Dorothy, 'The Legend of the Holy Grail, its Sources, Character and Development', in *The Holy Grail* or *Grand-Saint-Graal* (London, 1905).

Klenke, Amelia, *Chrétien de Troyes and 'Le Conte del Graal'* (Madrid and the Catholic University of America, 1981).

Kolb, Herbert, *Munsalvaesche, Studien zum Kyotproblem* (Munich, 1963).

Kurz, Johann B., *Wolfram von Eschenbach. Ein Buch vom grössten Dichter des Mittelalters* (Ansbach, 1930).

Leroux de Lincy, Antoine J.V., *Histoire de l'Abbaye de Fécamp* (Rouen, 1840).

Lindsay, Jack, *Arthur and His Times* (London, 1958).

Marx, Jean, *La Légende Arthurienne et le Graal* (Geneva, 1974).

Matarosso, Pauline, *The Redemption of Chivalry: A Study of the Queste del Sant Graal* (Geneva, 1979).

Mergell, Bodo, *Der Graal in Wolfram's Parzival* (Halle, 1952).

Micha, A., *La Tradition manuscripte des romans de Chrétien de Troyes* (Paris, 1931).

Nelli, René, *Ecritures cathares* (Paris, 1968).

Newstead, Helaine, *Bran the Blessed in Arthurian Romance* (New York, 1966).

Niel, Fernand, *Albigeois et Cathares* (Paris, 1955).

Owen, D.D.R., *The Evolution of the Grail Legend* (Edinburgh, 1968).

Paetzel, Martin, *Wolfram von Eschenbach und Crestien von Troyes* (Berlin, 1931).

Partner, Peter, *The Murdered Magicians: The Templars and Their Myth* (New York, 1981).

Pauphilet, Albert, *Etudes sur la Queste del Saint Graal* (Paris, 1921).

Pollman, L., *Chrétien de Troyes und der 'Conte de Graal'* (Tübingen, 1965).

Ponsoye, Pierre, *L'Islam et le Graal: étude sur l'esotérisme du Parzival de Wolfram von Eschenbach* (Paris, 1958).

Puech, Henri-Charles, *La Queste du Graal* (Paris, 1965).

Ravenscroft, Trevor, *The Cup of Destiny: The Quest for the Grail* (York Beach, Maine, 1982).

Richey, Margaret F., *Gahmuret Anschevin: A Contribution to the Study of Wolfram von Eschenbach* (Oxford, 1923) and *Studies of Wolfram von Eschenbach* (Edinburgh, 1957).

Ringbom, Lars-Ivar, *Graltemple und Paradies* (Stockholm, 1951).

Ritchie, Robert L., *Chrétien de Troyes and Scotland* (Oxford, 1952).

Runciman, Stephen, *The Medieval Manichee: A Study of the Christian Dualist Heresy* (Cambridge, 1947).

Select Additional Bibliography

San Marte, A.S., *Parcival-Studien* (3 vols., Halle, 1861–62).

Schröder, Franz Rolf, *Die Parzivalfrage* (Munich, 1928).

Serrus, Georges, and Roquebert, Michel, *Châteaux cathares* (Toulouse, 1986).

Singer, Samuel, *Wolframs Willehalm* (Berne, 1917) and *Wolfram und der Graal: Neue Parzival-Studien* (Zürich, 1937).

Sumption, Jonathan, *The Albigensian Crusade* (London, 1978).

Waite, Arthur E., *The Holy Grail: Its Legends and Symbolism* (London, 1909).

Weber, Gottfried, *Der Gottesbegriff des Parzival* (Frankfurt, 1935).

Weston, Jessie L., *From Ritual to Romance* (Cambridge, 1920), *The Legend of Sir Perceval* (2 vols., London, 1906–9) and *The Quest of the Holy Grail* (London, 1913).

Wilmotte, Maurice, *Le poème du Gral. Le Parzival de Wolfram d'Eschenbach et ses sources françaises* (Paris, 1933).

Index

Index